Winetaster's Choice

JMB
Château de Rouet, the home of Roger Danglade
overlooking the river Dordogne.

Winetaster's Choice

The Years of Hysteria: Tastings of French, California and German Wines

Harry Waugh

Quadrangle / The New York Times Book Company

To my wife Prue whose industry and above all patience have been invaluable.

Copyright © 1973 by Quadrangle/The New York Times Book Co., in conjunction with the Wine and Spirit Publication Ltd. All rights reserved, including the right to reproduce this book or portions thereof in any form. For information, address: Quadrangle/The New York Times Book Co., 10 East 53rd Street, New York, New York 10022. *Manufactured in the United States of America.* Published simultaneously in Canada by Fitzhenry & Whiteside, Ltd., Toronto.

Library of Congress Catalog Card Number: 71-190483
International Standard Book Number: 0-8129-0399-4

Interior design by Anita Duncan

Acknowledgments are made for permission to reprint the following pieces: *Wine World,* "An Eye Opener"; "Les Forts de Latour." *Vintage Magazine,* "Fine Claret for Today's Drinking." *Wine Magazine,* Re: Henri Woltner, tasting of the 1968's (Vintage Journey in 1971); "Burgundian Beneficence"; "A Great Vintage for the Moselle"; "Rhine Wines"; "Hans von Schubert (Maximin Grünhaus)"; "J. J. Prüm"; "The 1969 Vintage, St. Emilion and Pomerol". *Bon Appetit,* "What to Drink and What to Buy in 1974"; "A Privation of Port".

Maps by Frank Walters

Drawings by Michael Broadbent

Contents

Introduction   vii

FRANCE, 1971, AND EARLY 1972   1
    Cassis and the Rhône   3
    Harvest in Beaujolais   10
    Savigny-les-Beaune and Nuits-Saint-Georges   17
    Côtes de Beaune and Côtes de Nuits   19
    Paris, and Tasting of the Cave Thevenot   21
    Bordeaux: Tasting with Emile Casteja   25
    Graves Tastings, Red and White   29
    The 1970 Vintage at Cruse   35
    Château Cissac   38
    Some 1969 Wines   41
    Tasting with Henri Woltner   44
    Cognac   49
    Burgundy, 1972   54
    Bordeaux, 1972: First Impressions of the 1971's   64
    The 1970 Saint-Emilions and Pomerols   71
    Les Forts de Latour   74

VISIT TO AMERICA AND CANADA, 1972   81

    California, 1972   83
       Mayacamas   84
       Château Chevalier   86
       Louis Martini   88
       Freemark Abbey   92
       Heitz Wine Cellars   95

Tasting of Petite Sirah	97
The Wine and Food Society of Southern California	100
Beaujolais in California	101
Chalone Vineyard	104
The Grand Cru Club	108
Miscellaneous Tasting	111
Chicago, 1972	113
Cissac Tasting	114
Dinner with the Koch's	117
1960 Vintage Port	118
Cincinnati, 1972	120
Cru Bourgeois and Cissac Tasting	122
Canada, 1972	126
An Eye-Opener, London, 1972	129

GERMANY, 1972   137

The Moselle 1971: a Great Vintage	139
Nähe, Rheingau, Rheinhessen, Pfalz	147
Maximin Grünhaus	150
Down the Moselle and J. J. Prüm	153

MISCELLANEOUS ESSAYS   161

Sundry Tasting Notes: 1961 Bordeaux	163
"La Noblesse" of the 1961 Bordeaux Vintage	164
Fine Claret for Today's Drinking	166
Two Exercises in Gastronomy	171
Interesting Meals	176
Episode Five	178
Some 1961 Clarets	180
A Privation of Port	183
An Epic Occasion	185
Burgundian Beneficence	190

WHAT TO DRINK AND WHAT TO BUY IN 1974   193

    Index   203

Introduction

The present subtitle, *The Years of Hysteria,* takes its name from the period in which this present book was written. Namely the past two years, 1972 and 1973, a period during which the price of French wine and particularly that from Bordeaux, rose to such an alarming extent.

Having recently returned from a lecture tour covering no less than twelve different states in America, it has been impossible not to note the strong resistance to these price increases on the part of both the retailer and the consumer. It is going to be intriguing to watch how over the coming twelve months this resistance will express itself in relation to the attitude of the wine growers of France.

Since so far the French have had the American import market very much to themselves, it will be interesting to see if these greatly enhanced prices will lead to the further introduction and perhaps consolidation of the less expensive wines from Italy and Spain.

Looking further ahead still, as a result of the widespread planting of fresh vineyards in California and elsewhere, the increased production should make an appreciable impression on the domestic market. On the other hand, according to an excellent map prepared by the *New Yorker* magazine, 68 per cent of the total wine sales are concentrated mainly in California and on the East Coast in the area around New York. What will happen, one wonders, when the inhabitants of states (other than Missouri) situated in the centre of this vast country begin to evince even a minor interest in table wine, is too frightening to contemplate.

Château Bouscaut, Graves.

France, 1971, and Early 1972

BORDEAUX

Cassis and the Rhône

Innundated as we were with vinous duties which cropped up unexpectedly at the last minute, as well as getting the manuscript of *Diary of a Winetaster* sorted out and dispatched to New York, we feared we would have no holiday at all in 1971. Eventually Dame Fortune came to our aid and we found ourselves with a week to spare in Cassis, not far from Marseille in the south of France.

By early September, the holiday crowds had departed homewards, leaving Cassis not exactly empty, but full enough for animation. Though naturally there has been building since the war, the very nature of the terrain is such as to defeat, or at least fend off the type of developer who has ruined the not too distant Riviera. The focal points of Cassis thus remain virtually unspoiled, the bay, the little port for the yachts and local fishermen and the crescent of ancient houses encompassing it, as well as the extremely narrow streets (at least enough to deter cars) form a delightful background. On the eastern side of the bay there rises the gigantic wall of red rock steep enough to defy any builders and which takes on such a fascinating colour under the setting sun. Around the port, there are a number of restaurants providing temptation and in fact one can eat rather well although none of these establishments are honoured with a rosette in the *Guide Michelin*. Cassis appears to be primarily a place for the lovers of sea food; the fishing boats set out in the late afternoon, returning soon after dawn with their catch, so what you eat is superbly fresh, loup, dorade, rouget, sard and so on. The cooking is regional and naturally bouillabaisse features on most menus, though it is advisable to order it in advance. Like as not with your dishes, in place of the usual mayonnaise, you will be given a sauce rémoulade containing all the lovely local herbs.

For those who like shellfish, there is a nice little place on the port which specialises in such things as mussels, clams, *oursins* and quite a variety of oysters, sufficient indeed to bring out the worst of one's gluttony. Oysters can be an expensive luxury so perhaps it is as well for me that my wife does not eat them, but she says she derives a vicarious pleasure by watching the delight, or is it the pleasure on my face as I consume them.

Both red and white wines are produced from the vineyards spreading over the hillsides behind Cassis, but according to our experience, most of them suffer from bad handling. So oxidised were one or two of the white wines that their dark colour immediately gave them away.

They must have a sale somewhere and one wonders why the public accepts them. While on this particular subject, at a recent tasting of supermarket wines, I heard a fairly prominent London restaurateur praising those which had what he called a good golden colour. I asked him why and he replied that is what his customers look for! Generally speaking, a sound white wine should be drunk while it is young and fresh and before it has had time to take on colour, which it does naturally as it ages. This does not apply, of course, to great dessert wines such as Château d'Yquem, which improve with age in bottle. One of the signs of severe oxidation in a white wine, is a golden, almost brown colour, this is the first give-away; after that the wine will have a mawkish, unattractive taste and smell.

I remember complaining to a wine broker once about what had originally been a fine white Burgundy, but which had been allowed to become oxidised by the time it was put into bottle at the domaine. His feeble excuse was that many French people like it to taste like that! Undoubted authorities on gastronomy as indeed the French are, this story says little for their proper appreciation of wine.

Among the least agreeable wines on our hotel list at Cassis was the Mas Calendal (E. Bodin) especially the white; in fact we had to work our way right through the hotel list to find what we wanted. The following are notes on the local wines we liked the best:

Hauts-Coteaux (Caillot-Freres), Appellation Contrôlée, domaine bottled, white.
A pleasant if not pronounced bouquet, agreeable to drink, if no more. The red wine from this grower was not so successful. We had to try a number of others before we fell upon the more palatable wine—if only the head waiter had advised us at first, it would have saved both time and money, but sadly, I do not think that he knew himself!

Domaine de Bagnol 1970 (Henri Lefevre), domaine bottled, red.
Good colour, nice bouquet, is light and easy to drink. This appears to be the characteristic of these local red wines, always provided they have been adequately bottled.

Domaine de Bagnol 1970 (Henri Lefevre), domaine bottled, white.
Good pale colour, not overmuch bouquet, but an agreeable fresh flavour. This was easily the best we came across.

Along with Bandol, Palette and Bellet, Cassis is one of the four districts in Provence which are honoured with Appellation Contrôlée.

Unfortunately, I did not have an opportunity to taste what I am told is one of the best white wines of Cassis, namely Domaine Paternal (Cathinaud), but after all, I was on holiday and not duty-bound.

From Cassis, we drove through typical Provençal landscape to Aix-en-Provence to spend a few days with Melvyn and Janie Master, who have made for themselves a heavenly home in a vineclad valley not far from this completely unspoiled, sun-drenched town. Melvyn, whose home is appropriately surrounded by vineyards (A.C., Côtes d'Aix), is rapidly building up a business which supplies direct from growers in France to importers in America. His wife, Janie, whose recipes appear from time to time in *Wine Magazine,* fully deserves her reputation as a cook. To take a fairly simple dish, such as Pommes Dauphinois, we found her rendering infinitely better than the Pommes Dauphinois which we tried within a week at restaurants, one bearing two rosettes and the other three, in the *Guide Michelin!*

Apart from rushed business visits, five years have passed since I was last in the Rhône Valley and such is the charm of this part of Provence that we are contemplating renting a house here next summer. Thanks to the bad weather during the spring, especially during the season of the flowering of the vines, which seemed to last forever, and subsequent disasters caused by violent hailstorms, there have been depressing reports from all over France and what appears to be abundantly certain is that the crop of 1971 will be very small, in some places as low as 50% of average. However being situated further south than the other fine wine districts of France, the Côtes du Rhône area does not suffer so severely from inclement weather conditions; as a result the quantity here is expected to be only about 15% less than usual. In fact, if one can judge by the grapes in the vineyards surrounding the house where I am writing, the vines appear to be burdened with healthy looking fruit, but this region is some sixty miles south of the more famous vineyards of Châteauneuf-du-Pape.

On our last day, Melvyn Master drove us north along the autoroute to call upon two of the best known firms in the area, Gabriel Meffre and Jacques Mousset. The establishment of Monsieur Meffre is set in idyllic surroundings at Gigondas, a district which of recent years has become noted for its quality and thus has recently been elevated to Appellation Contrôlée! Nearby are some high hills with such jagged peaks as to be almost indescribable, reminiscent rather of romantic Victorian novels and, as though that is not enough, on a nearby hillside nestles a fascinating mediaeval looking village. Monsieur Meffre told us that although the crop would be smaller, the grapes were all very healthy and thanks to the fine weather in August and September, there was no pourriture and he expected to commence his picking on 27th September. He said that he thought the quality would be very good, even better than in 1970 and that indeed is saying something.

Monsieur Meffre is the proud owner of Château de Vaudieu, one of the best known properties of Châteauneuf-du-Pape. At his establishment we tasted a number of his wines including the 1967 Château de Vaudieu which has great elegance and quality.

Monsieur Jacques Mousset to whom for some time I have had introductions from a number of Burgundian friends, lives in a huge nineteenth-century castellated building which has a somewhat incongruous appearance among the vineyards of Châteauneuf-du-Pape, but this is amply made up for by the views, because in almost every direction they catch the eye, embracing the village and remains of the old palace of the Popes. Jacques Mousset is the owner of one of the finest vineyards of all, Château des Fines Roches.

In times gone by, Châteauneuf had a great deal of tannin and was made to last, but to suit modern conditions, the fermentation only takes about ten days, after which the young wine is kept in wood for about a year before being bottled. This is one of the reasons why you can now drink the 1969's and 1970's from this district. In fact at this establishment the 1970's had not yet (September 1971) been put into bottle, but at many other wineries they had.

During recent years, it has become fashionable to drink white Châteauneuf-du-Pape and although there are some good wines under this label, I have not in the past been overfond of it, as I found it a bit too heavy for a white wine. However with the latest methods of vinification, considerable improvements have been made. It was during this present visit though that I came across an excellent white Côtes du Rhône, a lesser animal in the Almanack de Gotha no doubt, but it made a good impression. It would seem that this is a recent development and the first vintage I ever tasted was made by Monsieur Mousset. Both the bouquet and the flavour were attractive and the fruit acidity gave a delightful freshness.

Among the other wines of Monsieur Mousset which we tasted were:

Côtes de Ventoux 1970.
> Medium colour, a slight raspberry flavour. It was light, but pleasant and easy to drink. These Côtes de Ventoux come from the slopes of Mont Ventoux and are inexpensive everyday wines. Mont Ventoux is 6,000 feet high and also on its hillsides are to be found fields of lavender and other herbs

under cultivation; the air all around is impregnated with their perfume.

Côtes du Rhône 1970 (12% alcohol).
Nice colour and bouquet, medium body, rather on the light side.

Côtes du Rhône 1970 (12.5% alcohol).
Good colour, more fruit and flavour and much more quality. This extra half degree seemingly adds greatly to the quality.

Côtes du Rhône 1970 (13% alcohol).
Good colour, full bouquet, plenty of fruit and rather good quality, still some tannin so it should take about a year in bottle to develop.

Gigondas 1969.
Medium colour, lovely bouquet, round and full-bodied, still a little tannin. The wines of Gigondas are clearly superior in quality to those simply labelled Côtes du Rhône but the name can be confusing because at times the locals pronounce the "s" at the end of the word and at others they don't!

Châteauneuf-du-Pape 1970.
Deep colour, plenty of individuality on the nose, this will make a fine rich wine.

The 1971 vintage at Châteauneuf-du-Pape began two days ago on Sunday, 19th September, and although the quantity will be a little less than usual, very good quality is expected. The lesser wines of the Côtes du Rhône should also be of reasonably good quality but there the quantity is expected to be about 25% less. As elsewhere, the weather during spring was unfavourable with too much rain throughout May and also a certain amount in June, but afterwards throughout July, August and September, it has been very hot and almost too dry.

Bearing in mind there are not the great variations of climate in this region of the Rhône Valley as there are in other and more northern parts of France, this is roughly how the vintages stand over the past decade. Although less good than usual there were no really bad years as in Burgundy and Bordeaux such as 1963 and 1965; 1964-1969 inclusive were of average quality, but the best years were 1961, 1962 and 1970. Let us hope that 1971 will fall into the latter category.

Monsieur and Madame Mousset had invited us to lunch at the château and before the meal offered us Louis Roederer 1964. Louis

Roederer always makes fine wine, but for some reason this bottle seemed to taste more delicious than usual. With it we nibbled this season's olives; picked only a fortnight before they had been prepared by Madame Mousset herself and this was the first time I had ever tasted such fresh ones. It seems that you crush them lightly, then soak them in salt water impregnated with fennel, thyme and rosemary. The result on this occasion was better than any olives you can buy in a shop. All of these herbs grow wild in Provence and if you go for a ramble in the country you will find the air laden with their perfume.

The succulent meal which followed had also been cooked by Madame Mousset and it may be of interest to relate some of the wines which accompanied it:

Tavel, Domaine de Vestides 1970 Domaine Bottled.
> The colour was quite pale, the wine light and beautifully balanced. I am no authority on Rosé wines or, in fact, a great admirer of such, but this was certainly the finest I have ever tasted. In my notes at the time I wrote "just like a blessing!"

During the conversation Melvyn Master mentioned that Jacques Mousset owned some vines in Juliénas, so yet another bottle appeared on the table, his 1970 Julienas, domaine bottled. This had a good colour, the unmistakeable bouquet of a fine Beaujolais and a delightful flavour, excellent quality.

Bois de la Garde 1969, Côtes du Rhône. Domaine Bottled.
> Good colour, pleasant bouquet, not very full-bodied.

Châteauneuf-du-Pape, Fines Roches 1962 (14% alcohol).
> Deep colour, very rich bouquet and a heavenly full-bodied wine with just the right amount of breeding to balance the weight.

Châteauneuf-du-Pape, Fines Roches 1955.
> A fine colour, just beginning to turn brown at the edges, a delightful bouquet showing great finesse. Very rich flavour, almost unctuous. This was a great bottle.

Whilst on the subject of great bottles, we had two exceptional wines at Melvyn's table during our stay. The first, a white wine from Condrieu:

1968 Viognier Condrieu (Georges Verney) Domaine Bottled.
> Good colour, could have more bouquet, but what a flavour! Although, of course, it is heavier, I could have mistaken this for a fine Moselle. The fruit acidity was delightful and it left a lovely taste in one's mouth. This was the first time I have

ever tasted the wine of Condrieu and it was quite a revelation. Unlike most white wines, Condrieu needs a year or so in bottle to be at its best. In this respect it is similar to the white Ch. Laville-Haut-Brion of Bordeaux which also improves greatly with bottle age. The grape used for Condrieu is the Viognier and the production is very small. I found this particular 1968 far superior to Château Grillet which, on the few occasions when I have tasted it, has usually proved a disappointment.

The other great wine from Melvyn's cellar was:

Châteauneuf-du-Pape, Mont-Redon 1949 (from a magnum).
The colour was beautifully dark, the bouquet so rich and full that it almost bowled one over. The flavour was similar. A really great wine which for sheer quality would stand up to and beat many a fine 1949 from either Burgundy or Bordeaux.

Wednesday, 22nd September

We left Aix in a crashing thunderstorm and the torrential rain made driving difficult. Nevertheless this autoroute now open all the way to Paris is a godsend to those of us who have to get about France on business. Our objective was the Beaujolais, about 3½ hours drive north and by the time we arrived the sky was a cloudless blue. We deposited our baggage at the Hôtel Chapon Fin in Thoissey and set off immediately for Fleurie where we left the car by the church and stumped off on foot for a good walk in the hills above the vineyards. Fleurie is one of the districts which has been scourged by hail this summer and the effects were visible amongst the vines, although the remaining fruit appeared to be in good condition. It is difficult to describe or to restrain one's enthusiasm over the walks up in these Beaujolais hills where there are few, if any cars to worry one and the air is so pure. Apart from its pleasure, walking is the perfect antidote for people who have to taste a lot of wine and, at times, succumb to the delights of French cooking!

We had a rendezvous at the Chapon Fin, at Thoissey with Bill and Marjorie Finlayson, old friends of mine who live in Toronto, Canada. That night for dinner we were all guests of Robert and Marguerite Sarrau and enjoyed ourselves to the full with the specialties for which the Chapon Fin is so noted, ballotine de canard, frogs' legs, écrevisses à la nage and so on.

Thursday, 23rd September
Harvest in Beaujolais

Here in the Beaujolais the weather had again been so uncertain during the spring that the flowering season was erratic, consequently the quantity is only expected to be about average. One of the results of the uneven flowering was *millerandage* which means roughly that finally there are both small and large ripe grapes on the same bunch. On this occasion the disadvantage of a smaller crop is balanced by the fact that the tiny grapes have more skin in proportion to their juice and this helps to give a better colour and more tannin to a red wine.

The weather in the Beaujolais was wonderful throughout July, August and specially in September, and this caused the grapes to ripen early and evenly. Thus we have an early vintage, often an augury for good quality. In common with the vineyards of the Côtes du Rhône there has not really been sufficient rain, so there is less acidity than usual, but you cannot have everything.

The Beaujolais of this year should have a good colour and bouquet with plenty of body and enough tannin to make it keep well. The quality should be even finer than in either 1969 or 1970, so what more can one wish! Owing to the slight weakness of acidity it will be difficult this year to find good wines *en primeur*, i.e., those to be drunk between November 1971 and March 1972. A careful choice will have to be made from those available but this will be past history by the time these notes appear in print. (*N. B.* This was borne out when in January 1972 I attended a tasting in London of some twenty *vins nouveaux* all from different sources. In spite of the present vogue, apart from one or two, they were rather disappointing.)

At eleven o'clock we had a rendez-vous with Robert Sarrau at Château des Capitans, his own property, a vineyard which is one of the best in the commune of Julienas. At vintage time here it is very much a family affair, Robert's wife, son, daughter and even his father-in-law all assisting. The vintage was in full swing with about thirty Spaniards together with some young friends of Robert's daughter all picking away in the sunshine. The Spaniards were very gay, singing and posing animatedly for photographs.

After a successful harvest such as this, the gentle bubbling of the must in the *cuves* must sound like sweet music to the ear of any proprietor and this year it appears that the strength may be as high as 13% alcohol. Robert said it is certainly the best wine he has ever made and the quality may even equal that other fabulous year for this district, 1947! The production of each vineyard is strictly controlled by law; for example, the limit at Château des Capitans is 40 hectolitres per hectare and anything surplus has to be sold *déclassé* as simple Beaujolais. In 1970, a huge crop, 80 hectolitres per hectare were made, so a great proportion of his wine had to be sold off as ordinary Beaujolais. Double the normal quantity is really straining the capacity of the vines but with this vintage of 1971, the quantity is estimated to be exactly in accord with the normal limit, i.e., 40 hectolitres, and this means that all the goodness has been concentrated in the smaller crop.

Together with the family we sat down to lunch with the *vendangeurs* and what a good meal it was! Tomato salad vinaigrette with masses of chopped parsley served in vast bowls, roast beef and a macédoine of delicious vegetables and then cheese, finishing up with some apple and quince puree. Many, many are the times when I have fared considerably worse! A great experience this with the cooking better than you'd get in any average restaurant and an atmosphere such as one could not buy.

Appetising as the food was with the *vendangeurs*, we had to restrain ourselves because those great gourmets, the Finlayson's, had invited both the Sarrau's and ourselves to dine with them at Troisgros at Roanne, a restaurant which has been described recently by one of the pundits as one of the two or three greatest in the world. The journey to Roanne was a labour of love, because Roanne is about sixty miles from Villefranche-sur-Saône. Added to which it was nighttime and made worse by a thunderstorm so the winding road up through the foothills of the Auvergne mountains seemed as tiring as any of those climbing up into the Alps. There is the well-known expression used in the *Guide Michelin* "il vaut le detour" and on this occasion if not a "detour" it was certainly worth the disagreeable journey.

There are a variety of menus at this temple of gastronomy; we chose the 55 franc one because it appeared to combine most of the specialities. We began with an excellent paté de Grives, rich and almost exotic of flavour. In many restaurants the paté de Grives comes out of a tin, but this, of course, was homemade. One baulks somewhat at the idea of eating the thrushes that have such a lovely song, but one is permitted perhaps to console oneself with the thought of the damage they do among the vines. One of the finest dishes I have ever eaten was Grives sur brochette and that was many years ago in that fine restaurant, La Mule du Pape in Châteauneuf-du-Pape.

Then came what to me was the *pièce de resistance,* one of the dishes for which Troisgros is so famous, Escalope de Saumon a l'Oseille (sorrel).

So often I have heard gastronomes going into ecstasies over this dish and clearly they were justified in doing so. So delicate, yet with such a flavour, the sauce was fabulous and I have seldom tasted one to equal it. In France, in season, there is much talk of the *saumon de la Loire*, but to my mind it is not a patch on the salmon we eat in England. Purposely therefore, I asked Monsieur Gros the provenance of his salmon and learned that it came from Norway. If I remember correctly, Norwegian salmon can be first class, especially the smoked variety, for this is less heavily smoked than ours in England and is sometimes served with a most delicious dill sauce.

The white Burgundy, Meursault 1969, made by Michelot Buisson, formed the perfect accompaniment, a fine bouquet and a wonderful flavour. When really well made, a Meursault *tout court* can equal many a Perrières or a Charmes. I know Monsieur Michelot well and for some fifteen years while I was with Harveys, bought his wine in every good vintage.

The Charollais au Fleurie a la moelle which also had a heavenly sauce of a deep rich reddish brown, was well matched by a 1966 Volnay les Caillerets from the cellars of the Society which owns the famous Clos de la Pousse d'Or. Incidentally this name has an intriguing translation in English, but in this rarified atmosphere of high gastronomy this is not the place for such frivolity! The Volnay had a most distinguished bouquet and a delicious flavour.

The final courses were cheese, then fraises de bois with strawberry ice cream, but knowing my capacity I managed to resist these temptations!

I had scribbled my notes on the only paper I could find, the frilly thing from the bottom of the bread basket and when he came to our table this so interested Monsieur Jean Gros that he picked it up and signed it forthwith! He then invited us to visit the cellar below, an invitation that we were not slow to accept. Beautifully arranged and without being too large, this cellar contains a really fine selection of wine, all the great clarets including Latour 1949 and naturally a splendid collection of Burgundy. In the latter case, it is not necessarily the great names which count so much but the firms and growers from whom the wine comes. The Burgundy in this cellar had clearly been selected with considerable discrimination.

To be thoroughly commercial for a moment, our host, Bill Finlayson, told us later that the bill for six people including coffee and huge Havana cigars came to under a hundred Canadian dollars. I can think of many places both in London and New York where you pay far more and fare infinitely less well and I am sure the same can apply to Paris.

Friday, 24th September

We bade farewell to the Finlaysons who were setting off for Zurich, Constantinople and Tokyo before returning home to Toronto. Prue and I moved to one of our favourite hotels of all, Les Maritonnes at Romanèche-Thorins, not that it is luxurious or anything like that, but because to us it epitomises the charm of the Beaujolais. We called on our friends Louis Jacquemont and Georges Duboeuf who both, most conveniently, have their offices and cellars in Romanèche-Thorins. It was Louis who kindly supplied me with much of the information regarding this unusually good vintage of 1971.

Georges Duboeuf, whom I mentioned in my last book, *Diary of a Winetaster,* is a *négociant* who specialises in only the finest Beaujolais, buying from the leading growers such as Monsieur Bernardot of Fleurie and Monsieur Descamps of Morgon. For his wines of the 1969 vintage, he gained many awards including thirteen gold medals and he fared equally well with his 1970's. Domaine bottling is comparatively rare in the Beaujolais but thanks to his mobile bottling plants which he designed himself, the greater part of the wine he sells is domaine bottled. With the exception of La Maison de Truffe, that mouthwatering grocer's shop in the Place de la Madelaine, Paris, he supplies his wines only to the great French restaurants such as Lasserre (Paris), Troisgros (Roanne) and Paul Bocuse of Lyon. In England they are distributed by that well-known establishment on Piccadilly, Robert Jackson Ltd. (famous as the original suppliers of Earl Grey tea) where they are enjoying a meteoric success.

Saturday, 25th September

In the shops in the Beaujolais, in fact, all over Burgundy attractive tastevins made of pottery are displayed for sale. The proper tastevins are the silver tasting cups which all Burgundian wine growers and *négociants* use for the appraisal of wine. They have a small handle and the curves and ridges formed into their shape enable the authorities to assess the colour of a wine, the indentations on one side being specially formed for judging the colour of red and those on the other for white. These pottery replicas make delightful ornaments and are useful for butter or jams for the table, or for nuts and olives at apertif hour. Sometimes they are even supplied with a lid to make attractive mustard pots.

Since these might add a splash of colour to the *Semaine Bourgignonne* which Jackson's of Piccadilly were to organise, my wife and I drove through the vineyards of the Macônnais to call on a young potter who has set up his establishment literally among the vines. There we discussed the tastevins, the mustard pots and some attractive wine pitchers, typically Burgundian. In the small local restaurants where the wine is included in the menu, very often it is served in such pitchers.

We returned by another route through the aptly named village of Rocher Vineuse and the picturesque district of Pouilly-Fuissé as far as Juliénas where we parked the car. It was a truly glorious morning as we began our ascent up through the vineyards to Pruzilly; on all sides were to be seen colourful groups of *vendangeurs,* both men and women, gathering in the last of the vintage. The unpicked grapes looked in splendid condition and since they have all been brought in under excellent conditions the prospects of the 1971 vintage appear more promising than ever. It is mainly the women and the children who snip the bunches with their scissors and a back-breaking task it is too; then when the hods on their backs are filled with the precious purple fruit the men carry them away and cascade the grapes into huge tubs on the waiting trucks and carts. Only occasionally nowadays does one see horses in the vineyards and never any longer those colourful, patient oxen of yore. This invigorating walk up hill and down dale took us for about seven miles along quiet country roads past gardens with trees laden with red, red apples and hedgerows alive with berries of every shade and description including some of a turquoise hue such as we had never seen before, all of these signs anticipating as it were, the approach of autumn.

We had had every intention to be abstemious and avoid lunch altogether, but when we returned to the car and found it parked across the way from a small restaurant called Chez La Rose, such was our appetite, the temptation was too great to resist. Promptly we ordered two Kirs; this is the local aperitif which consists of a little Cassis, a liqueur made from black currants, and topped up with chilled white Burgundy. A Kir makes a most refreshing and a not very alcoholic drink. A point to remember nevertheless, is the better the quality of the wine, the better will be the result! That great personality, the late Jack Harvey, always said the same about sherry in relation to cooking.

We chose the cheaper menu at 20 francs which turned out to be unusually good. An excellent terrine, followed by andouillettes, cooked piquantly with a mustard sauce to which a dash of wine vinegar had been added, the best andouillettes I have so far tasted; then a delectable entree in the form of *champignons au bois.* This is the season for wild mushrooms and (unlike the English, who now only seem to eat the cultivated variety) during September, the French being proper gastronomes, go out into the woods to search for them. There must have been three or four varieties and they were cooked to perfection. All these good things were washed down by a *pot* of 1970 Juliénas; in fact, because it was so delicious, a second one soon made its appearance upon the table! In the country villages of the Beaujolais it has always been the custom to serve the local wine in what they call a *pot*. This is a bottle made of heavy glass which contains 46 centilitres instead of the normal 72, or whatever it is a normal bottle contains.

Unlike my wife I am not a great cheese addict, but here, up in the hills behind the Beaujolais, they make the most delicious creamy goat's cheese imaginable. Since it should be eaten really fresh, i.e., within a few hours of being made, even in the great Paris restaurants it is not quite the same thing; this with some cream and lots of sugar made a fitting finish to a well earned repast. At times a meal such as this makes more of a lasting impression than something rich and rare in many of the grander establishments. Somewhere there lies a moral to this story, for if you wish to skip a meal it is dangerous to contemplate a good walk before the allotted time and what is more, ensure you leave your car far from enticement. The combination of a really good appetite and a lovely little restaurant within arms' length forms a temptation too great for most of us mortals to resist! The answer most probably is to defer your dieting until you return home.

While on this nice subject of food, having spent some four days in the Beaujolais, I feel I have now done my annual duty as far as the local specialities are concerned, grenouilles, ballotine de canard, jambon de Morvan, andouillettes (these are made from the entrails of a pig which sounds revolting, but as you see can be delicious) escargots, quenelles de brochet and of course, poulet de Bresse truffe aux morilles. When you come to think of it, this is not a bad range for just one district. The only thing I have not had this time is the special sausage from Lyon, which is accompanied so well by slices of firm boiled potato. Now perhaps you will understand one of the reasons why my wife and I look forward to our walks among these lovely hills, otherwise with all these temptations literally under our noses, life would be a burden.

On a number of occasions I have suggested that readers, those as fond of their tummies as we are, should consider a holiday in this earthly paradise and the time to do so is during the late summer following a good vintage such as 1972 because then you will have the 1971 vintage at your disposal; a vintage that some people consider to be the finest for twenty years. If you wait until 1973 you will have mainly the 1972's to drink and after three fine vintages in succession, it is tempting providence to trust that they will be equally good. From this you will gather that the local inhabitants prefer to drink most of their Beaujolais before it is twelve months old.

Sunday, 26th September

What a godsend the new piece of the autoroute is proving. Last year, nerve wracked, we had to battle our way daily up the highly dangerous RN 7 with constant threats from the volatile and violent French drivers. Now all is comparative peace and the journey takes but an hour.

On this occasion we changed our allegiance in so far as hotels are concerned, for instead of the Lameloise at Chagny, of which we are so fond and ostensibly in order to economise a little, chose the Hostellerie du Vieux Moulin at Bouilland, just beyond Savigny-les-Beaune and about ten miles from Beaune itself. Its situation is a sheer delight, alongside a stream running through an enchanting valley. The village, full of old houses, is tiny and blessedly untouched by progress, for in the road, pecking for food are to be seen those lovely old fashioned grey speckled hens, a sure sign of the lack of traffic. The roads are narrow and uncluttered by cars, the greatest danger perhaps being at night time with the cows meandering on their way home in the dark.

We found the vintage three parts gathered in. Here again, thanks to the exceptional weather in July, August and September as in the Beaujolais, the 1971 vintage is earlier than usual. It is not often that one finds such favourable circumstances and in spite of all the derogatory remarks I have expressed on "The Vintage of the Century" it does seem that for once 1971 may be in that category at least for red Burgundy; even the weather during the picking of the grapes has been all that one could wish for.

The sad thing however is that the vintage will be very small, in some places desperately so and this means high prices. It is not until some weeks hence (from the time of writing) that the prices will be established at the Sale of the Hospices de Beaune and I would not be surprised if all previous records are passed.

Although the vineyards of the Côte de Nuits were affected adversely, those of the Côte de Beaune suffered disastrously from hailstorms, e.g., during one single afternoon, 19th August, there were no less than three serious such storms in quick succession, and I have been shown pathetic photographs of the aftermath with entire bunches of battered grapes torn off and lying on the ground. The vineyards of Volnay, Pommard and Beaune suffered up to around thirty per cent but it was as serious as up to eighty per cent in Santenay, Mercurey and white wine districts.

Quite apart from the actual loss of volume, when hailstorms occur as close as a month to the time of the vintage, the taste of the red wine can be affected seriously owing to the bruised and dried grapes which must inevitably go into the pressing and it is not until the wine has finished its fermentation that the growers can verify whether or not the taste has got into the wine. By December no doubt, the growers will know whether their red wine has "weathered the storm". Fortunately white wine does not suffer quite so much from such disasters, because the skins are separated from the juice at the time of the pressing.

To return to a happier theme, thanks to the fabulous weather during July, August and September with a minimum amount of rain, the grapes this year are much smaller than usual and this should ensure that the colour will be darker than in former vintages. One of the weaknesses of recent vintages in Burgundy has been the greater proportion of juice to the skins, hence the rather light coloured wine of the present day. The grapes are extremely healthy too with no sign of *pourriture*. You can always tell when there is *pourriture* about, because when the bunches are brought into the *cuvier* and are poured out from their huge tubs a cloud of what looks like smoke curls up, but this year where I was, at any rate, there was none to be seen.

In normal years it is permitted to add a little sugar to the must at the time of fermentation and this also happens in Bordeaux; otherwise the wine of poor vintages would be disagreeable. The operation is called "chapitalisation," but with the 1971 vintage no such aid will be necessary because the must was measuring 13-15 per cent alcohol without added sugar. With the wine still bubbling away in the vats it is too early to be absolutely definite, but on all sides I heard growers say it is going to be the best vintage for red burgundy since 1947 or even 1945.

Monday, 27th September
Savigny-les-Beaune and Nuits-Saint-Georges

The Hostellerie du Vieux Moulin is extremely comfortable and the cooking first class. The proprietor, Monsieur Raymond Heriot, is most helpful and does not try to persuade one to eat vast quantities and choose too many dishes. When the time comes to pay the bill I do not suppose it will prove any cheaper here than at Lameloise in Chagny, but whatever happens, it has been a good excuse!

The long dining room is pleasantly decorated in a simple fashion and the specialities are certainly worth trying: tourteau au caneton, a ballotine of duck *en croute* served hot and particularly the quenelles de truite, sauce cardinale, as well as poussin de Bresse truffée aux morilles. These delicious sauces sound ominous but they were all so light that they had no ill effects and this surely is the hallmark of fine cooking. Every dish was presented to the table in a gleaming copper casserole which kept us guessing what our fellow gourmets were about to enjoy; that, of course, is part of the fun of dining in a first class restaurant!

We called on Robert Paillard, our broker friend in Santenay, who gave us further details of the damage caused in this neighborhood by the hailstorms and it seems that fate has dealt some extremely hard blows upon the *vignerons*.

As we walked together up through the village to call upon Louis Clair, Robert described the illness which had befallen the former during the summer. However he has made a remarkable recovery and it was an unexpected pleasure to find him on his feet and well enough to lead us down into his cellar to taste some of his 1969 and 1970 vintages.

The difference in quality between the 1969 and 1970 vintages was most marked. The 1970's in this cellar, at any rate, lack the depth and body of the 1969's and yet, such is the shortage of wine in Burgundy that they opened for sale at the same high price. One shudders to think what is going to happen to the 1971's, the figures have not a chance of being anything but astronomical!

Here again, loads of black grapes were being brought in but, alas, they looked very different from those I had seen on the Côte de Nuits. One could not avoid seeing the quantity of dried and battered objects going through into the press. *Misericorde*!

Later on in the day we tasted a few white wines with Maurice Gentilhomme, a firm in Nuits-Saint-Georges and these are the notes on them:

Saint-Aubin 1970.
> A fresh, fragrant bouquet, good fruit and flavour with a nice clean finish.

Saint-Aubin 1969.
> Great elegance of bouquet and perhaps a more developed flavour than the 1970, probably owing to the extra bottle age.

Saint-Romain 1969.
> Very full bouquet, quite a full bodied wine.

Meursault 1970.
   Attractive clean bouquet, fresh and clean with good fruit acidity. Leaves a pleasant taste in one's mouth.

Puligny-Montrachet 1970.
   Charming bouquet, a nice mouthful of flavour and it finishes well.

Meursault 1969.
   A lovely bouquet which lingered and a deliciously full flavour.

The above had all been well bottled and one cannot always say that of all white Burgundy. The wines of Saint-Aubin which come from near the districts of Chassagne-Montrachet and Santenay have not been well known in the past but they have some quality and are now becoming more popular. They remain comparatively inexpensive but for how long that will last is another question! In view of the increasing world demand other hitherto comparatively unknown districts are coming to notice.

Tuesday, 28th September
Côtes de Beaune and Côtes de Nuits

At 10:00 A.M. my wife and I presented ourselves at the establishment of Henri de Villamont in Savigny-les-Beaune for a tasting of the 1969 vintage. There we were met by Monsieur S. Haeni and his son, and Monsieur Feurty. I was pleasantly surprised to learn that already their grapes had been picked and gathered in safely. An early vintage such as this is always a good sign.

Since 1969 was the best vintage for red Burgundy for a number of years, I was anxious to see, some two years later, how the wines had turned out, but not all of them had yet been put into bottle.

Côte de Beaune: 1969 Vintage

Côte de Beaune-Villages.
   Pale to medium colour, a pretty nose, rather light but agreeable.

Côte-de-Nuits-Villages.
Good colour, nice full bouquet, good fruit, good quality.

Chassagne-Montrachet (red).
Medium colour, pretty nose, on light side but nicely balanced.

Savigny-les-Beaune.
Good colour, distinctive bouquet, has elegance and character.

Santenay.
Good colour, attractive bouquet, plenty of fruit and flavour, well-made.

Mercurey, Clos l'Evèque.
Fairly light colour, nice nose, light but elegant.

Aloxe-Corton.
Medium colour, full bouquet, has more body and more fruit than the others so far. Needs time to develop.

Volnay.
Medium colour, elegant bouquet, on light side but good quality. Needs time.

Beaune 1er Cru.
Good colour, nice full bouquet, full-bodied and round. Very good quality.

Volnay-Santenots.
Good colour, full fruity nose, a fine big wine for a Volnay. Will make a very good bottle.

Pommard Epenots.
Good colour, distinguished bouquet, round and full-bodied and finishes well. This is a wine which will keep.

Pommard Avelets.
Medium colour, nice nose, plenty of fruit and quality.

Côte de Nuits: 1969 Vintage

Nuits-Saint-Georges.
Medium colour, delightful bouquet, not a big wine but should keep well.

Chambolle-Musigny.
Good colour, nice nose, round with considerable charm.

Vosne-Romanée.
>Medium colour, a nice spicey nose, full-flavoured and well-balanced.

Echézeaux.
>Good colour, rich bouquet, full and round. Will make a good bottle.

Gevrey-Chambertin les Cazetières.
>Good colour, deep bouquet, good fruit and a lot of breeding. Quite powerful. Will make a fine bottle.

Gevrey-Chambertin.
>Good colour, lovely full nose, good fruit with considerable finesse.

Grands Echézeaux.
>Medium colour, lovely deep bouquet, full of fruit and quality. Heaps of breeding here. Will make a fine bottle.

Charmes-Chambertin.
>Good colour, attractive bouquet. Has fruit and body as well as distinction, is what the French term *harmonieux*.

Each of these wines came from individual growers and each had its own character and style. Among the Côte de Nuits my favourites were the Gevrey-Chambertin les Cazetières and the Grands Echézeaux.

In Beaune there is an excellent restaurant called l'Auberge Bourguignonne and there we lunched with Monsieur Feurty. Should you happen to go to it, two dishes that I suggest you try are the coquille St. Jacques and the jambon à Lie, the latter being hot ham cooked in the lees of wine.

Wednesday, 29th September to Sunday, 3rd October Paris, and Tasting of Cave Thevenot

Here we are in Paris for four days for the World Convention of the International Wine & Food Society. It is seldom that I visit Paris, a city I normally have to avoid like the plague on account of the expense and on this occasion it again lived up to its reputation. To be honest, London can nowadays be just as expensive, if not more, but there of course we feed at home.

The weather was superb from the first day to the last and there can be few more pleasant places than Paris under an early October sun. I made sure of my share of Belon oysters and fruits de mer before the Convention began because I knew we were destined mainly for classical French cooking. While on this particular subject, some of the most intriguing and familiar sights of Paris are the oyster openers who hold sway on the pavement outside many of the restaurants. Seafood must be a great pleasure for the Parisien because near the entrance of so many restaurants are displayed heaps of scrumptious shellfish such as Belon, Marenne and Claire oysters, clams, shrimps, mussels all decorated with masses of seaweed. The oystermen are clad just as they must have been a hundred years ago and in the naughty nineties, either a long blue or even a bright red smock and on their heads the traditional peaked French cap, all of which adds greatly to the scene. Incidentally, I am told these men are highly paid. The French have a nice touch when they serve oysters and shellfish because usually they present them on a bed of fresh seaweed. All this helps to get the gastric juices working nicely!

The first day, Wednesday, was spent on Committee meetings. The Convention really began on Thursday evening when we attended a delightful reception in the garden of the Maison de l'Amerique Latine. Here in a huge illuminated garden we met many old friends and drank innumerable glasses (at least I did) of Laurent Perrier Champagne and this was followed by a delectable buffet supper when we drank Georges Duboeuf's Beaujolais Blanc and Fleurie, both 1970 and both suitably chilled. Each of these wines were gold medalists and the epitome of the best Beaujolais can produce.

The following day, Friday, my wife and I "played hookey" because I had been told of a fabulous cellar of top-class Burgundy and we had to drive out of Paris to taste the wines. We found them even better than we had been led to believe. All were made from the grapes from very old vines, they had a colour such as you do not see in modern Burgundy with a bouquet and flavour that was remarkable. There was a richness too, reminiscent of fine prewar red Burgundy.

All domaine bottled, they came from the cellar of the widow of the late Monsieur H. Thevenot, who owned vineyards in the commune of Aloxe-Corton, such as Corton, Corton les Bressandes and Clos du Roi. This cellar was brought to my notice by the same friend who unearthed the Dr. Barolet Collection. Later on, these all appeared at one of Christie's sales.

We stayed for lunch with our young host and hostess, Monsieur and Madame Jean-Pierre Bloud. Incidentally Jean-Pierre is the manager and owner of Château de Moulin-à-Vent, one of the finest of all properties in the Beaujolais. Having wine in his veins as it were, he has recently started a business selling to private customers and since he will only handle the best quality, his affairs are prospering. So many people think they have to sell lots of rubbish to succeed but this is not at all the case; there is a crying need for firms, even a few, who can be relied upon for quality. There is a decided disadvantage though to Jean-Pierre's business, because at the weekend people drive out from Paris by the score to pick up a case of this or that, and since it is virtually a one man business poor Jean-Pierre and his wife have little time off, especially as they have a young family to look after.

Notes on the Tasting of the Cave Thevenot

Corton-Charlemagne 1963.
   Pale golden colour, a good fruity nose, quite rich, fresh, clean and well developed. Finishes well. Very good for its year.

Aloxe-Corton 1962.
   Good dark colour, rich bouquet, full-bodied with plenty of fruit. A nice "long" wine, very good quality.

Aloxe-Corton 1959.
   Good colour, rich bouquet. Unusually good, heaps of fruit, is round and complete. Will improve.

Aloxe-Corton Fournères 1955.
   Good colour, but turning a little brown. Fine bouquet, although a shade tired. Has fruit and is complete but is beginning to show its age.

Aloxe-Corton Fournières 1959.
   Lovely colour, a very rich bouquet, round and full with considerable character. Well made and splendid quality.

Aloxe-Corton Fournières 1962.
   Good colour, less dark than the 1959, but a nice nose with a touch of richness. Not a big wine but well balanced and of good quality.

Le Corton 1961.
   Lovely deep colour, heavenly bouquet, full, round and rich. A great powerful wine.

Corton-Bressandes 1962.
   Fabulous colour, great breeding on nose. Heaps of fruit, round

and deep with a good finish. This is better than the 1961 Bressandes.

Corton-Bressandes 1961.
Lovely deep colour, splendidly rich bouquet, full, round and of good quality.

Corton-Clos du Roi 1961.
Magnificent colour, lovely rich nose, powerful with heaps of fruit, a fine finish.

Corton-Clos du Roi 1962.
Lovely colour, delightful rich bouquet, a powerful full, round wine. Fine quality.

Seldom, these days, does one come across red Burgundy with such a deep colour as these, seldom does one find such richness and quality.

Friday was the night of the *grand diner* at the Georges V Hotel, a very gay occasion. How these chefs manage to produce a good meal for 250 people is past comprehension. The two wines of the evening were Château La Mission-Haut-Brion 1949 (from half bottles) and Latour 1949. I personally preferred La Mission which I thought superb (although admittedly some members complained that the bottles varied). At our table it was at the peak of perfection and alongside, splendid as it was, the Latour gave the impression that it would be better in five years' time.

On the Saturday we had a fatiguing journey to Epernay to be entertained royally by the Champagne Shippers and we only returned in time to change for dinner. This was our evening for the great restaurants of Paris and since our party was so huge, it had to be split up. The restaurants in question were Lucas Carton, La Tour d'Argent, Lapérousse, Prunier, etc. We ourselves had a very gay evening at Maxim's where we stayed on to dance afterwards. At Maxim's we had one of the dishes of my life, coquilles St. Jacques à la nage, served with "beurre battu." For those who do not know and I certainly didn't, this is a most glorious type of scallop stew, certainly a dish I shall never forget.

Bordeaux: Tasting with Emile Casteja

Duty called, so regretfully we had to leave the Convention on Sunday and make our way by car to Bordeaux. As it turned out, we missed the highlight of the Convention, the visit to Versailles and the most successful dinner of all at Le Doyen, off the Champs Elysees.

Monday, 4th October

In Bordeaux, at the new Aquitania Hotel we were the guests for three days of Joseph Berkmann, a delightful Austrian and the owner of the "Genevieve" group of restaurants in London. It is an unalloyed pleasure to know a restaurateur who really loves wine and one who is not guided by the branded names so dear to the restaurant trade. Also in Joseph's party were his partner Maarten Van Keulen and his wife and two other lovers of claret, Mr. and Mrs. R. Bottomley.

At eleven o'clock we arrived at the office of Borie Manoux where Emile Casteja had prepared a tasting for us of the 1970 vintage.

This is the list of wines, all of the 1970 vintage:

Château Le Pape Blanc.
> Pale golden colour, fresh bouquet, with an attractive fruity flavour. A good example of how the vinification of white Bordeaux has been improved of recent years.

Château Le Pape Rouge.
> Good dark colour, the distinctive Graves bouquet, full, round and finishes nicely.

Château Beau-Site (Saint-Estèphe).
> Good colour, a nice fruity bouquet, good fruit, good finish, good quality. It is not at all surprising that this wine has won a gold medal.

Château Beau-Rivage (Saint-Estèphe).
> Nice nose, full bodied.

Château Batailley (Pauillac).
> Good deep colour, full fruity bouquet, lots of flavour and is well-bred. Fine quality.

Vieux Château Peymouton (Saint-Emilion).
Good dark colour, pleasant bouquet, good fruit, well-balanced.

Chapelle Trinite (Saint-Emilion).
Very dark colour, distinctive bouquet, good fruit, well made.

Château La Fleur du Roy (Pomerol).
Good colour, full attractive bouquet, a delightfully rounded wine.

Domaine de l'Eglise (Pomerol).
Good deep colour, a distinguished bouquet with a distinctive flavour. Fine quality. As Emile Casteja said, here one could pick out the special "iron" taste of Pomerol. Sometimes with a Pomerol, the iron of the soil gets through into the flavour of the wine and although this may sound like a detraction it isn't in fact.

Château Trottevieille (Saint-Emilion).
Lovely dark colour, a full bouquet, heaps of fruit and flavour. A wine of considerable character and by far the best of this tasting.

Château Beau-Site, Château Batailley and Château Trottevieille belong to the family of Borie-Casteja which owns the firm of Borie-Manoux. Architecturally Château Batailley is one of the more attractive houses of the Médoc and because it is the summer house of the Casteja's, has the felicity of being inhabited. In contrast, many of the empty châteaux of the Médoc have a sad deserted appearance. Batailley is not far from Latour and I often walk around there during my early morning peregrinations.

We drove off to Libourne to lunch at Loubat, the good restaurant I have often mentioned before, where we drank 1967 Château Trottevieille, attractive flavour, of good quality and ready to drink now.

After a brief visit to the *chai* and vineyard of Trottevieille, where the grapes were being gathered, we went on to Château Ausone, always the show place of the district, for not only are the cellars (hewn from the rock) of considerable interest, but there are splendid views from the terrace across the valley towards Châteaux Pavie and Troplong-Mondot. Nevertheless it always saddens me to visit this enchanting property because the wine produced is nothing like its potential or former self. Château Ausone bears a name famous all over the world but whenever it crops up in conversation, the inevitable comment is regret that the quality is not better. According to the "form book", Château Ausone should be as good as if not better than Cheval Blanc but this nowadays is far from the case.

Thanks, alas, to my grey hairs, I remember that Ausone 1934 opened at a higher price than any of the first growths of that vintage.

All around the château there are fascinating little by-ways, and while exploring these suddenly we came across the mushroom caves. (I have always heard of this mushroom industry, if one can call it such, but never before in all these years had I actually seen where they are grown.) The town of Saint-Emilion is noted for the quarries which have been hewn out beneath and they stretch for miles. The quarrying began, I believe, in Roman times and it is from these subterranean caverns that the stone came for the construction of what was until quite recently the only bridge across the river Garonne to the city of Bordeaux. This bridge, known for over 150 years as the Pont Neuf, was built in the time of Napoleon Bonaparte. Many of these caves are used for storing wine as at Château Ausone, but there is also this flourishing business which supplies mushrooms for the Paris market. The man in charge told us that they stretch for two kilometres, which is roughly a mile! It was an eerie experience following him with his lamp through the silence and total obscurity and it conjured up nightmare experiences of being lost in there with no light or help of any kind.

Tuesday, 5th October

Our activities began with a tasting of inexpensive wine with Patrick Danglade at Messrs. Duclot in Bordeaux.

Château Gaby 1970 (Côtes-Canon-Fronsac).
   Beautiful colour, a full bouquet, good fruit, well-balanced with a nice finish. This is certainly a wine to buy.

Château Canon-de-Brem 1969 (Côtes-Canon-Fronsac).
   Medium colour, quite a nice nose, medium body. Usually I enthuse over Canon-de-Brem but 1969 was not a great year for the wines of the Fronsadais district.

Château La Valade 1967 (Côtes de Fronsac).
   Quite a good colour, a pleasant welcoming bouquet, medium body with a rather nice flavour.

Château La Dauphine 1967 (Côtes-Canon-Fronsac).
Quite a good colour, interesting bouquet, good fruit and flavour.

Château Villars 1967 (Côtes de Fronsac).
Medium colour, quite a nice nose but is too thin with a sharpish finish.

Château Gaby 1966 (Côtes-Canon-Fronsac).
Good colour, nose a bit 'off' but heaps of fruit. It was unfortunate to strike a bad bottle because this 1966 Gaby is clearly a good wine.

Château Rousset 1966 (Côtes de Bourg).
Good deep colour, a good bouquet, heaps of fruit and is well-balanced. Still undeveloped but should have an excellent future.

Château Bourdieu La Valade 1967 (Côtes de Fronsac).
Good colour, quite a nice nose, plenty of fruit, good quality.

The only outstanding wine among the above was the Château Rousset. (*N.B.* Ch. La Valade and Ch. Bourdieu la Valade are separate vineyards but belong to Monsieur B. Roux and Mlle. Roux respectively, Bourdieu la Valade being the smaller of the two.)

We all trooped off to lunch at a bistro on the quays called Restaurant de la Gironde where we ate clams, deliciously cooked tiny pale coloured moules marinieres, so much better than the large orange hued ones that are served up in England, and our first partridge of the season. The 1964 Château La Lagune was surprisingly good even if it did finish a little short. The partridge, incidentally was much too "high," at least for my taste! An interesting feature of this restaurant are the lockers in which the different Bordelais *négociants* keep their own wines and this relieves the owner from financing much of his cellar.

Having sampled that morning some of the wines from the Fronsadais area we drove there to try some more at the châteaux and direct from the cask.

Château La Dauphine 1970 (Côtes-Canon-Fronsac).
A splendid dark colour, a lovely fruity bouquet. It is full and round and finishes well.

Château Canon-de-Brem 1970 (Côtes-Canon-Fronsac).
A deep colour and a most distinguished bouquet, round and full-bodied and of remarkable quality, better, if anything, than La Dauphine.

The vintage in this district finishes before that of the Médoc and all the grapes of 1971 had been gathered satisfactorily, but there are pluses and minuses with regard to the crop. The weather in the Bordeaux area has not been anything like so good as it was in Burgundy. Thanks to the universally bad weather in June the crop on the east bank of the Dordogne is only about three quarters of the normal. Apart from a few storms it was lovely in July though the hailstorms reduced the crop still further. August with just enough rain was not bad. At the beginning of September there was a cold spell, but afterwards it became infinitely better.

All the same, the prospect of making good wine in these districts remains from satisfactory to very good. Thanks to the thick skins of the very ripe and healthy grapes, the colour should be dark, the acidity normal, from 4 to 4.50 and the wines should be nicely rounded. In the good districts there will be no need for "chapitalisation" and that is always a good sign.

To give an example of the smallness of the 1971 crop, at Château Rouet, the family home of the Danglade's, they have only made twenty hectolitres per hectare whereas the normal quantity is forty-five. On account of the huge crop in 1970 and the exceptional quality of the wine, the growers were permitted for the purposes of appellation contrôlée an excess of up to sixty hectolitres per hectare.

Wednesday, 6th October
Graves Tastings, Red and White

A day set aside for the red Graves, a somewhat underestimated district as regards to quality. The leading château is Haut-Brion, rightly classified as a first growth and where such good wine is being made these days; then virtually across the road is the highly successful Château La Mission Haut Brion and, in so far as quality is concerned, these are followed fairly closely by Haut-Bailly and Pape Clément.

It seems to me there is room for improvement among some of the other classified growths that produce red Graves; improvement such as so obviously is in progress at Château Bouscaut. To sell claret these days is as easy as falling off a log, but when the châteaux in question increase their quality, not only will the public benefit, but the price demanded for each vintage they produce could go up even more.

At Château Haut-Brion we found the harvest had already been

gathered in under ideal conditions and although the crop was about half the normal size, Jean Delmas, who manages the property, told us he expected the quality of his 1971 to be even better than 1970, an exciting comment, because his 1970 is a great success. There is a splendid array of stainless steel fermenting tanks at Haut-Brion and a number of other improvements have been made for bringing in the grapes and separating the stalks from the bunches before they are pressed. Château Haut-Brion was the first in Bordeaux to experiment with stainless steel tanks with a thermostatically controlled cooling system, and it was from here that we got some of our ideas for Château Latour. It all seems common sense now, but at the time of the installation people were saying that Latour would never be the same again and the criticism must have been even worse for our "pathfinders" at Haut-Brion. Now, of course, the new system has proved itself over and over again. Modernisation has at least some benefits to bestow upon us, but its initiation requires both courage and foresight, particularly when it is a question of wine.

In the *chai* a most instructive tasting of the 1968, 1969 and 1970 vintages had been prepared for us.

Château Haut-Brion 1968.

Medium colour, distinguished bouquet, plenty of fruit and well-balanced. This had been bottled in January 1971 and has proved to be one of the very best of this indifferent vintage. This is saying something, because successes do not abound amongst the 1968's!

Château Haut-Brion 1969.

Good colour, a fruity, well-bred bouquet, rounder than the 1968 and again a success for its year. In general 1969 was a better vintage than 1968, but not nearly so great as it was made out to be at the outset. It is too early yet to say categorically how these 1969's will turn out. In any case though these two vintages from Haut-Brion demonstrate not only the distinction of this noble vineyard but also the ability of the management to overcome poor conditions.

Château Haut-Brion 1970.

A splendid colour and a beautifully rich bouquet, a big round wine that will undoubtedly make a great bottle.

Before leaving we paid our respects to Mr. Weller who has been in charge of this property ever since his relation, Mr. Clarence Dillon, purchased it in the late twenties.

Jean Delmas is also the manager of Château Bouscaut of Cadaujac, also in the Graves district. This potentially fine vineyard which produces both red and white wine had been allowed to go downhill until it was purchased recently by a most enlightened American syndicate. The new owners have had the foresight to obtain the advice and services of Jean Delmas and since they are sparing no expense to improve everything to do with the vineyard, this will be one of the properties to watch in the future. Through improved vinification, a difference in the quality of the wine is already discernable and once the new plantings of Cabernet Sauvignon have come of age the true potential of Château Bouscaut will be patent for all to see.

In the *chai* of Château Bouscaut, Jean Delmas had prepared for us an interesting tasting of the red and white Graves of 1970, and to meet us had invited Monsieur Jacques Marly, the proprietor of Château Malartic-Lagravière, who is the President of *l'Union des Crus Classées de Graves*.

1970 Vintage: Red Wines

> Château Malartic-Lagravière (Léognan).
> Good colour, attractive bouquet, medium body, pleasant flavour.
>
> Château Bouscaut (Cadaujac).
> Good colour, nice full bouquet, good fruit and flavour and it finishes well. This will make a good bottle.
>
> Château Carbonnieux (Léognan).
> Good colour, fruity bouquet, quite a big wine but of lesser quality than the Bouscaut.
>
> Château Haut-Bailly (Léognan).
> Good colour, fine, well-bred nose, lovely flavour, is it of blackberries? This big wine was clearly the best at this tasting. They are making good wine nowadays at Haut-Bailly.
>
> Domaine de Chevalier (Léognan).
> Good deep colour, distinguished bouquet, good fruit and finishes well.
>
> Château Pape-Clément, Pessac.
> Deep colour, very good bouquet and a delightful flavour. Will make a lovely bottle.

1970 Vintage: White Wines

> *Château Bouscaut* (Cadaujac).
> Distinguished bouquet, good fruit, pleasant flavour.
>
> *Château Malartic-Lagravière* (Léognan).
> Grapey bouquet, full-bodied and flavoury. The flavour of the Semillon grape is clearly discernable.
>
> *Château Carbonnieux* (Léognan).
> Good bouquet and flavour.

Architecturally, Château Bouscaut must be among the most elegant of all the houses around Bordeaux and in the garden behind there is a lovely swimming pool. Madame Delmas had arranged a delicious lunch for us and these are the red wines that accompanied this succulent meal:

> *Château Bouscaut 1964.*
> Good colour, nice bouquet and plenty of flavour. This is one of the successful 1964's. In view of the sad story of some of the 1964 Médocs, one is inclined to look suspiciously at the red wines of this vintage.
>
> *Château Bouscaut 1928.*
> Still a good colour, although going what the French call "tuillé," in other words, turning a little brown. The bouquet was excellent and not showing its age. This was in excellent condition and has fared far better than many others of the same great vintage. If ever there were a wine to show the true potential of Bouscaut, here it is. I feel sure it will not be the fault of the new owners nor that of Monsieur Delmas if, in say ten years' time, Bouscaut has not been brought back to a high standard in accordance with its potential.

Although a "dodgey" subject, this matter of the potential of the châteaux fascinates me. The soil always remains the same but it is the men who change and even in my lifetime I have seen châteaux, as it were, go up and down the scale.

Among the pluses, one of the most striking successes is the rise of Ducru-Beaucaillou, a wine which before the war lay somewhat in the doldrums (in 1929 for instance, when so many fabulous wines were made, the Ducru was a grave disappointment). Its rise can only be due to the present owner, Monsieur Jean-Eugene Borie. Château Palmer, which was nothing special in the inter-war years, has now emerged into the top flight. Beychevelle, which was a top seller before the war in England, has had its ups and downs recently, but certainly if one can judge by the 1970 vintage, it is right on form again.

These changes for the better often occur after a change of ownership. Malescot is a case in point and so certainly is Lefon-Rochet where they have made an excellent 1970. When Lafon-Rochet changed hands in 1959 there was too large a proportion of Merlot vines and it is only now after ten years when the comparatively recently planted Cabernet Sauvignon vines have reached maturity that the tangible result can be seen, or should one say, tasted! From now onwards Lafon-Rochet should get better and better. Grand-Puy-Lacoste is another property which produces fine quality with great regularity. Being a fifth growth, Grand-Puy-Lacoste cannot perhaps expect to beat the *grands seigneurs* but in spite of its lack, shall we say, of "blue blood" i.e., fifth growth versus first or second, very often it gives some of them a good run for their money. For future purchasers, the 1970 Grand-Puy-Lacoste is also worthy of consideration.

Such prewar experience as I had, did not enable me to study thoroughly the *crus bourgeois;* more is the pity for this is a fascinating field. The *crus bourgeois* have no famous 1855 classification to carry them through, they rise and fall on their own merits, fundamentally the merits of their proprietors. It is always more exciting and more of a challenge to sort out and to discover these lesser known châteaux. The trouble nowadays is that a few of the better known *crus bourgeois* are becoming, and deservedly so, as expensive as some of the classified growths.

It is most appropriate that Château Gloria, the *cru bourgeois* which has made such a name for itself since the war, should be the property of the President of the *Comité Interprofessionelle de Vins de Bordeaux,* that is to say, Henri Martin, one of the great wine authorities of France. On several occasions, in blind tastings, I have put Gloria above even some of the second growths and once again, this was certainly the case with the 1970 vintage. There are two sides to every coin though because friends in America complain that when I first began to write about Gloria and de Pez they could buy them at a reasonable price, but now they have become too expensive! I have been a fan of these two châteaux for many years. I shall not forget easily the computer-maker who told me that he had put my tasting notes in *The Pick of the Bunch* through one of his machines and that Château Gloria had emerged on top. It makes me wish I had shares in that château!

Château Lanessan is another in the same bracket and so is Château Cissac whose quality is still unrecognised except in England. I know that in a recent blind tasting of the 1970's of this category I put it ahead of Château de Pez.

The less said about the minuses perhaps the better and if I were discreet I would say nothing at all! Both Léoville-Poyferré and Rausan-Ségla produced superlative 1929's and were pre-eminent on English merchants' lists before the war, but since then they seem to have fallen rather by the wayside and one seldom hears of them producing anything really special even in a great vintage. Rauzan-Gassies is usually rather disappointing too and although it is better now, Calon-Ségur has at times lapsed from grace. It might be appropriate here to mention the médocs of 1964 where the grapes were picked too late, but this I hesitate to do because of disagreeable repercussions. Your wine merchant should be able to tell you, although I have been astonished to see them being sold so often in American liquor stores. Presumably the owners live too far from Bordeaux to know what is going on. In Saint-Emilion it is good to know that Clos Fourtet, which for years has been going through a bad period, has made an excellent 1970 and that Ausone, for so long disappointing, has produced a fine 1971.

We dined that night with Monsieur Emile and Madame Casteja at their delightful home, Château Batailley, and to our great pleasure the other guests were David and Margot Pollock and their daughter Susan. Apart from delicious food, the wines were of special interest. Château Batailley 1953 of which Emile reminded me I had bought hundreds of cases for Harveys in the old days, turned out to be one of the best of that so charming vintage and what is more it still remains utterly delightful when so many of its fellows, including the first growths, are on the downward slope. The other was Emile's birth year 1921, rather an off-vintage but this bottle had retained all its vigour.

Instead of driving back all the way to Bordeaux (there are nasty patches of fog at this time of the year) David and Margot persuaded us to stay the night at Latour and since we were moving there the following day in any case, we did not need much persuading!

Between Friday, 8th October and Tuesday, 12th October we remained quietly at Château Latour visiting properties and watching the 1971 vintage being brought in under cloudless blue skies.

Having driven up through France, through the Rhône Valley, the Beaujolais and the Côte d'Or of Burgundy, it has been possible to obtain a fairly good idea of the prospects for the red wines of 1971. Although the quantity produced in the three places mentioned would be much reduced in comparison with 1970, the quality seemed appreciably better than usual but, as I had rather feared, the prospects for Bordeaux though good, appeared somewhat less assured than in 1970.

While the 1971's are still fermenting and bubbling away in their vats, it is far too early to make prognostications but it has been difficult to ignore the quiet optimism of some of the proprietors as they discuss the new wine. A number of them think it may even be as good as 1970. All the same a sad lesson was learned in 1969 when so many growers were led to believe the quality was far superior to what in fact it turned out to be, hence their caution while assessing the quality of their 1971's. Of one thing we can all be certain and that is, because of their scarcity the 1971's will be expensive.

On arrival at Château Latour, I was pleasantly surprised by the number of grapes on the vines, nothing like so many as last year of course, but they all looked extremely healthy. Perhaps as a result of the appalling weather conditions in June, the vineyards have been attacked this summer by red spider and in order to obliterate this scourge constant spraying was necessary. The visual effect of red spider at this time of the year is the dull brownish colour of the vine leaves so it was easy to pick out the vineyards which had been carefully tended. For instance at Latour, looking across the tops of our vines, they appeared like a sea of green, a refreshing sight in comparison with the colour of so many of the vineyards of the Médoc. This is merely a question of good husbandry, i.e., spraying the vines at the right time. Splendid weather continued throughout the picking period and lasted right up to the 12th October by which time all the grapes at Latour had been safely gathered in.

The reduced quantity, similar in many cases to 1969, is what worries, in particular, the smaller growers, some of whom even with greatly increased prices, wonder if they will cover their expenses. The trouble with a difficult vintage, as 1971 was to begin with, is that more work than usual is required among the vines, much more spraying for example, thus such a vintage costs more to produce than an easy one like 1970.

Monday, 11th October

The 1970 Vintage at Cruse

I drove into Bordeaux to visit the house of Cruse and there met Edouard Cruse, Francois Samazeuilh and other members of the Cruse family. Edouard and Francois had prepared an elaborate tasting of the 1970 vintage, no less than twenty-two wines; such a number is more than

I like to tackle at one time but beggars can't be choosers. In order to avoid repetition, I am incorporating the results of today's tasting with others I have been privileged to attend during this visit to Bordeaux.

First Tasting, October 1971

1970 vintage

> *Beychevelle* (Saint-Julien).
> Dark colour, pretty nose, good fruit and body, has elegance and great charm.
>
> *Ducru-Beaucaillou* (Saint-Julien).
> Dark colour, good nose, full of fruit, well made. A fine wine.
>
> *Las-Cases* (Saint-Julien).
> Dark colour, good full nose, plenty of fruit, round but prefer Ducru-Beaucaillou.
>
> *Pichon-Longueville-Baron* (Pauillac).
> Medium colour, delightful fragrant nose, medium body, distinctive flavour, has character but needs time.
>
> *Pichon-Longueville-Lalande* (Pauillac).
> Very dark colour, lovely nose, good fruit and body. Rounded and rather nice.
>
> *Lynch-Bages* (Pauillac).
> Very dark colour, smell of fruit, blackcurrant? Full, round great charm with some tannin. Fine quality.
>
> *Calon-Ségur* (Saint-Estèphe).
> Medium colour, nice nose. Good fruit, well-balanced. Good quality and truly representative of this chateau.
>
> *Montrose* (Saint-Estèphe).
> Very good colour, full, fruity nose. Strong and powerful, perhaps a little coarser than some of the others.
>
> *Brane-Cantenac* (Margaux).
> Good colour, fragrant nose, medium body. Well-made and distinguished.
>
> *Cantemerle* (Macau).
> Good colour, pretty nose, distinctive flavour and medium body.

La Lagune (Ludon).
   Very good colour, strong smell of blackcurrants. Big, round wine. Fine quality.

Giscours (Labarde).
   Extremely deep in colour, attractive full bouquet. Round and full bodied. Fine quality.

Grand-Puy-Lacoste (Pauillac).
   Deep colour, good bouquet, a lovely big wine.

Malescot (Margaux).
   Deep colour, still purple. Very good bouquet. Good fruit and body.

Les crus bourgeois of 1970

Chasse-Spleen (Moulis).
   Very deep colour, splendid bouquet, round and full with lots of individuality. This has great quality and must be among the best médocs of its year.

La Tour-de-Mons (Soussans).
   Deep colour, splendid bouquet, full-bodied and has great style. Very well balanced.

Siran (Labarde).
   Medium colour, good bouquet, medium body and rather thin in comparison with some of the others.

Gloria (Saint-Julien).
   Good colour, very good bouquet, delightful flavour, very good quality.

de Pez (Saint-Estèphe).
   Dark colour, fine bouquet, good fruit and finishes well.

Phélan-Ségur (Saint-Estèphe).
   Good colour, nice fragrant bouquet, medium body.

Poujeaux (Moulis).
   Very deep colour, lovely bouquet, lovely flavour, fine quality.

Bel-Air Marquis d'Aligre (Soussans).
   Deep colour, good bouquet, good fruit.

Lanessan (Cussac).
Deep colour, very good bouquet, round and full-bodied, plenty of tannin. Excellent quality.

The *crus bourgeois* of the Médoc appear to be better than usual in this fine vintage of 1970. Naturally, some are better than others but with a few exceptions, it seems one can buy them more or less with equanimity. Among the wines mentioned above, I thought the Chasse-Spleen quite outstanding, with Lanessan, Gloria and de Pez not far behind. Had I the means, I would quickly acquire a case of each of these four châteaux.

Lunching later in the new dining room at the Quai des Chartrons with other members of the family we drank some unusually good wines:

Château Grand Barail Lamazelle 1967.
Good colour and bouquet, attractive flavour and already very easy to drink.

Château Giscours 1929.
A lovely colour, it has that so typical and very special 1929 bouquet and such a delicious flavour. For a bottle (as opposed to a magnum) this has kept remarkably well.

Château La Conseillante 1929 (magnum).
Deep colour, lovely bouquet, heaps of body and no sign of age. A great bottle of a great year.

After the morning's tasting, a tiring affair, even if one does spit out all the wine, and this delectable luncheon, I had to be particularly careful during the forty mile drive back to Latour!

Tuesday, 12th October

Château Cissac

The morning was spent with Louis Vialard on his property at Château Cissac in the commune of that name just inland, that is river-wise, from Pauillac. As I think I have mentioned before, Château Cissac has been in the Vialard family for more than 100 years. This is a true Médocain family, one of the very few still inhabiting their château the year round.

Louis is rather a rare bird at the time of this particular vintage, he is the only person whom I have found so optimistic. When I called there the picking was still in full swing, but he spared the time to drive me through his property to show me his vines. His grapes all appeared to be most healthy and I could see he was not exaggerating about the quantity of them, the crop was indeed heavier, much more so than I had seen elsewhere.

Louis had had trouble with his manager during the summer and had to dispense with his services. Perhaps it was as well, as it turns out, for he had personally supervised the work in the vineyard and thus has only himself to congratulate on the abundant crop. Château Cissac is a *cru bourgeois* which, at the time of writing I think I am right in saying, is hardly known at all in the United States. Louis Vialard is one of the few proprietors who still make their wine in the old fashioned manner, so its characteristics are a good dark colour and considerable depth of body. In one respect it is not unlike Latour and La Mission-Haut-Brion, because since the method of vinification is basically the same, it takes longer to mature than many of its fellow wines.

Louis considers his 1970 vintage the best he has ever made and since in tastings of this vintage, I had been particularly impressed by Château Gloria and Château de Pez (two properties in the top flight of the *crus bourgeois*) I had asked him to arrange a blind tasting of his own 1970 against these two undoubted successes. All three have an equally good dark colour and this is the result:

de Pez 1970 (Saint Estèphe).
Good bouquet, full, fruity and finishes well. Very good quality.

Cissac 1970 (Cissac).
Good bouquet, a full-bodied deep wine, some tannin. This should make a good bottle.

Gloria 1970 (Saint-Julien).
Lovely bouquet, excellent flavour. It has a special charm all of its own. Very fine quality for a *cru bourgeois*.

The Gloria was the best of the three and this is not really surprising in so far as I am concerned, because at times in previous blind tastings I have put it above some of the much more famous châteaux of its commune. Where the making of wine is concerned there is no doubt that Henri Martin is a bit of a genius. His Château Gloria was hardly known twenty years ago and look at it now!

Second, easily second and, so far as I was concerned, a pleasant surprise (I did not have to make polite noises to my host!) came Château Cissac which at least at this stage of its career, had infinitely more depth than de Pez. Later on when I discussed this with an authority on the wines of the Médoc, he warned me that very often about a year after the vintage, de Pez goes through a rather "hollow" period and then resumes its old form. Nevertheless, taking all this into consideration, on this occasion the Cissac had showed so much better and I do not feel that when it is a year or so older it will drop back too far in the race.

Among the best *crus bourgeois,* in the past, I have put at the summit such wines as Gloria, de Pez, Lanessan and sometimes Liversan and it looks as though Cissac, which I have not really come across until recently, should be among them.

It is interesting to study a family such as this at vintage time for it is completely involved. Madame Vialard sees to the food of the pickers and the son and two daughters were busy helping the *vendangeurs* and showing visitors around. Incidentally intending visitors would be well-advised not to consider going to Bordeaux at this particular period, a period which naturally sounds the most romantic. It is the culminating point of the whole year's work, a moment when the efforts of all concerned are fully concentrated upon getting the grapes in safely and attending to the vinification so there is little time to look after the visitors, who on all other occasions are most welcome. At Latour every member of the staff is so occupied at this period that regretfully we have to discourage visitors as much as possible.

During lunch we tried three vintages of Cissac:

> *1969:* Medium colour, an agreeable bouquet, not a big wine, but already pleasant to drink. With more maturity this will make quite a nice bottle.

The 1969 vintage is somewhat of an enigma; it emerged on the scene accompanied by paeons of trumpets, but about six months later disappointment set in. Although most of the 1969 Médocs are now safely in bottle, it will probably be better to wait another twelve months before a proper assessment can be made of them.

> *1959:* Good dark colour, a lovely bouquet, a fine vigorous wine, which the French term "un vin solide" and it finishes well.

When it appeared on the scene, 1959 was hailed as the year of the century and it was really with the 1959's that the American market made its first real impact on Bordeaux. The great names were ordered regardless, and consequently prices which up to then had always been fairly normal, or so we thought, rocketed to the sky and alas, from the English buyers' point of view, have never descended. Gone for ever are the good old days! Now with hindsight, it can be seen that the 1959's are not all so great as they were made out to be, for some of them are inclined to finish a little flat.

> *1943:* A good colour but going a little brown, a fragrant bouquet, it still has heaps of fruit and body and, for its year, has kept remarkably well.

The 1943's filled a gap admirably immediately after the end of the war. It was rather a light vintage, charming while young but it did not last very well and most 1943's have long since been drunk up. Those that now remain are usually rather frail old ladies!

A tasting of Château Cissac in America is described below, pages 114-117.

Wednesday, 13th October

Some 1969 Wines

Sadly my wife and I packed our bags, our stay at Château Latour having come to an end, but there was nevertheless a fascinating day in store for us; a visit to Jean-Pierre Moueix at Libourne. As usual Jean-Pierre had arranged one of his instructive tastings, this time the 1969 vintage of Saint-Emilion and Pomerol. Our last tasting with this notable château proprietor had been three months before when we had the unforgettable experience of tasting the 1970's from this region. These words are used intentionally because 1970 is a great vintage for Saint-Emilion and particularly for Pomerol, the best in fact for many years. Now that I have had an opportunity to study the 1970 médocs, although this may be putting too fine a point to it, I have a feeling that, relatively, the last named may not be quite so successful.

Life has its ups and downs and one cannot always have the pleasure of tasting tip-top vintages, so sometimes it is the turn, though not so agreeable an experience perhaps, of some of the lesser years. The summer and autumn of 1968 had been so bad that few, if any 1968's of Saint-Emilion or Pomerol were bottled at the châteaux. This near disaster was followed by 1969, another disappointment especially for the merlot vines, but certainly better than 1968 and at least considered worthy of château bottling. Two years in succession without any good wine to sell would have been a tragedy for the growers! It is difficult to say how the 1969's will turn out, but with regard to quality, they may be in line with the 1960's or 1962's from these same districts, when neither vintage was a great success.

So here are the 1969's, not a great year admittedly, but they have their merits. It must not be forgotten that when wines are still about a year or two old they are often disturbed and affected adversely at the time of the following vintages. This is one of those things of nature which are hard to explain.

1969 Vintage: Saint-Emilion (Blind Tasting)

The Wine	Characteristics	Placing
Corbin Great Growth	Medium colour, quite a good bouquet, it is complete and has fruit but could be more plump	7
La Clotte Great Growth	Medium colour, quite a nice nose, more fruit, body and quality than Ch. Corbin	3
Pavie-Macquin Great Growth	Rather a light colour, not much bouquet, is light but has some charm	4
La Gaffelière First Great Growth	Quite a good colour, a fairly full bouquet, well-balanced, has both style and breeding	1
Magdelaine First Great Growth	Quite a good colour, good bouquet, full-bodied with plenty of fruit. Some tannin	2
Figeac First Great Growth	Quite a good colour, a "winey" nose, on light side with a disappointing finish. Perhaps it is the fact that it is vintage time which has upset this wine. It should be tasted again some months thence	6

1969 Vintages: Pomerol (Blind Tasting)

The Wine	Characteristics	Placing

de Sales
   Secondary
   First Growth
	Rather light colour, a nice bouquet, not full-bodied but it is smooth and agreeable	3

Gazin First Great Growth	Rather light colour, bouquet satisfactory, has fruit and body but is less attractive than Ch. de Sales	4
La Conseillante First Great Growth	Light colour, a nice nose but seems somewhat thin and hungry	6

Some 1969 Wines   43

1969 Vintage: Pomerol (Blind Tasting) (continued)

The Wine	Characteristics	Placing
La Fleur-Pétrus First Great Growth	Good colour, attractive full bouquet, has good fruit and is well-made, fine quality for this vintage	2
Trotanoy First Great Great	Medium colour, full bouquet but not so good as that of Ch. La Fleur-Pétrus. Good fruit and balance, has more depth than all the others. A lovely round wine	1
Vieux Ch. Certan First Great Growth	Quite a good colour, pleasantly full bouquet, but lean and lacking charm	5

Finally, it was the turn of the Grands Seigneurs, Pétrus and Cheval Blanc and although they also were tasted "blind" it was easy to tell the one from the other.

Pétrus 1969. First Great Growth (Pomerol).
   Good colour, finely bred bouquet, has heaps of fruit and body and is well-balanced, some tannin, a nice "long" wine.

Cheval Blanc 1969. First Great Growth (Saint-Emilion).
   Has perhaps more elegance and depth of bouquet and more body than the Pétrus but of the two, I think I preferred the Pétrus.

Before closing down as it were, we tried two other blind tastings, Pétrus against Trotanoy and Cheval Blanc against La Gaffelière. Pétrus with its extra depth was twice the wine of Trotanoy and similarly Cheval Blanc, being so rich and round had much more weight and depth as well as a finer after-taste than La Gaffelière.

Lunching later at Château Videlot and as delightfully as ever, we had the good fortune to meet Christian Moueix, the younger son of Jean-Pierre, with whom I share so many happy memories of California. There is excitement in the family because his father has just bought for him a first growth Pomerol, Château La Grave-Trigant-de-Boisset. This is a fine vineyard which produces a lovely round wine and one that I often used to buy in my Harvey days. The earliest vintage I ever tasted was the 1929 and it was so fabulous I have never forgotten it. The last I bought for Harvey's was 1955 and it turned out better than most of its contemporaries of that year. Under the skill and dedication of Christian this will undoubtedly be a property to watch in future vintages.

The wines at lunch were of more than usual interest, 1961 Château Cheval Blanc to begin with, dark of colour and still a little hesitant, or should I say resistant, but of such fine quality. A few more years are still needed for it to reach its best. The *pièce de resistance* was a fantastic bottle of 1947 Château Lafleur, the best vintage for Pomerol since the war. So rich and so powerful was it that it reminded me of vintage port! The fabulous 1947 pomerols had a power and a richness all of their own, so let us hope the 1970's will emulate them.

The intensive tasting and perhaps also that bottle of 1947 Lafleur made us late for a rendezvous in Saint-Emilion with George Rainbird and Dr. and Mrs. Ian Cathie. George is President of the International Wine & Food Society and Ian Cathie is a fellow member of the Management Committee. At Château Ausone we talked for a few minutes with Madame Dubois-Chalon, the wife of one of the co-owners of the property and we also visited Cheval Blanc and Pétrus.

The vintage in this district had finished during the previous week and all the grapes had been gathered in under good conditions. It will be interesting to see how the 1971 vintage turns out for this neighbourhood. That the crop will be very small (hence very expensive) is certain but whether the quality will match that of 1970 must be doubtful. When in July 1971 I tasted the 1970 pomerols and made notes on them I scribbled "this must be the best vintage for the Pomerol district since 1947"—a target difficult to equal.

Thursday, 14th October

Tastings with Henri Woltner

A *bonne bouche* had been stored up for the end of our 1971 visit to Bordeaux, for the Woltner's had asked us to spend our last two days with them at Château La Mission Haut Brion, a particularly kind invitation in view of Hélène's recent illness, and it was a relief to find her looking so well.

As usual, Henri had prepared an instructive tasting, if not necessarily an agreeable one. One has to take the rough with the smooth for not all the Bordeaux geese are swans, in other words, the poorer vintages have to be tackled along with the others. On this occasion it was the turn of the 1968 vintage, truly one of the weaker brethren! In the decade of the 1960's, there were three weak links, 1963, 1965 and 1968 and I still remember the painful occasion when in 1969, I had to taste the 1965's and so acid and so generally unattractive were they at that time, I could not bring myself to write about them. Time is a great healer, however, and when on the evening before (October 13th), we had tried 1965 La

Fieuzal against the 1965 La Mission Haut Brion, I was agreeably surprised. La Fieuzal, being lighter, was naturally ready to drink at this moment, but of course, given time, La Mission will make the greater bottle. The 1965 La Mission Haut Brion is clearly one of the successes of that disappointing vintage.

However unattractively the 1968's are presenting themselves at this particular moment, given, say, a couple more years in bottle, it may be that they will have discarded some of their now so obvious acidity and possibly may afford us some pleasant surprises. All the same, from the results of this tasting, some of *les Grands Seigneurs* of 1968 already appear to be greatly over-priced.

1968 Claret (Blind tasting)

Nénin (Pomerol).
Medium colour, not much bouquet, light and rather thin, not much here. 10/20
(*N.B.* Very few 1968 Pomerols were bottled at the château.)

Beychevelle (Saint-Julien).
Medium colour, slightly fuller bouquet, more body than the Nenin, but not much charm. 12/20

Cos d'Estournel (Saint-Estèphe).
Weak colour, bouquet rather thin and disappointing. This is slightly better though with more fruit. 12 plus/20

Ducru-Beaucaillou (Saint-Julien).
Medium colour, pleasant bouquet, well-balanced and easily the best so far in this tasting. This must be one of the rare successes in 1968! 14/20

Gruaud-Larose (Saint-Julien).
Good colour and bouquet. Is well-balanced but has a poor finish. 13/20

This is disappointing because when I tasted the 1968's in October 1969, Gruaud-Larose was one of the best. Young wine can be temperamental at times and this may be going through a bad phase.

La Tour-Haut-Brion (Talence, Graves).
A better colour than most, and a big fruity bouquet. This is bigger and more full-bodied than the others so far tasted. 13/20

La Mission Haut Brion (Talence, Graves).
Good colour, an attractive bouquet, has good fruit and body but there is still some acidity to lose. 15/20

Lafite (Pauillac).
Medium colour, a fragrant bouquet, lacks charm and could have more body. 13/20

Cheval Blanc (Saint-Emilion).
Medium colour, a fuller, rounder bouquet, different style, but it was slightly oxidised and although it did not have the green-ness of some of the others, the oxidised taste came through. 11/20
(*N.B.* The label on this particular bottle differs from the normal because it does not bear the words "Premier Grand Cru Classé."

Mouton-Rothschild (Pauillac).
Medium colour, quite a good bouquet, not so big as usual for Mouton and lacks charm. 13 plus/20

Margaux (Margaux).
Rather weak colour, plenty of finesse on the nose, has elegance but less fruit than the Mouton. 13/20

Latour (Pauillac).
Good colour, a full bouquet and for its year is comparatively full-bodied and powerful (I feel it would be invidious for me to put marks against this!)

Haut-Brion (Pessac, Graves).
Good colour, distinguished bouquet, good fruit, well-balanced and good for its vintage. 15/20

As a summer, 1968 was notorious for lack of sunshine, therefore not all the grapes were fully ripe at the time they were picked. The effect of this has been to make many of the 1968's taste rather green and green-ness, which must not be confused with acidity, will never disappear.

(*N.B.* All wine has a certain amount of acid. If too little, it can be flabby and uninspiring, if too much, it tastes rather sharp.)

The growers who had sufficient labour at hand to delay the picking until the last minute, were able to benefit from slightly riper grapes. It must be remembered however, that a moment comes when the sap ceases to rise in the vines and no matter how long the grapes are left unpicked after that time, there can be no further improvement with regard to ripeness.

Also, owing to the excessive rainfall, there was a considerable amount of *pourriture,* or mouldy grapes, from which the merlot vines suffered most of all. Hence, of course, the scarcity of château-bottling in the districts of Saint-Emilion and Pomerol.

This *pourriture* was so universally bad that Henri Woltner told me he had a team of women going through his vines for ten days before the vintage, employed solely on cutting out the rotten bunches. This may account partly for the success of his two 1968's in comparison with some of the others. Under such circumstances the extra cost entailed and a corresponding reduction of his crop was well worth while. Henri was not the only grower who took this precaution for some others acted likewise. Since this elimination of rotten bunches was practised very little just before the vintages of 1963 and 1965, it may turn out that some of the 1968's will age a little more gracefully than did similar wines of 1963 and 1965.

As it is, the 1968's are light wines, both in body and colour and at the moment they are singularly lacking in charm. For all this, I suppose, the person chiefly to blame is the "clerk of the weather." Had the grapes been riper at the time of the vintage, the 1968's would, no doubt have become palatable earlier (as appears to be the case with the 1969's) so it looks as if we may have to wait until 1973 and perhaps even later, before we can begin to appreciate this rather dismal vintage.

I would here like to say how grateful I am to Henri Woltner for arranging this tasting for me, which, if not too agreeable as a task, was immensely instructive. As though to make up for the hardships of the morning he produced two simply fabulous wines for dinner, which incidentally, were the choice of Prue, my wife. Personally, I would never have dared to ask for such a gem as his 1947 La Mission Haut Brion!

Château Ausone 1947 (Saint-Emilion).
Good colour and a heavenly bouquet. Easily the best Ausone I have drunk for many years. Coupled with a delicious sweetness, it has kept very well.

Château La Mission Haut Brion 1947 (Talence, Graves).
Very dark and a splendid rich bouquet. A wine of almost incredible flavour and richness.

1947 coming so soon after 1945, was also hailed as a great vintage, as indeed it turned out for the wines of Saint-Emilion and Pomerol, especially the latter. More often than not, to taste young wine from the cask is a disagreeable exercise, but I remember how attractive the 1947 médocs still in cask tasted in their early days. Apart perhaps, from the 1953's, I cannot remember any vintage to equal them in so far as charm is concerned at that early stage of their career. Although then, the 1947 médocs were delightful when they were young, they did not, for me at any rate, fulfill their early promise and what few first growths I possessed of this vintage, I was able to dispose of many years later at huge and to my mind undeserved prices, at Christie's!

The 1947 Château Cheval Blanc has always been regarded as the outstanding wine of its year, indeed by many has been considered as the outstanding claret of the century. Be that as it may, I am not at all sure that La Mission Haut Brion is not as great, or even greater, having more finesse and polish. Tastes and opinions vary, of course, but if not greater, I would certainly put it in the same class. Alas, few of us still have bottles of either wine in our possession, so comparisons will have to remain academic!

Before I conclude the account of this visit to Henri Woltner, here are the tasting notes on the most recent vintages of his wines (as in October 1971).

La Tour-Haut-Brion 1969.
    Good colour, nice bouquet, has good fruit but still some acidity.

La Mission Haut Brion 1969.
    A good dark colour, a fine bouquet, fuller and rounder than La Tour Haut-Brion and although it also has a trace of acidity it is well balanced.

La Tour-Haut-Brion 1970.
    Very deep colour, a fine full bouquet, a great mouthful of fruit and fine quality. What a difference after the 1969 vintage.

La Mission Haut Brion 1970.
    Colour almost black. Heavenly bouquet, and as good a 1970 as I have so far tasted. Wonderful quality.

We were told that the 1971 has an equally dark colour and at that moment Henri Woltner hoped the quality would be between 1959 and 1961.

Friday, 15th October — Departure!

Cognac

The road northwards from Bordeaux to Angoulême is one of the worst I know, so it was a relief to branch off on to the delightful, even if narrow, country roads which lead to the Cognac district.

Although I have visited this region many times, I have never so far mentioned it in my writings simply because, similar to Scotch whisky, cognac is usually sold as a branded article and thus to me, at any rate, the subject is uninspiring. I suppose one could say more or less the same thing about Champagne, but apart from the excellent standard non-vintage wines, the succeeding vintages give the *grands marques* considerable interest.

Unhappily for the lovers of fine things, one or two of the cognac firms abused the use of vintages, so some years ago a law was passed by the French Government virtually forbidding the mention of a vintage on any bottle. Such legislation is sad indeed, because branded names take all the glamour from cognac. Half of the fun in life lies in the chase of whatever it may be and for me, at any rate, the search for rare old vintage cognac, however difficult the task, continues to provide an excitement and a challenge and at times even produces results which are more than gratifying.

Briefly, cognac is distilled from the produce of white grapes grown in a strictly limited area and the predominant vine planted is called the Saint-Emilion, though this has nothing to do with the red wine from the district of that name near Bordeaux. The wine itself, low in alcoholic strength, is thin, acid and disagreeable to drink and soon after the fermentation has ceased is distilled into alcohol. Everything thereafter is most strictly controlled by the Government. For instance, it is not permitted to move a cask of cognac from one *chai*, or cellar, to another without official approval, and twice a year the stock in each *chai* is carefully checked by Government officials.

In the past, the vine planted was mainly the Folle Blanche, but its use has been almost discontinued owing to its susceptibility to inclement weather. Nowadays, it has been supplanted by the Saint-Emilion, a much sturdier plant, more resistant to the dreaded *pourriture*.

The finest cognac of all is Grande Champagne, but partly because it ages so slowly, is the most expensive. The second, Petite Champagne, which though exceedingly good, is lighter and perhaps a little less distinguished than the Grande Champagne. There are other well-known districts such as the Borderies and Fins Bois and one comes across them from time to time on the lists of the old established English wine merchants such as Berry Brothers, Harvey's and Avery's. So far as I know only a few firms in America like Sherry-Lehmann list fine vintage cognacs, for there, by and large, the branded article holds sway. Thus in general, much of the romance has departed from the sale of this commodity.

Our objective was the home of a very old friend who is both a grower and a distiller, a man who must have some of the finest, if not the finest stock of great cognac in the world. Since he is idle about speaking English and since some twenty-five years ago my French was indifferent to say the least, our friendship grew out of conversations which consisted mostly of smiles and nods. Now, I am thankful to say, both of us have at least made some progress in each other's tongue!

The continuing fine weather of this "sun blessed" autumn enabled us to see the countryside of cognac at its best. The rolling hills and the unspoilt landscape were a relief after the flatness of the Médoc and once again we found ourselves in the midst of the *vendange*.

As one follows the sun, so during these five weeks in France have we followed the vintage, all the way through the Rhône Valley, the Beaujolais, the Côte d'Or, Champagne, Bordeaux and now still it continues in the Cognac district. The harvest for the red wine had finished in the Bordeaux area by 15th October, but in Charente it begins later, so, here we were, once again in the midst of it all. From the visual point of view the vintage in Charente is more picturesque than the other districts we have already visited for apart from the beautiful country all around us, there are still no tractors to be seen, only delightfully nostalgic horses pulling their loads of grapes back to the farms, many of which are very old and of quite romantic appearance. Almost immediately after our arrival, we were taken to one of these farms in the Petite Champagne district, where we watched the progress of the grapes through the press and here, unlike in other wine districts, the stalks and all go into the pressing. In their varied shapes, the copper stills can be unexpectedly attractive. At this particular farm there are two distilling rooms, a modern set where the heating is carried out by gas and, in an adjoining room, there stand the elegant eighteenth century stills, far lovelier in their form and a joy to behold. These ancient stills are only used infrequently, because they are fired by "old fashioned" coal and our guide, the son of our host, told us it had once been part of his job as an apprentice to maintain them for the distilling period and what a dirty job it had turned out to be!

In the nearby *chai* we tasted some of the young entry and here we had a surprise because the owner, a tremendous enthusiast for quality, has retained a few rows of folle blanche vines. We were able therefore to taste the folle blanche 1970 vintage against the Saint Emilion 1970. As he explained, to keep these folle blanche vines is a pure luxury. Both cognacs had a very pale straw colour and each had a young but already developing bouquet. While comparing the 1967 vintage, the colour in each case was already a shade darker and the bouquet more mature and it was evident the distilled spirit was just beginning to cast off some of the brashness of youth. Very young cognac is so potent that it can only be judged by its bouquet and fragrance, but young as it was, the bouquet of the folle blanche seemed to have even more finesse than that of the Saint-Emilion.

As the cabernet sauvingnon is the vine "par excellence" of the Médoc, so is the folle blanche in the Charentais district, that is to say that the distillation of the wine made from this vine has a finesse, an elegance which is difficult to equal. By this, there is no inference that the cognac produced from the Saint-Emilion has no finesse, because that depends greatly upon the soil in which the vine is planted; the quality can indeed be just as good, but the delicacy of the bouquet may be just that little less; it is all really a matter of nuances, such as the difference between Lafite and Pétrus! Nevertheless, one cannot compare the quality of the vines of the Médoc with those of Charente, because with cognac there is the transformation of the product wherein the art of distilling is so skilled that it can make a very considerable difference to the cognac produced.

As with other wine regions, a much reduced crop is expected this year. For instance, whereas six casks of cognac were made from these few rows of folle blanche vines in 1970, only two were expected in 1971. That wretched month, June 1971 has a lot to answer for, the despair of the wine growers all over France was great as during the critical flowering season, they watched the incessant rain and tempestuous weather destroy the prospects of the nascent crop. As those same storms swept over England, in a lesser and more selfish vein, I thought of all the recently hatched partridges and young wild pheasants being drowned, as indeed they were! This year fewer than ever of those succulent partridges will grace our dining tables. Gastronomically, it is not so serious for the pheasants, because it is possible nowadays to rear them artificially, under broody hens or in incubators.

The next stop was a typical Charentais farm of ancient origin in the heart of the Grande Champagne district. Here, in the *chai*, were hundreds and hundreds of casks of the finest Grande Champagne imaginable, all sleeping and maturing slowly through decade after decade and under conditions of almost poetical peace and solitude.

Lying there were all the vintages from the present day, going as far back as half a century. During its lifetime, fine cognac passes through many casks, new oak for the first six months in order to give it a special bouquet and flavour and it is then transferred to older and older casks as it continues to age. In the final stages the casks are of such age that they impart no more bouquet or flavour to the spirit within. It depends, of course, upon the individual characteristics of the cognac in question, but after some fifty or sixty years in wood it has no more to gain, so the time comes to transfer it to large glass demi-johns. Once inside these huge glass jars, the quality and strength remains constant and the loss through evaporation is greatly reduced.

Thus fine cognac can be captured at its peak of perfection, both from the point of view of maturity and of alcoholic strength, the latter being at around 39-40. Being too strong, young cognac has to be broken down with distilled water to make it palatable, but as cognac continues to age in cask, often it will lose strength of its own accord and the ideal moment for bottling comes when, through natural processes, it has lost the required amount and at the same time reached the maximum of maturity.

One cannot say, of course, that the oldest cognacs are necessarily the finest. In this respect they resemble perhaps, the great pre-phylloxera clarets of the nineteenth century; a few are still fantastic, but generally speaking, the others are, shall we say, interesting, but often disappointing. To allow one's mind to wander through even higher flights of fancy, would it not be interesting to have a somewhat similar reference library of some of the great beauties through the centuries, but tastes may have changed and there too, we could be disappointed.

Under the family home which was formerly a monastery, we entered the superb seventeenth-century cellar with its splendid gothic arch and there, in that hushed and monastic atmosphere, we stood and almost worshipped. Here lie the great cognacs, those of the finest quality imaginable and here they spend their last days in wood before the time comes for their transfer to the perpetuity of the glass demi-johns. The brandy we tasted here, or rather sniffed, because that is how you treat fine cognac, was the Grande Champagne vintage 1914 and how utterly delectable it was! It is difficult to believe that in these modern days such a treasure trove, i.e., whole casks of priceless cognac of varying vintages should still exist in their pure and natural state. In the niches on the walls and hanging from the ceiling, are huge cobwebs which are supposed, please don't ask me why, to aid the maturing of ancient cognac.

The last time I entered this cellar, some years ago, I was privileged to taste the Grande Champagne vintage 1906 and a finer cognac I have yet to come across. There is no point in keeping these rarities indefinitely in cask for there is a fear of them becoming woody, so now the 1906 had been transferred, or should I say promoted, to an adjoining cellar which I call the "holy of holies." Before leaving, I whispered an offering of thanks to the god Bacchus for providing us mortals with such unbelievable nectar.

This "holy of holies" is quite a large room fitted with racks which are laden with as much as a hundred demi-johns of what must represent the finest stock of cognac in the world. Some are wicker covered, others with canvas and many suitably encased in the cobwebs of long dead spiders.

All this put me in mind very much of that exciting moment, when in Beaune I first descended into the cellar of the late Dr. Barolet and gazed with awe and rapture upon the countless untouched bins of prewar Burgundy. Never again, I know, will I be blessed with the opportunity of discovering such a collection of fine old burgundy and I also know never again will I have the "entree" to such a fabulous variety of pure unblended vintage cognac. For me, this was indeed another Aladdin's Cave!

My host pointed to a number of old demi-johns which he has known all his life because they belonged to his father before him, the oldest I believe was the vintage of 1832. One could spend hours browsing through this unique library of mostly nineteenth century vintages, for each container has its own particular style and character. Among those we were privileged to sniff was my old friend, the Grande Champagne 1906; I say old friend, because I have been lucky enough to taste it before on a number of occasions—in fact, I was presented with a bottle of this nectar as a wedding present! Two others which bowled me over (not literally) were both of the 1893 vintage, one of them being the same as Sir Winston Churchill used to enjoy after the war.

It was thus on this rather rarified and ethereal plane that our "Vintage Journey" came to its fitting climax.

Thursday, 17th February

Burgundy 1972:

Reluctant sightseer as I am, I seem to have scored a couple of "firsts" today. This, my second journey to Burgundy within three weeks began in London at 5:50 this morning when Julian Cotterell, the managing director of Jackson's Piccadilly, came to collect me in his Bristol. We picked up his friend David Whately and set off for Dover, but because there was no traffic at that early hour in London we discovered we were arriving too early. This gave us an opportunity to see a bit of Canterbury, a town I have hitherto only rushed through on my way to catch a boat. So much of our time do we spend on sightseeing abroad that we are inclined to neglect altogether such delights as the old streets of Canterbury and above all its Abbey. Luckily, as it turned out, we approached the latter the wrong way, i.e., through the precincts of Kings School with its charming old buildings, passing through a cloister looking even more ancient than the Abbey which itself dates back to 1067!

After crossing the Channel, the Bristol took the autoroute in its stride until we turned off towards Compiègne and this is where the second "first" took place. I have childhood memories of Compiègne because my grandmother, although English, was born and brought up nearby. On several occasions since then I have passed through by car but never had I stopped to visit the railway carriage in which the Germans officially surrendered at the end of World War I. This time we did and it was certainly worth while. Apart from the carriage itself there are innumerable photographs of that war, grisly but interesting. It was however a little disconcerting to learn later on that this was only a replica, the original having been destroyed by the Germans in 1940.

Friday, 18th February

We passed the night at Hôtel l'Etoile at Chablis. Many years ago the Etoile had a rosette in the *Guide Michelin* but unfortunately lost it, so we did not expect too much, but as often happens on such occasions, we had the best meal so far, for on the 20 franc menu was a terrine, quenelles de brochet with an excellent sauce and an entrecôte. We tried two half-bottles of Chablis Bougros from the same grower and found the 1966 far superior to the 1967; all the same, the bottling of these wines by a local *négociant* could have been a lot better. These were followed by a local red 1967 Bourgogne Irancy, which, although only *un petit vin* turned out to be well above expectations and certainly much better than the 1966 Château Grand-Corbin-d'Espagne and the 1967 Château Fombrauge we had already tasted on this journey. Neither of these clarets had been château bottled and it seems the bottling of the local French *négociants* is no better than similar bottling in England. After dinner we got into conversation with the patron, who is also the chef, and spent a fascinating fifteen minutes in his spotless kitchen admiring the huge array of shining copper pans and other utensils.

An instructive morning was spent in the cellars of Monsieur Jean Claud Simonet, a noted grower of Chablis. It seems that there have been three good vintages in succession, 1969, 1970 and 1971 and in that order for quality. As emerged from the tasting which followed, the 1970's are very good, if not of quite the same calibre as 1969, but the 1971's were still too undeveloped to appreciate properly. Monsieur Simonet described them as rather big wines, good but not great and, on account of the small crop, they are considerably more expensive than were the 1970's at a similar stage in their career.

Blind Tasting of Four Wines of the 1970 Vintage (Domaine Simonet)

> *Chablis Montmains,* Premier Cru
>> Clean fresh bouquet, good fruit and flavour, very dry, very good.

We had bought this same wine for Robert Jackson's the year before and so promptly ordered some more.

> *Chablis Mont-de-Milieu,* Premier Cru
>> Fresh, fruity bouquet, a little rounder than the Montmain.

> *Chablis Fourchaume,* Premier Cru
>> Delightful bouquet, heaps of fruit, very good flavour.

> *Chablis Montée de Tonnerre,* Premier Cru
>> Unusually fragrant bouquet with a delicious taste to match.

To begin with, I was quite led away by the charm of the Montée de Tonnerre, but finally came back to the basic quality of the Fourchaume. Incidentally, one of the characteristics of La Fourchaume is a tiny hint of fresh mushrooms in the bouquet. Once this had been pointed out, it was more easy to distinguish! The other anecdote, or whatever it is, pertaining to this tasting concerns Mont-de-Milieu whose name derives from the fact that in the Middle Ages the frontier of Champagne and Burgundy ran through this vineyard.

Monsieur Simonet had two vintages of Irancy in his cellar, 1969 and 1970. We tried them both but they were too thin to be appreciated in our northern climate.

The 1971 Vintage

Chablis Montmains, Premier Cru
   Distinguished bouquet, good fruit but a sharper finish.

Chablis Vaillons, Premier Cru
   Pretty bouquet, attractive flavour.

Both Les Clos, Grand Cru and Mont-de-Milieu, Premier Cru of 1971 were still fermenting so we were unable to form any impression. Then followed a quick tour along the steep hillside and through the vineyards of the wines we had been tasting as well as those of Blanchot, Valmur, Vaudesir and Bougros. Great progress has been made since I first used to come here just after World War II. Like some of the vineyards of the Napa Valley in California, Chablis suffers severely from frost. The damp atmosphere rises from the river, it freezes and disaster ensues. In California much of the frost damage is avoided by the water sprinkler system, the water freezes on the vines but by so doing protects them from the worst excesses of the frost. From all appearances, here in the vineyards of Chablis, the calor gas system is used and these rather unromantic white containers dot the hillsides, but provided they keep the frost at bay, appearances are not so important.

If you prowl around the little town, in spite of the devastating enemy bombing during the war, there are still some fascinating old buildings to be seen. One of these sixteenth-century houses, an old monastery, was for sale so David Whately promptly put in a bid for it, having first ascertained that it had an unusually good cellar!

We had fully intended to leave earlier but since it was now lunch time we returned for a light meal at the hotel and how fortunate for us that we did. Having frugality in mind we only ordered one grilled andouillette each but as they were unusually appetising we could not resist a second helping! I have eaten andouillettes in many places and not always liked them, but never have they been so delectable as those made and cooked by Monsieur Bergerand of L'Etoile at Chablis.

With the new autoroute it is now but an hour's run from Chablis down to the Côte d'Or. We called on my old friend Raymond Javillier in Meursault who had rather gloomy news to relate concerning the white wines of 1971, for whereas he usually makes about 120 casks, his production last year was down to 30 and he told us of another grower with an average of 150 casks who had only made seven.

In so far as the red wines of 1970 are concerned Raymond considers those of the Côte de Beaune are on the whole more successful than those of the Côte de Nuits. In 1970 there was considerable over-production on the Côte de Nuits but because of hail and other vicissitudes, on the Côte de Beaune, the excessive production had been limited to a certain extent and therefore the quality was better.

All the same, by careful picking and choosing among the red 1970's there are some good wines to be found and somewhat unexpectedly, in many cases these are more satisfactory than many of the much vaunted 1971's. While I was on the Côte d'Or at the time of the 1971 vintage hopes of great quality were soaring, so much so that people were talking optimistically of the best vintage since 1947 and 1945, although at that time it was realised that much of the crop had been damaged by hailstorms during the late summer, more especially on the Côte de Beaune. However, the weather during July, August and September had been so fabulous that grapes were completely ripe and I learned that there would be no need to chaptalise. Chaptalisation means the addition of sugar to the must in order to bring up the alcoholic strength and to make poor wine more palatable; it is practised frequently in Burgundy and to a certain extent in Bordeaux. For instance, in Bordeaux when the vintages of 1963, 1965 and 1968 were so poor, chaptalisation was essential. Not unnaturally, growers are inclined to be reticent as to the quantity of sugar they add to their wine.

Throughout the winter I had heard reverberations, but it was not until I arrived in Burgundy in February 1972 that I learned that only about 20 per cent of good wine had finally been made; what had not been spoiled by the hail had been ruined by the growers themselves! In this year of all years when there was no need to chaptalise, many of them had done so regardless, with the result that much of the 1971 vintage had volatile acidity. Since a great deal of this wine has already changed hands at higher prices than ever before, one wonders what will happen and who eventually will receive it!

We passed what was left of the afternoon in the cellars of a grower in the Mercurey district, a man who makes his wine in the old fashioned manner, that is to say, he leaves his fermented wine on the skins for a longer period than is usual, the resultant wine being darker and more robust than is now customary.

During our stay on the Côte d'Or we put up at my favourite hotel there, Lameloise at Chagny, upon which I have frequently commented before, but without boring the reader with endless accounts of meals, here are at least two of the specialities of the Lameloise which are really worth trying the next time you go there. Ecrevisses à la nage—these are cooked in a delicious thin soup, really a bouillon; you get into a proper mess tackling this dish, but it is well worth while! Feuilletés de truffles— here is an entire truffle wrapped in bacon and set on a bed of paté-de-foie-gras, the real stuff, not the usual imitation and the whole thing is encased in a lovely light pastry.

Unfortunately, the same praise cannot be given to the wine list which includes a preponderance of *négociants'* wines and too many of the present day anaemic red Burgundies. This is strange, for of all places, you would expect the Lameloise to have an outstanding wine list. In consequence, I usually confine myself to the local Rully for the white wine and Georges Duboeuf's Beaujolais for the red.

Saturday, 19th February

The village of Chassagne-Montrachet lies on the far side of what used to be the main road to Paris and formerly you almost took your life in your hands in attempting to get across to it. One of the leading growers who lives in Chassagne is Monsieur Delagrange-Bachelet whose wine I have been buying for over twenty years. Down below in his cellar, we tasted his 1971 vintage of Chassagne-Montrachet les Caillerets, les Morgeots and his Bâtard-Montrachet. None of them had finished their fermentation, but the underlying quality was unmistakeable.

Madame Delagrange joined us upstairs for a *vin d'honneur* in the form of a bottle of 1969 les Caillerets, the same as Jackson's are selling in London. I had not tasted it for over a year and my goodness, how splendidly this has developed in bottle.

In Raymond Javillier's cellar we tasted three of his 1971's, but they too were still fermenting; the quality though appeared to be good. Already the bouquet of his recently bottled Meursault les Tillets 1970 has developed considerable character. It is round and full-bodied and should be very nice to drink in, say, 1973.

We ended our day on a high note in the village of Puligny-Montrachet where we called on the Domaine Leflaive, for there you find some of the best white Burgundies of all. I always feel secretly rather flattered when I visit this property, for the diminutive *maître de chai*, who makes up for his lack of size by masses of personality, always addresses me as "Monsieur 'Arrie"!

The first two wines were already in bottle and how excellent they were!

> *Bienvenue-Bâtard-Montrachet 1969.*
> A remarkable bouquet, full-bodied, but with such finesse and such freshness withall.
>
> *Bâtard-Montrachet 1969.*
> Superb bouquet, tremendous depth of flavour, fabulous quality.
>
> *Bienvenue-Bâtard-Montrachet 1970* (in wood).
> Splendid bouquet, which of course will develop still further, and a simply delicious taste.
>
> *Bâtard-Montrachet 1970.*
> Lovely bouquet, a heavenly flavour, this will make a great bottle. When one tastes wines of this quality it is hard not to over-do the superlatives.
>
> *Puligny-Montrachet 1971.*
> Still fermenting, but clearly of good quality.
>
> *Puligny-Montrachet, les Pucelles 1971.*
> Also fermenting, but first class.
>
> *Bienvenue-Bâtard-Montrachet 1971.*
> Too much fermentation for comment on this.
>
> *Bâtard-Montrachet 1971.*
> As the fermentation was almost finished one could see this is going to be a great wine.
>
> *Chevalier-Montrachet 1971.*
> Fine bouquet, great finesse and quality.

Where white Burgundy is concerned, or all white wine for that matter, so much depends on its handling and the standard of bottling. Everything is relative, of course, but when I think of the six or seven examples of the 1967 Montrachet which I tasted with the Berkeley Wine & Food Society in California in April 1971 and how disappointing they were (with the exception of the wine from the Domaine de la Romanée-Conti), I cannot help feeling how much better are these great, but less prestigious wines of the Domaine Leflaive.

Monday, 21st February

It was now the turn of the red wines, but on arrival I quickly realised that February 1972 is not the best of moments to be looking for them. Here are but a few of the reasons why the moment was unpropitious:

(a) Like everywhere else, the 1971 crop was lamentably small and had been made even smaller by violent hailstorms late in the summer. Thus the scarcity of the 1971's and their great reputation has sent the price rocketing.

(b) Although 1970 was a prolific vintage for red wine, there was really too much of it, being one of those occasions when the vines overproduced thereby reducing quality. Very careful selection was therefore required and happily one of the better results of this visit was to be able to find some attractive, fairly full-bodied 1970's.

(c) The best of the 1969's have all been sold, a pity because this is a fine vintage.

(d) 1968 was a bad year for red Burgundy.

(e) 1967 was only moderate with regard to quality.

(f) Such as are left of the 1966's are certainly not the best.

All the same and as will be seen, the picture was not too gloomy. In Gevrey-Chambertin, we called on the firm of Thomas-Bassot, a small family business, but one of the few really reliable ones. These are the wines we tasted, all of the 1970 vintage and all, naturally still in cask.

1970 Vintage: red wines in wood

    Savigny-les-Beaune.
        Medium colour, nice nose, on light side, but an agreeable flavour.

    Aloxe-Corton.
        Medium colour, nice nose, attractive flavour, should turn out well.

    Vosne-Romanée.
        Medium colour, good nose, very good flavour, fairly full-bodied.

Chambolle-Musigny.
> Medium colour, attractive bouquet, lovely flavour, the best so far.

Gevrey-Chambertin.
> Medium colour, good fruit and depth, some tannin.

Gevrey-Chambertin 1er cru.
> Medium colour, lovely bouquet, lovely flavour, considerable quality.

Nuits-Saint-Georges les Poulettes 1er cru.
> Medium colour, fine bouquet, delightful flavour.

Clos de la Griotte-Chambertin.
> Splendid colour, wonderful nose, outstanding flavour.

Clos des Ruchottes-Chambertin.
> Good colour, attractive bouquet, full-bodied yet elegant, fine quality.

Tuesday, 22nd February

Travelling with Julian Cotterell adds a new dimension to my continuing vinous search in France, for being managing director of Robert Jackson, that exciting grocer's shop in Piccadilly, London, he has naturally other objectives than solely that of wine. For instance, among the places upon which we called during this visit to the Côte d'Or was a big mustard factory and later on we were to visit an intriguing pottery specialising in kitchen ware.

Among the many things we were looking for was a really good Crème de Cassis (the blackcurrant liqueur) for which the province of Burgundy is so famous. Crème de Cassis forms, of course, the base of the delectable Burgundian aperitif called Kir, or, if you prefer, *Cassis au vin blanc*. Depending naturally upon the size of your glass as well as your personal taste, you put about a dessert spoonful of Crème de Cassis into a fairly large sized wine glass and top it up with a chilled white Burgundy. The traditional wine used for this purpose on the Côte d'Or is an *Aligoté*, but to my mind it is just as pleasant with a Macôn Blanc or something similar. There is cassis and cassis, however, and one of the secrets of the success of your aperitif is the quality of your base; the better the ingredients, the better your pre-prandial drink will be.

This aperitif, incidentally, takes its name from the late Canon Kir, who, for many years, was the mayor of Dijon and the popularity of his favourite drink has spread the world over.

The buying of Crème de Cassis is not so simple as it sounds, because it is a liqueur which has to be made from freshly gathered blackcurrants and, in spite of its alcoholic strength, from 16 to 20 per cent, it is better if consumed within a year of production. It is not a good thing, for example, to leave your bottle half empty for too long as after a month or so, it tends to become oxidised, all the more excuse then to pour yourselves an extra Kir! Cassis can also be mixed agreeably with vermouth etc., and is especially good when poured over a vanilla icecream or added to a blackcurrant sorbet. In a number of restaurants in Burgundy where blackcurrant ices are very popular, they are served together with a miniature bottle of cassis and the result is simply delicious. Another version of an aperitif made with cassis is what in the Beaujolais is known as a *Tassée;* this consists of a very little cassis with an equal quantity of Liqueur de Framboise (raspberry) topped up with red Beaujolais.

It was this matter then which led us to a family business in Nuits-Saint-Georges called Vedrenne Pere et Fils, who, we had been informed, make a Supercassis. To our surprise, we found there a whole gamut of liqueurs and syrups which are made on the premises and there are also stills for the production of marc de Bourgogne and other items. It was interesting to learn that after the original stock of cassis is made from the freshly picked blackcurrants, the rest of the fruit is preserved in alcohol in huge containers for production during the remainder of the year, the emphasis being that cassis is always freshly made. There are various qualities from 16 to 20 per cent, but the fact is that the better your cassis, the better your Kir. Among the other liqueurs made by this family are Kirsch, Fraise, Framboise and Prunelle de Bourgogne. The latter is made from the kernels of wild plums. We were persuaded, not unwillingly, to taste the whole range of these liqueurs and believe me, even after spitting it all out after each sip, we were in high spirits by the time we departed.

Wednesday, 23rd February

At Romanèche-Thorins in the heart of the Beaujolais, we passed an instructive morning tasting "the young entry," a whole selection of the 1971 vintage and some of these 1971's are exceedingly good. Many firms have their "stock blends" covering the range through Beaujolais, Beaujolais-Villages, Fleurie and so on and that's that, but what is so much more interesting here with Georges Duboeuf is that his wines are all individual and unblended, thus you have the opportunity to make your choice between half-a-dozen different Fleuries, an equal number of different Morgons and so on, all from individual growers, most of which, more often than not, have won first or second prizes. Blends are for mass sales, but however good they may be, they lack that extra interest for the true Beaujolais enthusiast.

We found that many of these 1971's were already in bottle and most of those which were not would be bottled by the end of April. One of the reasons why Beaujolais, so called, is such indifferent stuff on the English market is because in order to save expense, it is shipped over in bulk under the Appellation of Bourgogne Rouge, a name which certainly does not guarantee it to be Beaujolais, and secondly, it is usually shipped nearly a year after the vintage, thereby losing one of its primary charms (providing it is genuine Beaujolais) its freshness.

The "Insight" column of the London *Sunday Times* has recently exposed the sale of so-called Beaujolais by two of the best known distributors of wine in London, and they finally had to admit it was not the genuine article at all! Whatever other effects it may have, the English entry to the Common Market will put a stop once and for all to such malpractices. It has been all too easy in the past to print labels, a practice very much to the disadvantage of the serious merchants who sell the genuine wine.

Thursday, 24th February

It took us about two hours' driving through lovely country to reach the pottery whence Julian purchases some of his supplies for the shop. It was the first time I had ever been taken over an important establishment of this calibre; one could see every kind of vessel in all stages of preparation. Lunching later with the owners in their home, we were given some really fine home-made *paté de foie gras*, which reminds me that next February we have plans to search for the best makers of this luxury not only in and around Strasbourg in Alsace, but also in the Dordogne Valley and Les Landes near Bordeaux. Many authorities on the subject will tell you that the pâté from Les Landes is the best of all.

Whilst on this diverting subject of gastronomy, I had always wanted to eat a meat at Paul Bocuse near Lyon, but somehow have never had the opportunity. This restaurant, together with Troisgros at Roanne and the Auberge de Lill at Illhaeusern, is considered by many to be one of the finest restaurants in France and that, of course, means the world. It was therefore with alacrity that we accepted Georges Duboeuf's invitation to dine there. By this time, Julian's enchanting wife, Harriet, had arrived and she and I at least, guzzled the superb fresh *pâté de foie gras* followed by small lobsters (à la nage) served in their bouillon. It is all too seldom that I, at any rate, ever see *pâté de foie gras* in London, so as may be seen, no opportunities are allowed to slip by when I am abroad.

On arrival, we were welcomed by Paul Bocuse himself and he promptly ordered for us one of his house aperitifs, which is a glass of champagne to which has been added a teaspoonful of Liqueur de Framboise. Provided your champagne nose is not tilted too high in the air, this is a drink which is well worth trying!

Bordeaux, 1972: First Impressions of the 1971's
Tuesday, 21st March

As instructed, I arrived at the Kensington Air Terminal at 8 o'clock only to find that the Travel Agent had not taken into account the recent change from winter to summer time—how welcome that extra hour in bed would have been! Due to a schedule mix-up, instead of arriving in Bordeaux at 11:30 A.M. it was near 4 o'clock when eventually I got there. Knowing what was in store for me, I had made no plans for the evening, but I could not resist going to the Auberge Basque alongside the market to enjoy some of my favourite sea food. The huge platter of every kind of shellfish was as good as ever and this was followed by one of the best red mullet I have ever eaten. Gastronomically, one's first day in France is always the best!

Wednesday, 22nd March

At the offices of Duclot in the rue Constantin, Patrick Danglade and Jean-Francois Moueix had arranged a tasting which was altogether too much for one morning so we divided it into two sessions. A comparative tasting, blind, of course, of some of the 1967's in the morning and then in the late afternoon what was, for me, to be my first look at the much discussed 1971's; much discussed of course, on account of their ridiculously high price.

1967 Vintage

Pavie (Saint-Emilion).
Good colour, a pleasing bouquet, has good fruit and is rather nice, still a little severe, but is mellowing. 13/20

Brane-Cantenac (Margaux).
Dark colour, a full fragrant bouquet, a lovely flavour and quite a mouthful of wine. Still some tannin. 15/20

Beychevelle (Saint Julien).
Good dark colour, attractive bouquet, full, round and complete. 17/20

Figeac (Saint Emilion).
Medium colour, nice nose, not a big wine but quite good nevertheless. 15/20

Vieux Ch. Certan (Pomerol).
Good colour, delightful bouquet, plenty of fruit and flavour. Very good quality. 14-15/20

Calon-Ségur (Saint Estèphe).
Good colour and a nice full bouquet, considerable fruit and quality. 17/20

Rauzan-Ségla (Margaux).
Medium colour, attractive bouquet, a big wine with a special flavour, rather backward. 12/20

According to the average placing of the three of us, they came in this order, Calon-Ségur, Beychevelle, Figeac, Vieux Ch. Certan, Brane-Cantenac, Pavie and Rauzan-Ségla. I suppose it is as the wines are tasting or even how one is tasting oneself on a particular day, but usually I find I place Brane-Cantenac 1967 higher up the list.

The Great Wines of 1967

Mouton-Rothschild.
Good colour, lovely bouquet, beautifully balanced, supple,

charming and complete, may be ready comparatively early. 17/20

Margaux.
Good dark colour, bouquet sweet and delightful, a fine big wine. Margaux came out very well in this tasting. 18/20

Latour.
Very dark colour, powerful bouquet, very full-bodied, great flavour but backward. 17 plus /20

Cheval Blanc.
Very good colour, fine bouquet which I mistook for Haut-Brion (how wrong can one be!) well-made, good fruit and some tannin. This should be both delightful and easy to drink. 17/20

Haut-Brion.
Dark colour, full bouquet, both rich and strong of flavour, fine quality but still backward. 17/20

Ausone.
Medium colour but such a pretty bouquet, lighter of body than the others but nevertheless most elegant. 15/20

Pétrus.
Dark colour, a huge powerful bouquet and a great big full-flavoured wine as well, really fine quality. 19/20

It is a pity that Lafite was not present but this, for what it is worth, is the order in which we placed them: Pétrus, Margaux, Latour, Mouton, Haut-Brion and Cheval Blanc level, and then Ausone.

The late afternoon session, the 1971's, began with some of the wines from the Fronsadais, a district which, in these days of vastly increasing prices, assumes greater and greater importance to myself and my personal friends.

1971 Vintage

De Carles.
Unusually dark colour, very good nose and is rich, round and complete. 16/20

La Dauphine.
Dark colour, good bouquet, a fine rich, full-bodied wine.

Though still fermenting a little, it was easy to discern the underlying quality. 18/20

Canon-de-Brem.
Lovely colour, splendid bouquet, full of fruit and flavour, fine quality. 19/20

Little did I imagine that these 1971 wines from the Côtes-Canon-Fronsac would be so good. Since 1970 was about the best vintage for this district for the past twenty years I had expected to find the 1971's on a lower plane. Perhaps they are in fact, I don't know, but I could not help being impressed by these three.

A few 1971's from the Médoc

Gloria.
Full bouquet and heaps of fruit, charming. 16 plus/20

La Tour-de-Mons.
Good colour and bouquet, has fruit but is still very closed up. 12/20

Boyd-Cantenac.
Medium colour, quite a nice bouquet, heaps of flavour. 14/20

Beychevelle.
Good colour, pleasant bouquet, lots of fruit and some tannin to lose. 16/20

Haut-Batailley.
Good colour, bouquet not yet developed but full and round, very good. 17 plus/20

La Lagune.
Good colour, attractive nose, round and delightful. 17/20

Pichon-Longueville-Baron.
Good colour and bouquet, not properly developed yet, could have more charm. 16/20

Lanessan.
Very good bouquet, fine quality, both rich and round. 18/20

Phélan-Ségur.
Nice bouquet, good quality. 15/20

I was not the only one to pick out the Lanessan as the best in this tasting. There is no doubt that from time to time, at blind tastings, the *crus bourgeois* can emerge with flying colours.

On account of the absurdly high prices, quite involuntarily, I have been rather prejudiced against these 1971's, but have found myself quite agreeably surprised. The colour of those I have tasted today has been darker than I had expected and the quality much better. Naturally, it is too early to say much now only a few months after the vintage, but they have considerable quality and though naturally not so great as the 1970's, they look as though many of them will turn out rather well.

Thursday, 23rd March

Jean-Francois Moueix drove me to his father's offices in Libourne and there I met Jean-Pierre Moueix, his second son Christian and his nephew Jean-Jacques. Since there was so much to be done in all too short a time, we went straight into the tasting room and there I found a mighty tasting prepared for me.

While I was in Bordeaux during the time of the 1971 vintage I had somehow imagined that it would be a better vintage for the wines of the Médoc than those of Saint Emilion and Pomerol, but when I saw the dark colour of the first batch of wines for tasting, I realised I might have to change my mind.

1971 Vintage: Saint-Emilion

Pavie.
A nice deep colour, good bouquet, body and flavour. This should make an excellent bottle. 16/20

Clos Fourtet.
Good colour and bouquet, but has less charm, in fact is a little thin in comparison with the others. 14/20

Magdelaine.
Medium colour, good bouquet with plenty of fruit and flavour. 15/20

La Gaffelière.
Dark colour, a fine bouquet and though still fermenting a

little, is round and full-bodied. Once again La Gaffelière has made a very good wine. 17/20

It is too early, of course, to make an accurate assessment of the wines of this vintage, but this for the moment is the order in which I placed them: La Gaffelière, Pavie, Magdelaine and Clos Fourtet. I have a feeling that the Magdelaine may present itself better later on in the year and I hope that the same applies to Clos Fourtet. After going through a disappointing period for a number of years Clos Fourtet blossomed out beautifully in 1970.

1971 Vintage: Pomerol

Lafleur.
Very good colour, a nice fruity bouquet, has medium body, some tannin and a lovely flavour. 15/20
This may not appear a very high rating, but on this occasion, in spite of its high quality, leeway has to be left to include the great wines of Pétrus and Cheval Blanc.

La Fleur-Pétrus.
Dark colour, fragrant bouquet, round with a delightful taste, has just a little more depth than Lafleur. 16/20

La Conseillante.
Very good colour, fine bouquet, is full of fruit and has a most delicious taste. 16/20

Vieux Ch. Certan.
Very dark colour, full bouquet, good fruit with more depth than La Conseillante. 17/20

Latour-Pomerol.
Very good colour, pleasing bouquet, good fruit but mellow and easy to taste. 17/20

Trotanoy.
Very dark colour, deep bouquet, a huge round wine which should make a splendid bottle. 17-18/20

If it were not for the outstanding 1970's which we were to taste virtually alongside, I would be writing even more enthusiastically about these wines. Some of them are indeed first rate although when compared with the great 1970's, they appear to have just a little less charm and depth.

The Great Wines of 1971

Ausone
Very dark colour, unusually dark for Ch. Ausone. A big rich bouquet and a great powerful wine. 1971 appears to be a fine vintage for Ausone and how comforting it is to be able to write enthusiastically about it once more after all these years. 18/20

Cheval-Blanc
Dark colour, very good bouquet, rich, round, full-bodied and delightful. 19/20

Pétrus
Very dark colour, considerable finesse of bouquet, has lots of fruit and depth combined with charm. 18 plus/20

In past vintages, to sort out the three great wines at a blind tasting at this particular stage in their career has been comparatively simple, but today, for the first time it was more difficult. Usually and not only on account of its lighter colour, it has been fairly easy to pick out Ausone immediately but to complicate matters on this occasion, the Ausone was just as dark as the others! It was also difficult to decide between the Cheval-Blanc and Pétrus, but finally I placed them in this order, Cheval-Blanc, Pétrus and Ausone. These are early days, of course, for the 1971 vintage and there may be slight changes in, say, six months' time, but whatever happens it is splendid to know that Ausone is back again where it should be, in the top league.

Before leaving the 1971's we tried two other variations, we tasted blind a Gaffelière versus Cheval Blanc and Ausone, and Trotanoy (always one of my favourites) against Pétrus. The Gaffelière has undoubtedly splendid quality, but by comparison with the others, it lacks that extra weight. The Ausone though with far more power and depth than La Gaffelière and of excellent quality and substance, was again beaten by the Cheval-Blanc, but then what an opponent to be up against! The Trotanoy with its lovely nose, its richness of flavour and undoubted quality gave the Pétrus a good run for its money, but finally the extra depth and quality of the latter turned the scales.

The 1970 Saint-Emilions and Pomerols

It was an unexpected pleasure to be able to taste all these wonderful wines again after a lapse of some nine months. They are much more mature now than when I tasted them in June 1971 and in every case have borne out their promise of almost a year ago. In spite of the soaring price of the 1970 vintage, lovers of fine, full-bodied claret will come to no harm by buying a case or so of some of these outstanding Saint-Emilions and Pomerols.

Referring to my notes on these wines which appeared in the 1972 Springtime issue of *Wine Magazine*, I see that I have switched the order of La Gaffelière and Magdelaine, putting this time the latter in the lead; among the Pomerols, the Latour-Pomerol and La Fleur-Pétrus have changed places, but only just!

1970 Vintage: Saint-Emilion

Pavie.
A fine dark colour and an attractive bouquet. A lovely full-bodied wine. This is showing very much better now than some nine months ago. 16/20

Magdelaine.
Very dark colour, lovely bouquet, a big round wine which will make a splendid bottle. 18 plus/20

Figeac.
A fabulous colour, a great rich bouquet. Not quite so big as the Magdelaine but here is another which is showing so much better than in June last year. 16 plus/20

La Gaffelière.
Very dark colour, fine bouquet and of great quality. This too should make a great bottle. 18/20

1970 Vintage: Pomerol

Lafleur.
Very dark colour, almost black, a lovely bouquet, it has heaps of fruit but is still suffering a little from 'growing

pains.' This should be tasted again in a few months' time. 15/20

La Fleur-Pétrus.
Colour almost black, splendid bouquet, full-bodied, full flavoured with a delightful taste. 18 plus/20

La Conseillante.
Colour almost black and a terrific bouquet, good fruit but this too needs time. 17/20

Vieux Ch. Certan.
Very dark colour, fine bouquet, well-made, well-balanced, considerable tannin. 18/20

Latour-Pomerol.
Black colour, very deep bouquet, full, round and a heavenly flavour, a great wine. 19/20

Trotanoy.
A fabulous colour and a fabulous nose, with taste and quality to match. A masterpiece. 19 plus/20

Still, it appears that the pomerols of 1970 are greater than the Saint-Emilions, even so I would be thankful to settle for some of the latter. Those collectors who have managed to buy some of the Latour-Pomerol and the Trotanoy are both wise and fortunate.

Ending on a simply tremendous note, here are the tasting notes on the Grands Seigneurs of 1970.

Ausone.
Fine dark colour, a good nose but seems a little drier than the others and is not quite in the same class.

Cheval Blanc.
A lovely dark colour and an equally lovely bouquet, this has more weight and quality than the Ausone.

Pétrus.
Very dark colour, a superb bouquet, enormous depth of flavour and really fabulous quality.

There was little dispute over the order—Pétrus, Cheval Blanc and Ausone.

Friday, 24th March

A further tasting of the 1971 vintage, this time with Emile Casteja, the head of the firm of Borie-Manoux situated in the Cours Balguerie-Stuttenberg. This confirmed once again the quality of the vintage.

1971 Vintage

>*Château Baret* (Graves).
>Medium colour, pleasant bouquet, good fruit.
>
>*Château Batailley* (Pauillac).
>Very dark colour, a fine bouquet, heaps of fruit and flavour, this will make a good bottle.
>
>*Château Beau-Site* (Saint-Estèphe).
>Unusually dark colour, a big, fruity bouquet, full-bodied and powerful, this too will make a good bottle.
>
>*Chapelle, de la Trinite* (Saint-Emilion).
>Medium colour, attractive bouquet, round and full-bodied.
>
>*Château Beau Rivage* (Bordeaux Superieur).
>Very dark colour, plenty of bouquet, good fruit.
>
>*Domaine de l'Eglise* (Pomerol).
>Good colour, fine bouquet, heaps of fruit, a lovely mouthful of wine, will make a good bottle.
>
>*Château Trottevieille* (Saint-Emilion).
>Medium colour, lovely bouquet, supple, charming and well made.

Saturday, 25th March

Spending the weekend at Latour, I found the vines a good week behind in their development. It is to be hoped they will catch up and produce an abundant crop for that is what is so badly needed in Bordeaux. At the moment, world demand seems to have outstripped production.

As usual at these weekends, I seize the opportunity to taste the young wine and here are my notes on the two last vintages.

Les Forts de Latour 1971.
Good colour, full, very fruity bouquet, still very young, but lots of fruit and plenty of body.

Château Latour 1971.
A good dark colour, a depth of bouquet showing finesse and breeding, a fine big wine with heaps of fruit. Of far finer quality than I had dared to hope.

Les Forts de Latour 1970.
Very dark colour, a lovely scented bouquet, very good fruit, medium to full-bodied.

Château Latour 1970.
Exceedingly dark colour, splendid bouquet, a powerful full-bodied wine. Still very backward but will make a great bottle.

The highlight of the weekend though was the tasting of the 1966 and 1967 vintages which had been arranged by our manager, Monsieur Jean-Paul Gardère, in order to see how our Les Forts de Latour compared in those vintages with the other *crus classés*. Since I have written an article about this tasting, one which, by now, will presumably have appeared in the American Magazine, *Wine World,* it may be easier for all concerned, if I include it here.

Les Forts de Latour

The purchase of Château Latour took place late in 1962, but the grapes of that crop were picked and the wine made under the supervision of the former manager, Monsieur Brugère, who had been responsible for the vineyard for over forty years but who, being then over eighty years of age, was about to relinquish his duties. The two brilliant managers who took his place in the direction of the vineyard were Henri Martin and Jean-Paul Gardère.

Henri Martin is, of course, none other than the owner of Château Gloria (Saint-Julien) which entirely through his own efforts, has had such a resounding success over the past decade, so much so that his wine, a *cru bourgeois*, now commands a higher price than many of its peers among the *crus classés,* second growths included.

Jean-Paul Gardère, likewise a friend for well over twenty years, is a Médocain wine broker of great distinction and it is thanks to the unremitting efforts of these two unusually able and energetic men that

Les Forts de Latour

Château Latour continues to progress from strength to strength. It gives me considerable personal satisfaction that in a way, I was instrumental in these two outstanding men assuming the direction of the property.

Their competence was quickly challenged, because they had the misfortune to commence with a really bad vintage, namely 1963. In a way though, this proved to their advantage and also to the château for it is now generally accepted that under the worst conditions possible when, in fact, some of the other châteaux did not declare a vintage, they produced what is recognised to be easily the best 1963 and one which, although it may not have a very long life ahead of it, is drinking remarkably well at the moment. In this manner quickly they established their reputation.

At the château, there are two large framed maps of the vineyard, the earlier one being dated 1822 and the more modern, 1898. From these it is clearly discernable that two outlying pieces of the original vineyard namely, La Pinada and the Petit Batailley, both situated between the vines of Pichon-Longueville-Lalande and Batailley had been allowed to run wild. In 1963, one of the first objectives of the new management was to uproot the scrub and the gorse bushes and prepare the ground for the re-plantation of vines. Since these two pieces of land lie some two miles away from the main vineyard one can perhaps understand their abandonment to nature for in the days before motor transport, the distance involved must have been a consideration. At the time of writing, the vines of La Pinada and Petit Batailley are some eight years old and henceforth every year their produce will become better and better.

Also from the maps it was discovered that through the years "the mice" had been nibbling away at the western edge of the main vineyard, the part close to the main road leading from Bordeaux to Pauillac and it was resolved as far as possible to re-purchase these small strips of land. No doubt that from time to time they may have been given to former life-long employees in lieu of a pension. As these small pieces of land were slowly re-purchased, it was exciting to discover from their title deeds that some of them bore the name of Les Forts de Latour.

The name for the second wine was at hand and almost heaven sent, Les Forts de Latour, for during the Middle Ages and during the English occupation of Guyenne, an English fortress is reputed to have stood on the site of the present winery. At the time of the English defeat and withdrawal, this stronghold was captured by the brilliant French commander de Guesclin who promptly razed it to the ground. It is also reputed that the tower which is the emblem of the vineyard was built from the stones of the ancient fortress and from this, of course, comes the name, Château Latour. There are no actual records of this because the great vineyards of the Médoc were not planted out until the middle of the seventeenth century.

It has long been the policy of some of the leading châteaux to have a second wine sold under a separate label, because in every vineyard, whether it be great or small, there is always a certain proportion of wine made from the young vines. In France it is permitted to sell wine with Appellation Contrôlée once the vines have attained four years of age, but in the early years the produce from these young vines is not nearly so good as that from older ones. It is only from eight to ten years of age that they really begin to show their true potential. For many years now there has not been a second wine at Latour so it was decided to launch one in order to incorporate the produce of the young vines from the main vineyard and when those vines were old enough, also from the grapes of La Pinada and Petit-Batailley. This had the added advantage of ensuring that henceforth only the very finest *cuves* would go into the *grand vin*.

Since the quality from the lesser *cuves* of 1966 was so good, this appeared to be a good moment to start bottling the second wine and from that time onwards there has been a bottling of Les Forts de Latour as well as the *grand vin*. The problem then arose as to when Les Forts de Latour should be placed on the market and because this would be an entirely new wine it was decided to give it a year or so of bottle age before so doing. There was a further consideration, the fact that the wine having some maturity, would enable us to compare it with regard to quality with others of similar vintages. The quantity available of the 1966 vintage being somewhat limited, it was also agreed to offer the 1967 at the same time. Having resisted a certain amount of pressure to produce them earlier, it was finally decided to offer these two vintages to the trade during the course of 1972, but first it was deemed necessary to hold a blind tasting with the aid of a panel of competent authorities to see how Les Forts de Latour of 1966 and 1967 would compare with some of the well-known châteaux of the same years.

This tasting was duly arranged on Saturday, March 25th, 1972 in the Salle de Reception at Latour. Amongst the tasting panel were Jean-Eugène Borie, the owner of Ducru-Beaucaillou and a number of wine brokers from the Médoc. All that we knew of the twenty-eight anonymous bottles was that Nos. 1 to 14 were the 1967 vintage and Nos. 15 to 28 the 1966's, and that somewhere in each group was included a bottle of Les Forts de Latour. The marking was 20/20 for colour, 20/20 for bouquet and 20/20 for flavour, totalling a possible 60/60. For what they are worth, the points shown below are my own.

Vintage 1967

Wine	Characteristics	My Placing	Score	Group Placing
La Lagune	Good colour, agreeable bouquet, attractive flavour, good quality	9	45/60	5
Ducru-Beaucaillou	Good colour, nice scented nose, heaps of fruit, fine quality	7	47/60	4
Léoville-Las-cases	Medium colour, nice nose, full of fruit and well-made	10	45/60	12
Les Forts de Latour	Good colour, finesse on nose, very good flavour	3	50 plus/60	1
Pichon-Longueville-Baron	Medium colour, pretty bouquet but excessive acidity	14	42/60	14
Gloria	Good colour, bouquet not giving much, still rather hard	13	44/60	9
Beychevelle	Good colour, plenty of bouquet, good fruit	12	44/60	3
Pichon Longueville-Lalande	Good colour, pretty bouquet, elegant and attractive	8	47/60	6
Montrose	Good colour, big, full but rather hard bouquet, a very big wine, still has considerable tannin	4	49/60	8
Grand-Puy-Lacoste	Good colour, elegant bouquet, good fruit, but lacks charm	11	45/60	13
Léoville-Poyferré	Good colour and bouquet, well made with quality	5	49/60	10
Lynch-Bages	Good colour, delightful bouquet, good flavour	6	48/60	11
Calon-Ségur	Good colour, deep concentrated bouquet, powerful with considerable fruit	1	54/60	7
Brane-Cantenac	Very good colour, lovely bouquet, reminiscent of cedar, very well made	2	51/60	2

Vintage 1966

Wine	Characteristics	My Placing	Score	Group Placing
Calon-Ségur	Pale to medium colour, pretty bouquet, on light side but will be easy and agreeable to drink	14	41/60	13
Léoville-Las-cases	Medium colour, fair bouquet, good fruit and body but seems a little coarse	13	44/60	12
Pichon-Longueville-Lalande	Good colour, fruity bouquet, good fruit but a trace of acidity to lose	12	46/60	5
Gloria	Very good colour and bouquet, attractive flavour	8	49/60	2
Brane-Cantenac	Medium colour, good bouquet, well-made but still rather hard	Equal 10	47/60	6
Les Forts de Latour	Very dark colour, rich bouquet with great finesse, very good flavor	6	51/60	4
La Lagune	Very good colour, full bouquet, but lacks some charm, still plenty of tannin	9	48/60	Equal 7
Pichon-Longueville-Baron	Very good colour, bouquet average, but has good fruit	Equal 10	47/60	11
Montrose	Very good colour, plenty of bouquet, good fruit and flavour	8	47/60	13
Lynch-Bages	Good dark colour, lovely rich bouquet, a big powerful wine	2	53/60	2
Ducru-Beaucaillou	Good dark colour, big full bouquet, lovely taste, good quality	3	52/60	Equal 7
Léoville-Poyferré	Dark colour, good bouquet, fine quality	5	52/60	Equal 9
Beychevelle	Dark colour, lovely cedar bouquet, fine deep wine, still some tannin	1	55/60	1
Grand-Puy-Lacoste	Good colour, nice fragrant bouquet, heaps of fruit and a very good flavour	4	52/60	Equal 7

Not unlike the cook who tastes the soup with her spoon, over the past five years I must have tasted Les Forts a number of times, yet I did not pick it out in either of these groups! As may be seen this test was somewhat severe and it was with delight (I refuse to say surprise) that I found it emerging with such success.

Naturally in the future there will be good vintages and bad but that is something from which we all have to suffer. One thing is certain, however, as the vines of the two outlying vineyards grow older the quality is bound to improve. It would seem that Les Forts de Latour has got off to a good start.

With John Movius of the Los Angeles Chapter of the Wine and Food Society.

H. Brand Cooper, Alden G. Pearce, Robert Anstead, and myself in the kitchen of the Bel Air Country Club.

After the Petit Sirah tasting, Oakland, California, May 1972.

Autographing after a lecture in Daneville, California.

The arrival of the vintage.

Château La Mission-Haut-Brion.

The grape.

The chai.

The tasting table.

Polite spitting!

Tasting the 1970 vintage with Henri Woltner.

With Dr. Otto Loeb the great authority on wines of the Moselle.

Tasting the 1968 clarets with my wife.

View from Château Ausone.

*Visit to America and Canada, 1972*

● CALISTOGA
● Sterling Vineyards
● Hanns Kornell
Schramsberg ●
● Old Souverain Cellars
Stony Hill Winery ●
N
Freemark Abbey ●
NAPA VALLEY
Christian Bros. Cellars ●
● Charles Krug
Beringer ●
● Joseph Heitz
ST. HELENA ●
Sutter Home ●
● Louis Martini
● Beaulieu Vineyard
● RUTHERFORD
Inglenook ●
Robert Mondavi ●
● OAKVILLE

Friday, 30th March

California, 1972

Greeted by a superb morning, our hosts, Dr. and Mrs. Bernard H. Rhodes, drove us through the Napa Valley to Willows Ranch, Tehama County, where Fred and Diana Holmes had arranged a picnic. They have over 15,000 acres of lovely rolling country where they raise cattle and sheep and it makes our farms in England appear minute by comparison. Delightful as the picnic was the situation appeared grim, for there had been no rain for over three months and during what should ostensibly be the rainy season. It is said to be the worst drought since 1870! The grass, which at this season should be luxurious, was not even ankle high.

The Rhodes' spend every Easter with Tom and Martha May at their enchanting home at Martha's Vineyard, Oakville in the Napa Valley and once again Prue (my wife) and I had been included in this by no means ordinary invitation. There are many lovely homes in this beautiful valley, but this large and comfortable house was built for the May's to gain the maximum from the heavenly surroundings. The scenery is splendid in Alsace and also in my beloved Beaujolais country for there the charm of the ancient towns and villages also have so much to offer, but for sheer beauty the views in every direction in the Napa Valley are, to my mind, unsurpassed, many of them being simply breathtaking.

Close to the wooded hills on the west side of this valley the house is situated atop a small hill immediately overlooking Martha's Vineyard, a source of delight I have often mentioned before. Martha's Vineyard was originally planted out by Barney and Belle Rhodes and the cabernet sauvignon vines produce a wine whose quality in relation to others of the Napa Valley must surely correspond to a first growth claret. At vintage time all the grapes are sold to Joe Heitz who handles the vinification and after-care of this wine with enormous skill.

That evening there was a dinner party at which we met once again Fred and Eleanor McCrea of Stony Hill Vineyard, Louis and Elizabeth Martini of the noted Louis M. Martini, Captain and Mrs. Wendell Mackie, also wine producers. Staying here in the Napa Valley is not unlike being in Bordeaux or Burgundy, for practically everyone you meet is connected with wine.

On the Saturday evening we went to a square dance at the Lodi Farm Centre. The occasion was organized by Bob and Marge Mondavi and was a huge success. This is a square dance club which meets once a month for this purpose and as complete novices, Prue and I feared we might disgrace ourselves, but as it turned out we found many of the others present knew almost as little about the steps as we did. There was always someone to put one straight and I had never before realised what fun it could be.

On the morning of Easter Sunday the traditional egg hunt took place at Martha's Vineyard, dozens of coloured ones for the children and each grown-up had to look for his or her own. These eggs are blown and most skillfully painted by our hostess with scenes appertaining to the individual guest. If someone has moved into a new house, this is illustrated; for a sailing man there might be a yacht and for Dr. Adamson, a psychologist, his egg this year was decorated as a human head showing all the sections: wit, intelligence and so on. My own, designed by Tom May depicted a map of the world showing our route across the United States to the Napa Valley and marked Easter 1970, 1971 and 1972 to commemorate my three visits. Prue's was equally clever, utilising the attractive design for the jacket of my next book.

Monday, 3rd April

Together with the Rhodes' we moved down the hill the next day to the house of Fred and Diana Holmes who were on their way across the Pacific to Australia. As the Rhodes *had to* spend the day in Oakland, Prue and I sat in the garden by the swimming pool. It was as well we took advantage of the sunshine because the weather was about to break.

Mayacamas

Prue and I began our vinous explorations of 1972 on a high note, for on Good Friday Barney drove us up to Mayacamas to see Bob and Nonie Travers. It is quite a long ride up into the hills and the way somewhat difficult to find. This lovely mountain vineyard has already been described in *The Pick of the Bunch* but on arrival up there one never ceases to be staggered by the wonderful views in every direction.

This delightful young couple, Bob and Nonie, bought Mayacamas in 1968 after searching for a suitable property for over two years, but the time was not wasted because meantime Bob learned the art of making wine from no less a master than Joe Heitz. Having commenced his career in business and although successful, he soon realized it was not his metier and so turned his thoughts to becoming a wine grower. Now with Nonie at his side and two small children he appears to have attained his ideal in life. He still has to buy grapes from other growers to make his wine, but on each occasion you visit Mayacamas you see four or five more acres of land grubbed up and turned into vines. When you have only a minimal staff it is a slow business to create a vineyard, but these two young people have all the time in the world before them.

The winery, built in 1889, is an ideal place for the ornithologist, for all manner of birds inhabit the trees outside the entrance; it is a joy to see the crested bluejays darting from tree to tree and we were able to watch as well as listen to a woodpecker at work.

Chenin Blanc 1971

This is Bob's last vintage of Chenin Blanc, for henceforth he has decided to concentrate mainly on Cabernet Sauvignon and Chardonnay. In view of the quality of this particular wine it may seem a pity but I feel sure he is making the right move. It has a pretty, very fresh bouquet and a good full fruity flavour.

Chardonnay 1971

Attractive full bouquet, a big wine with plenty of fruit. This should turn out well.

Merlot 1971

The grapes for this had come from Barney Rhodes' vineyard situated in Zinfandel Lane in the Napa Valley. Good colour, powerful bouquet, very fruity flavour. A certain proportion of this will be blended into the Cabernet Sauvignon.

Cabernet Sauvignon 1971

Being young the bouquet has not yet developed, but it has a good depth of flavour.

At lunch with globe artichokes stuffed with shrimps remoulade, we drank the 1970 Chardonnay which though still young was most interesting and has a good flavour. With our cheese we tried first of all Bob's 1967 Cabernet Sauvignon—a deep colour, not a big wine but it has an attractive taste. Finally, the wine, which has already caused such a stir, his 1968 Zinfandel with an alcoholic strength of 17% by volume! A gorgeous rich bouquet easily one of the richest unfortified wines I have ever tasted. This is really a freak wine and one which may be very difficult to repeat; the alcohol was so high that it never underwent the normal malolactic fermentation. It is gratifying to know already I have a case of this most unusual wine tucked away in London.

Here are the notes that Bob Travers gave me concerning this remarkable wine: "We call it Late Harvest, but the grapes were actually picked in the second half of September 1968 and had reached a maximum of ripeness, so much so that there were a number of raisins among them. The sugar of the must read 17¼ (Balling), but the raisins did not dissolve until the fermentation was in progress, so we never got a higher sugar reading, but obviously much sugar was contributed by these raisins. No extra sugar or fortifying spirit was added. The juice was left on the skins just seven days and was pressed at 8 (Balling). The residual sugar in the wine is 0.4%. The fermentation (from crushing to completion) took exactly one month. We made just over 1,000 gallons of the 1968 Late Harvest Zinfandel (from about 6 tons of grapes). The wine was not fined and was bottled in June 1971, after 2 years and 8 months in a 1,000 gallon new American oak cask."

Château Chevalier

Tuesday, 4th April

Barney drove us northwards up the valley through Rutherford to St. Helena where we turned westwards up into the hills to visit the old winery called Château Chevalier. The house, copied from one in France, was built by Chinese labour in 1891, but the vineyard had been planted out about some twenty years before. The mass of tall variegated palm trees standing around the house gives the scene an almost tropical appearance.

The story of this property is a perfect example of what is happening here in the Napa Valley. The vines had been abandoned just after World War I on account of Prohibition, and subsequently the land. The new owners are doing and have done a remarkable job here for in only two years they have grubbed up the trees and the scrub that had been allowed to grow over the original vineyard. This was no mean task because according to their rings, many of the fir trees were over forty years old!

This is a real mountain vineyard, in a way not unlike Mayacamas, with precipitous slopes on which the young vines have been planted and the scenery in all directions equally superb. Gregory and Kathy Bissonette live here with their six children in idyllic surroundings. A stockbroker by profession, he has always wanted to own a vineyard, in fact has been interested in wine long before he had anything to do with the business. Since the stockmarket of San Francisco opens at 7 o'clock every morning, he has to be at his office very early but this leaves him time to return home to work on his tractor during the afternoons. The vineyard has become the joy of his life, so much so that his wife, Kathy, says that at the beginning she became quite jealous of his "beastly old tractor."

Certainly he has done a vast amount of work, clearing the ground, cutting out the terraces to plant the vines and finally the planting. There is a little patch of pinot noir but in the main the vineyard is planted with cabernet sauvignon and chardonnay, and I was interested to hear that a proportion of merlot has also been included. It really seems as though the Médocain system of blending a little merlot with cabernet sauvignon is finally catching on. For me, it has been fascinating to watch the development of this idea over the past few years and it will be even more interesting to taste the result in some ten years' time.

This property whose total surface, hill and dale, is about 300 acres, will, to begin with, have about seventy acres under vines, and it is hoped that later on a further seventy may be added. With such an acreage the winery will be entirely self-supporting, and thus all its produce will have the advantage of being sold under the heading of estate bottling.

We dined delightfully with Fred and Eleanor McCrea of Stony Hill. This vineyard which I have mentioned on previous occasions is situated high up in the hills overlooking St. Helena, and is noted for some of the finest Johannisberg Riesling and Chardonnay of all California. Such is the competition to acquire Fred's wine, that it is all sold immediately a vintage is offered and the average ration works out at about only a case per person! You therefore have to act pretty quickly if you want some Stony Hill wine in your cellar.

At dinner we began with a delicious 1967 Traminer, a lighter and to my mind a more attractive wine than the average Traminer from Alsace. With the main course we drank Fred's 1968 Pinot Chardonnay, a wine which has already acquired a great reputation. It was particularly fresh and charming. The special characteristic of the Chardonnays of Stony Hill is that they are very slow to develop (this 1968 certainly has some way to go to reach its best) and they last longer than most other wines made from this varietal.

Finally, with a delectable fresh fruit salad, we sipped Fred's new masterpiece, 1969 Semillon du Soleil. This delightful dessert wine made from sun-dried Semillon grapes is not at all unlike a light beerenauslese from Germany. Unlike the vineyards of Europe where everything has been tried and proved over the centuries, here in California there is so much to be tried, so much still to be discovered.

Louis Martini
Wednesday, 5th April

There have been signs of approaching rain during the past two days and now at last it has come and come in earnest, for as I look across the vineyards up to the wooded hills on the west side of the valley, great sheets of it are sweeping across the landscape. After the long drought, the vineyard proprietors are jubilant and as one of them has put it this morning "every drop is worth a dollar!"

It was still fairly pelting down as we arrived at the winery of Louis M. Martini at St. Helena. Our tasting was set in a small new house overlooking the vineyards which is being arranged by Louis' father, the founder of the firm and now over 85. Wine making as a career has clearly suited him, for a healthier man at that age it would be difficult to find.

When I arrived here in 1969 I found everyone excited about the quality of the 1968 vintage and first rate it was too, but it seems as though 1970 is even better. At this moment it would appear that a good vintage is coming in alternate years because neither 1969 nor 1971 are really much to write home about.

Louis Martini keeps his red wines in huge redwood tanks of around 5,000 gallons capacity (that is the equivalent of about 2,500 dozen bottles) for three or four years before putting them into bottle. He has a tremendous talent for blending and must be one of the most skillful in the industry either in America or Europe. The wines we were to taste this morning were of the 1970 vintage and although they have not yet been blended, give one a very good idea of their unusually good quality.

Louis Martini 89

1970 Vintage

> *Zinfandel* (from the mountain vineyard in Sonoma County, alcoholic strength about 13.5%).
> An impressively dark colour, a fine rich bouquet reminiscent of raspberries and a powerful flavour, in fact a real mouthful of wine. If I did not live so far away, I would like to have a case or so of this!
>
> *Pinot Noir* (from Carneros, at the lower end of the Napa Valley).
> Good colour for this varietal, an attractive bouquet and plenty of flavour. Later on this will be transferred to smaller oak casks.
>
> *Barbera.*
> Again a very dark colour, most fragrant bouquet, not a big wine and has some tannin. There is a delightful flavour which leaves a nice taste in the mouth. This also will be transferred to smaller oak casks for maturing. Clearly this is another success.

The two Cabernet Sauvignons which followed will eventually be blended together with Louis' usual skill, but I would dearly love to have a case of the mountain vineyard (Sonoma County) bottled off later this year. I would then keep it for five, six or even seven years and then what a splendid bottle it would make!

> *Cabernet Sauvignon 1970 Mountain Vineyard* (Sonoma County).
> Very, very dark colour, rich sweet nose, a gorgeous big, very rich wine. Only ten days ago I was in Bordeaux tasting the great clarets of 1970 (certainly the best vintage there since 1961) and this wine reminded me very much of them, not only for its fabulous colour, but also for its richness and complexity.
>
> *Cabernet Sauvignon 1970* (Napa Valley).
> Good dark colour, bouquet hinting of cedar wood or is it green pepper? Not a big wine, but it has an attractive fruity flavour. We tried mixing this with the other Cabernet and the result was successful.
>
> *A Merlot blend of 1968 and 1970.*
> I think I am right in saying that Louis Martini was among the foremost (if not the foremost) growers to plant out some

merlot vines. He has made this blend rather as an experiment and will give the wine about three years bottle age before sale. Medium colour, with a fragrant bouquet, on the light side and already very easy to taste. This may not be a long keeper, but will certainly have the advantage of developing early. An interesting wine, for I am sure I have never come across a bottle of pure merlot from Bordeaux.

Cabernet Sauvignon 1968.

A straight unblended wine—good colour, lovely bouquet, a delicious black currant flavour, has some tannin still but is of fine quality. It was bottled in February 1972 and surely will make a great bottle.

Cabernet Sauvignon 1968.

The same wine as above but blended 70% cabernet sauvignon, 20% merlot and 10% malbec. A good dark colour, great finesse as well as some sweetness on the bouquet. A big fruity wine with a whole range of flavours and it finishes nicely. This to me resembles much more a médoc than anything I have tasted here before. Louis himself describes it as a "Frenchy wine!"

Cabernet Sauvignon 1966 (Special Selection from Sonoma).

Good colour, full cedar or eucalyptus bouquet, delicious fruity flavour. Never fined and once filtered over; the operation of fining is, as in cooking, to clarify the wine and the best ingredient of all is white of egg (used at Château Latour), but there are other chemical varieties which are successful but less expensive. Although it clarifies, it must be admitted that fining can take some of the heart out of a wine and from time to time here in California one comes across wines which have not been fined at all, and with very good results. On the other hand sometimes at Latour, we fine twice; with only one fining as in the old days, the wine had so much "stuffing" in it that it took about twenty years to come around! Nobody nowadays is prepared to wait all that time before a wine is ready to drink. It was all right in the old days when people lived in great houses, planted out their woods and laid down wine for their children to enjoy.

Cabernet Sauvignon 1964 (Special Selection and a blend to be released on the market in, say, 1974).

Good colour, rich full bouquet, a fine powerful wine which in many ways resembles a fine claret, plenty of tannin still.

At Louis M. Martini, what in France are called the best "cuves" are set aside for bottle age and are then sold under Special Selection. It can be, of course, that in the interim the wine from the regular "cuves" tastes better than the Special Selection, but by and large they do not have quite the intrinsic quality, and the Special Selection which takes longer to develop emerges triumphant in the long run. This particular 1964 is a good case in point; it must have been tasting tough and resistant while the regular 1964 Cabernet Sauvignon was in its glory, a glory, let it be noted, never so great as the ultimate peak of the Special Selection.

As we were finishing this interesting and really instructive tasting, Louis' father came in and together we enjoyed a glass of champagne. My goodness, what progress has been made in the methods of wine making here in California. 1970 seems to have been just as good a vintage here as was 1970 in Bordeaux and it will be fascinating to see how these 1970's turn out; one thing which is absolutely certain, the colour is every bit as dark as that of the 1970's in Bordeaux. It would be interesting to take a bottle of each of the 1968 Cabernet Sauvignons mentioned above and put them into a blind tasting in Bordeaux and later on I would like to do the same thing with the splendid Cabernet Sauvignons of 1970.

The Martini home is the upper floor of an old converted winery, and is a joy to behold. For the walls of the principal room, skillful use has been made of the three foot thick stone walls. Liz Martini had prepared some delicious food for us, and to accompany it Louis thought we might be interested in some old vintages of white wine from his cellar, namely Mountain Dry Semillon 1951 and Mountain Johannisberg Riesling 1964, both of which had kept remarkably well, especially the 1951; the colour of the latter being as pale as a normal 1968 or a 1969.

The meal ended with the delicious Moscato Amabile, slightly sweet and slightly sparkling. This fresh light wine (only 10 per cent alcohol) makes an admirable finish to any meal. As so often happens, this attractive wine had been discovered by Louis and his father through a mistake in the cellar and so successful was the result, they decided to make it in earnest!

That evening we dined happily with Milt and Barbara Eisele at their ranch just north of Calistoga. Milt is another of these enthusiasts who has given up business in order to become a vineyard proprietor. They bought this property about four years ago and have now remodelled the interior of the house in a most delightful manner. This Napa Valley is very prone to frost, and so far as I can see, the only place in France to equal it for vulnerability must be Chablis. Poor Milt has been going through all the teething troubles, because among other things when he purchased the property there was no frost protection of any kind. Recently he coined a definition for unhappiness: "to lie in bed at night and listen to your neighbour's wind machines working and to know that you have none yourself!" All this is being installed, but for nights in succession both Milt and Barbara have been up until dawn among the vines, lighting and tending various heating devices to ward off the frost.

Staying as we are here in the Napa Valley during the critical spring season, smudge pots and other frost protection methods are to be seen on all sides. At least there was no fear at this particular moment, because it was still raining in torrents as we drove home.

Thursday, 6th April

Freemark Abbey

I have come to the conclusion that Prue and I are terribly spoilt for here in the Napa Valley the wineries open their doors to us for special tastings. I believe I am right in saying that the normal visitors are given to taste only the wines on sale, whereas we are honoured with their "young entry," in this case the 1970's and 1971's and this is much appreciated. For many years now I have been accustomed to tasting and buying very young wines of the previous vintage from the French vineyards and so these very young wines are not strange to me. For example, in order to obtain the best, that is the pick of the bunch from the Côte d'Or in Burgundy, you have to get out among the wine growers about the middle of November following the vintage and make your reserves before the mass of the buyers arrive for the auction of Les Hospices de Beaune. It is not easy at that particular time because many of the wines are still fermenting. One has to delve, as it were, beneath the surface and try to assess the quality.

Today the rain has ceased and the sky is clearing but at least the vines have had a good soaking. We were expected at Freemark Abbey where we always receive such a warm welcome. Freemark Abbey is a comparatively new winery but has access to old vines, not only of its own but others, such as the fabulous Bosche Vineyard. The direction here is a group of really dedicated men, Bill Jaeger, Chuck Carpy, Laurie Wood and Brad Webb. The last named is known as one of the great wine makers of California. Their aim is by no means mass production, but a small quantity of really first-class quality and it is quite evident they are achieving this ambition.

To begin with Jerry Luper, the young bearded wine maker, led us into the winery to taste the wines in wood.

Chardonnay 1971 (this has been in a small cask for about a month).
At the moment the bouquet is the best part, for it has a delightful fragrance. As for the taste, it is still too young and aggressive, but clearly as it matures it will develop into a good wine.

Pinot Noir 1971 (in a small barrel for only about three weeks).
The colour still rather pale, this is what is so odd about red wine for sometimes during its youth in cask it loses its colour and then gradually picks it up again. (I have seen this happen at Latour and that is one of the darkest hued wines of all.) Not much on the nose yet and though on the light side, has an agreeable flavour.

Just to prove this point about the colour, Jerry Luper let us taste the identical wine of the 1970 vintage which, he told us, was equally pale in colour at the same stage in its career.

Pinot Noir 1970.
Good colour and bouquet with plenty of fruit and flavour, well balanced, good quality.

Cabernet Sauvignon 1971.
Full bouquet, with lots of fruit but perhaps a trace of greenness.

Now that I seem to be alternating regularly between Bordeaux and California it is fascinating to find similarities. Owing to indifferent weather in the spring here in California, there was a late flowering of the vines and because of subsequent unfavourable weather the vines did not have the chance to catch up. The inevitable result was that some of the cabernet grapes were not as ripe as one would wish at the time of the vintage and unripe grapes lead to a certain amount of greenness in the wine. Almost the same thing happened in Bordeaux during 1967; there too, there was a late flowering and although many of the 1967 clarets are excellent, here and there, there is some greenness apparent, especially among the *crus bourgeois* (in fact I touched on this point in *The Pick of the Bunch*).

Merlot 1971 (Grapes from Barney Rhodes' vines).
A good colour and very nice bouquet; there is still some tannin but it has an agreeably round flavour. No doubt this merlot will be used for blending later on with the cabernet sauvignon.

Cabernet Sauvignon (Bosche) *1970.*
With this wine there has been blended 10% of Barney Rhodes' 1970 merlot. What a colour and what a fabulous bouquet. A beautiful dark colour with a fabulous Cabernet bouquet. A splendid powerful wine which will certainly make a great bottle.

Petite Sirah 1971.
Unusually deep colour, heaps of bouquet and a big full-flavoured wine, still has considerable tannin but makes an enormous mouthful. Unfortunately only 350 cases were made, so that will not go far.

Later in the tasting room, we sat down to try some of the recently bottled stock.

Johannisberg Riesling 1970 (bottled in August 1971 and on the market since April 1, 1972).
A nice pale colour, a fragrant, perfumed bouquet and a delicious flavour combining freshness with finesse. It leaves a pleasant riesling after-taste.

Then came two Cabernet Sauvignons both made from the grapes of the splendid Bosche vineyard. These emphasised the striving for perfection which is now so evident in the Napa Valley. I have touched on this subject in my last books but it is only during the recent years that the growers have considered the addition of a small proportion of merlot to the cabernet sauvignon to tone down some of the, if one may call it, aggressiveness, of the cabernet sauvignon. The blending of a small percentage of merlot has long been the practice in the Médoc at Latour we have roughly 20%) and I have often wondered why it was not done here. The local methods of maturing have of course been different in the past, the red wine being matured in huge redwood tanks for three or four years in order to soften it before bottling, whereas in the Médoc the red wine is only kept in its small oak casks from eighteen months up to 2½ years. If in the Médoc only pure cabernet sauvignon was used perhaps the wine there would have to be kept longer in cask. What interests me now so much is that each year when I visit the Napa Valley, there is more and more talk of blending a little merlot with the cabernet sauvignon. As is evident, things are still in the experimental stage and not all growers by any means have come round to this policy of blending.

> *Cabernet Sauvignon* (Bosche) *1968* (aged in small oak casks with the addition of 40% Merlot).
> A beautiful dark colour and a fine rich bouquet, quite a rich flavour and should be ready fairly soon.
>
> *Cabernet Sauvignon* (Bosche) *1968* (with 10% merlot).
> A lovely dark colour and an even richer bouquet. This great rich wine will make a fine bottle coming comparatively speaking up to first growth standard.

Who knows, one of these days, the great wines of this Valley will also be classified; presumably this would only apply to wine coming from single vineyards, but some of the Cabernet Sauvignons I have tasted during the past year or so are worthy of this distinction. The disadvantage, of course, lies in the minute production, so perhaps this is something to be considered in, say, twenty years' time.

Heitz Wine Cellars
Friday, 7th April

Last year, 1971, Joe Heitz provided for me a simply mammoth tasting of his red wines including those made from the famous Martha's Vineyard Cabernet Sauvignon. On this occasion it was the turn of the white ones.

> *Gewürztraminer 1971* (fined only yesterday).
> Nevertheless it has a pleasant hint of honey on the nose and flavour. This will be filtered and bottled very soon.
>
> *Johannisberg Riesling 1971.*
> Pale colour, a rather full bouquet and lots of fruit. At present it has what I describe as a heavy California taste, i.e., a pronounced earthy flavour, but by the time Joe, great wine maker as he is, has nursed it and polished it up, it will no doubt, emerge from the ugly duckling into a swan.
> As with everything else, there are good wine makers and not so good wine makers, but it is at establishments such as this where true craftsmanship and skill are so evident.

Johannisberg Riesling 1970.
Great finesse of bouquet, attractive, fresh, fruity and very well made. Here we have the answer to the above, the same wine but a year older, polished and finished to perfection.

Pinot Blanc 1971.
A fresh bouquet and a full, fruity flavour. This should make a good bottle.

Pinot Blanc 1970 (bottled July 1971 and to be released for sale in May 1972).
Fine bouquet, good flavour, well-balanced but a trifle lighter in character than the 1970.

Pinot Blanc 1969.
Taking on a little more colour, an attractive mature bouquet, considerable character but I preferred the 1970 and 1971. It appears the grapes from which this wine was made came from another vineyard.

Chardonnay 1971.
Quite a full rather heavy nose, but heaps of flavour, will make a good bottle.

Chardonnay 1970.
Very pale colour, good nose but needs time to develop, good fruit and flavour. Should be just right when offered for sale in about nine months' time.

Chardonnay 1969.
Pale golden colour, a lovely mature bouquet, a big full-flavoured wine.

Before leaving we tried the 1969 Pinot Noir which had only been bottled the day before. The colour is good for a Pinot Noir and there is a good full bouquet. It is round and full of flavour but needs about two years in bottle to smooth out its edges.

We lunched lightly at that amusing place called 1870 Vintage. This is an agglomeration of craft shops and the huge building or buildings derive their name from its original purpose, a winery built in 1870. With delicious sandwiches (we English have a lot to learn from the Americans about sandwiches) we enjoyed the great treat of no less than two vintages of Martha's Vineyard Cabernet Sauvignon, namely 1967 and 1966. Here are my notes on them:

Cabernet Sauvignon 1967 (Martha's Vineyard, 100% cabernet sauvignon).
A good dark colour and a fantastic range of smells, almost "perfumes" in the bouquet reminding me rather of the bouquet of Mouton-Rothschild or Lynch-Bages. An equally fine and most distinctive flavour, a flavour which locally is described as complex. This must be a Californian expression because I have never heard it used in Europe.

Cabernet Sauvignon 1966 (Martha's Vineyard, 100% cabernet sauvignon).
Similar in every way to the 1967 but deeper and more closed up. Although the 1967 may take the limelight over the next five or six years, I think the 1966 with its greater depth will triumph in the long run. It has been a real pleasure not only to taste again but to drink these real aristocrats of the Napa Valley.

If one may judge from these two wines, there is a similarity between the 1967's and the 1966's here and the same vintages of the Médoc. The 1966's are not immediately so attractive but finally have more depth and intrinsic quality.

Thursday, 13th April

Tasting of Petite Sirah

The Petite Sirah vine is reputed to have been brought from the Middle East to the Rhône Valley in France by the Crusaders, whence in the nineteenth century it appeared in California. The name "Petite Sirah" (why it changes its gender, I do not know) most probably is of American origin, because the vine grown in France that produces the great wines of Hermitage is called the *Syrah*. In his admirable *Encyclopedia of Wine,* Frank Schoonmaker, who, incidentally, seems to have a poor opinion of the quality of the California Petit Sirah (his spelling), suggests it is not the Syrah grape at all, but "a common variety called the Duriff, which was widely planted in the Rhône Valley a century ago, but is no longer permitted in any French vineyard entitled to an "Appellation Contrôlée." However, this varietal appears to be well suited to the soil of California, and firms like Concannon have had much to do with its development and the improvement of the wine itself and have thus added to its popularity.

The fairly comprehensive tasting under discussion took place in the Oakland home of Dr. and Mrs. Bernard L. Rhodes and a large proportion of the people present were members of the wine trade. There was considerable variation in the quality produced by the various wineries represented, ranging from very good to, in one or two cases, very bad indeed. Consequently the proceedings would have afforded a valuable object lesson for any budding student of wine. For example, among the poor wines, thrown in for good measure, there were some very positive examples of oxidisation and of volatile acidity. However, such mishaps are not exclusive to California, because they can be encountered all too frequently in Europe, especially among the wines sold in the London supermarkets. On the credit side, for those who prefer a fairly full-bodied "Burgundy type" wine, a well-made Petite Sirah, such as the Concannon 1965 or 1969, or the Mirassou 1967 or 1968, should meet their approval.

Although clearly the group did not agree with me over my findings on the Concannon 1965 and the Parducci 1965, wines I first tasted during my visit to California in 1969, at least it is comforting for me to find these two developing so well. I see from my notes that during the same visit, I also tried the Parducci 1967, but this, although pleasant, does not appear to have turned out quite so well as anticipated.

Group A: Vintages of 1965 and 1966

Wine	Characteristics	My Score	Group Placing
Parducci 1965 (Unfined)	Dark colour, rather rich bouquet, good flavour	15/20	Share 1
Concannon 1966	Medium colour, powerful bouquet, good fruit, but needs time	10/20	3
Mirassou 1966	Good colour, smooth rich bouquet, could have more charm	12/20	Share 1
Concannon 1965	Dark colour, fragrant bouquet, full and round, finishes nicely	16/20	4

Group B: Vintage 1967

Mirassou 1967	Colour dark, but not absolutely bright, a fragrant well bred bouquet, has both style and quality	15/20	1

Tasting of Petite Sirah

Group A: Vintages of 1965 and 1966 (continued)

Wine	Characteristics	My Score	Group Placing
Parducci 1967	Good colour, good bouquet, nice flavour, but a little hard	13/20	2
Papiano 1967	Colour beginning to turn a little brown, volatile acidity apparent both on bouquet and flavour	0/20	3

Group C: Vintage 1968

Wine	Characteristics	My Score	Group Placing
Souverain 1968	Good colour; too much, is it sulphur on the nose? But has fruit and tastes better than it smells	12/20	3
Mendocino 1968	Rather pale colour, an agreeable bouquet, but is thin and lacks charm	9/20	5
Barngo 1968 (Corti)	Very dark colour, poor nose, full-bodied, but badly oxidised	0/20	2
Concannon 1968	Good colour, well-bred bouquet, pleasant flavour, on light side	13/20	4
Evoe 1968 (Paul Broadhead)	Very dark colour, very rich bouquet, full but poor flavour	10/20	1
	N. B. Tasted this wine at a later date and it seemed much better, anyway it is an interesting effort for a "home-made" wine		

Group D: Vintage 1969

Wine	Characteristics	My Score	Group Placing
Mirassou 1969	Deep colour, pleasant full bouquet, fruity flavour but has too much acidity	4/20	3
Wente Brothers 1969	Medium colour, fairly good bouquet, full bodied, a trace of acidity, could have more quality	12/20	5
Gemello 1969	Good colour, poor nose, sharp and of mediocre quality	4/20	2
Freemark Abbey 1969	Deep colour, rich scented bouquet, good flavour	13/20	4
Concannon 1969	Good colour, rich scented bouquet, full-bodied and rich	16/20	1

Group E: four are non-vintage

Wine	Characteristics	My Score	Group Placing
Mirassou 1968	Good colour, very nice rather "peppery" nose, has considerable character. (N. B. This is a higher score than any 1968 above.)	15/20	Equal 1
Windsor N. V.	Good colour, nice bouquet, agreeable flavour	11/20	3
Nicolini N. V.	Very dark colour, deep bouquet, has fruit, but lacks breeding	11/20	Equal 1
Sonoma Vineyards N. V.	Good colour, quite good bouquet, but is rather fierce on the taste	6/20	5
Simi N. V.	Good colour, poor bouquet, has volatile acidity	0/20	4

From an entirely personal point of view, the 1965 vintage showed up best and, something which is difficult to understand, the 1968's (recognised to be a good vintage in California) were comparatively disappointing.

While studying some of the other tasting notes subsequent to the tasting, I notice that the word "peppery" is also used to describe the bouquet. Certainly, I noticed this myself with the Mirassou 1968, so perhaps, like the cedar or eucalyptus nose for Mouton-Rothschild and Latour, this is a characteristic of Petite Sirah?

Monday, 17th April

The Wine and Food Society of Southern California

The 270th meeting of this chapter was held at the lovely Bel Air Country Club, high up in the hills overlooking Los Angeles.

It was fortunate for me that my host at the Beverly Wilshire Hotel, the renowned Hernando Courtright, should have invited me for what must be the best and certainly the most amusing evening of the year, the occasion when the members, all male, cook the dinner themselves.

The Club had been taken over for the night and from the moment that I entered the kitchen, our assembly point, I knew I was in for a good evening for there was a marked sense of conviviality within these most appropriate surroundings. A good proportion of the members were on duty as chefs and were dressed accordingly, many looking quite impressive in their tall white hats. There we nibbled delightful tidbits such as tender snails on small squares of toast, fresh shrimps on artichoke leaves and so on. These were accompanied by an agreeable sparkling white Burgundy called Fragnya.

Our cooks, who from time to time, had to leave the dining room in order to attend to their own particular dishes, provided us with a really good meal, one worthy of the best of professionals. Here is the bill of fare: The terrine of veal and ham en croute stuffed with truffles and pistachio nuts and made by Grafton Tanqueray was as good as any I have eaten in France and the cold lobster which followed was easily the best decorated dish I have ever seen, great use being made of parsley and white flowers. The California lamb was accompanied by beetroot and sprouts hollandaise, and so good were the latter that I must try this rendering when I return to England. We finished with crepes in a delicious sauce.

As for the wines, the fine 1879 Sercial went well with the terrine and so did the 1969 Avelsbacher Hammerstein Feine Spätlese with the lobster; the 1966 Châteauneuf-du-Pape Petite Bastide (Diffonty) was dark of colour and full-bodied and this was followed by the 1966 Corton-Clos du Roi (Lionel Bruck).

Although men do cook in England and many of them remarkably well, it seems to me that this practising of the gastronomic art by the male sex is not so widespread as it is here in both Northern and Southern California. In spite of the serious attention paid to the cooking, an evening like the one just described has a gaiety and lightness of spirit that is hard to emulate.

Thursday, 20th April

Beaujolais in California

Why it should be so, I fail to understand, but never yet during my numerous visits to California have I tasted any really good Beaujolais. Can it be the journey, that long sea voyage through the Panama Canal, that is too tiring for the wine, though why Beaujolais should not travel so well as other red wines is difficult to comprehend. Suffice it to say that so far, any Beaujolais that I have tasted here on this Coast has been disappointing and what is worse, the tasting to be described here did little to retrieve this poor impression.

We also suffer in England from indifferent Beaujolais, but that is largely the fault of the English wine trade, because the bulk of it is brought over in containers without Appellation Contrôlée and over and above that, it is bottled in England with all the weaknesses attendant thereto. Most of it is bottled some six months later than the fine wines in the Beaujolais itself and thus, by the time it comes to the table, it has lost much of its freshness.

There are no such excuses for shipments to California, because at this particular tasting, all the wines had been bottled in the Beaujolais district and all of them bore the authenticity of Appellation Contrôlée. In addition, 1970 is certainly a good vintage and the wines were comparatively youthful. Beaujolais should be drunk while it is young and fresh, in fact, freshness is one of its chief attractions and that is why it tastes so good if served slightly chilled, gaining thereby a double freshness, the youth of the wine itself, coupled with the temperature at which it is served.

In order to capture this charm and freshness, it has to be bottled very early, that is to say (with the possible exception of a few of the more full-bodied wines such as Moulin-à-Vent) certainly within six months of the termination of the fermentation. There are two kinds of Beaujolais, the "vin nouveau" and the regular kind. The "vin nouveau" is a very light affair intended for immediate consumption and it appears in the French bistros as from the 15th November, just about a month after the vintage. It is not long lived however and it is advisable to finish it up before the end of March. I have described it as a gaily painted butterfly flitting briefly across the vinous scene and that is about what it is, something to cheer us up during the gloomy winter months.

The "vin nouveau" is becoming almost too much of a good thing in England, because in London during the months of November and December 1971, there were no less than thirty versions of this particular wine on sale and not all of them good, at that! At a blind tasting of some twenty of them arranged by an enterprising young man, Roger Aldridge, I found a number had too much acidity for my liking. The importation of this wine is certainly feasible in England, for it only takes about two days in a truck for it to arrive in London. I also believe that it is obtainable in great cities like New York as the journey across the Atlantic does not take too long, but until wine can be freighted at a reasonable cost by air, I cannot imagine any "vin nouveau" being sold successfully in California.

The bottling of what one could call the "regular" wine commences from January, following the vintage, onwards and most of it is safely in bottle by the end of April. In the Beaujolais region, the connoisseurs always drink the "wine of the year" (really, in fact, the wine of the previous year). For example in this year of 1972, they will be drinking the 1971's and they tend to regard anything else as too old. They are right too, because given a good vintage, Beaujolais has this special quality of freshness, but once it has been in bottle for about a year, somehow it seems to take on a different image.

We wine lovers have been lucky with our vintages during recent years; we have had three good ones in succession, 1969, 1970 and 1971. The growers on the Côte d'Or however have not fared so well because there was considerable overproduction of the red Burgundies, but down south in the Beaujolais, the vineyards did not suffer so much in this respect.

During the late summer of 1971, there was excessive hail on the vineyards of the Côte d'Or and this produced an ill-effect on what was going to be a fabulous vintage. There was hail too down in the Beaujolais, but not nearly to such a damaging extent. Although as a vintage, 1971 may not be an absolute world beater, it was nevertheless very good, in fact some of the 1971's are really excellent; so much depends, of course, on your source of supply. This should be amply demonstrated by the time these words get into print, in fact, by that time no doubt the 1972's should be in all the shops.

Tasting of nine 1970 Beaujolais
Arranged by the Berkeley Wine and Food Society
in the home of Mr. and Mrs. A. D'Anneo

Wine	Characteristics	My Placing	Points for	Group Placing
Chénas Château de Jean Loron Domaine Desvignes	Good colour, typical Beaujolais bouquet, not much body, but light and agreeable	3	30	2
Beaujolais-Villages (Louis Latour)	Medium colour, fairly full bouquet, good fruit and flavour	1	29	3
Chateau de Morgan Mons. Sauzy, Prop. (Thorin Selection)	Rather pale colour, dusty bouquet and similar flavour, disappointing	7	8	8

Tasting of nine 1970 Beaujolais (continued)

Wine	Characteristics	My Placing	Points for	Group Placing
Moulin-a-Vent de la Tour de Bief (Cave Georges)	Good colour, full bouquet, has fruit but is oxidised	8	19	4/5
Chiroubles (Beaujolais Producteurs)	Pale colour, something odd about the bouquet, but plenty of fruit and a nice flavour	6	2	9
Moulin à Vent de la Tour de Bief (Comte de Sparre)	Very good colour, good bouquet, a big, robust wine	2	49	1
Côte de Brouilly Ch. Thivin en Beaujolais (Geoffray)	Medium colour, typical Beaujolais bouquet, good fruit, but spoiled for me by its acidity	9	10	6
Moulin-à-Vent Domaine du Petit Chêne (Louis Max)	Pale colour, nice bouquet, not a big wine	5	9	7
Juliénas Cave Lacharme Depagneux	Dark colour, but rather an odd bouquet, full-bodied and rather hard	4	19	4/5

As usual, it was a blind tasting and although my own notes do not coincide greatly with the consolidated opinion, the general feeling was that this collection of Beaujolais was not exciting.

Friday, 21st April

Chalone Vineyard

You have to be quite a devoted disciple of the vinous calling to visit Chalone, for it takes a good 2½ hours drive southward from San Francisco before you even turn off up into the hills at Soledad. The name Soledad rings a bell because it is here in Monterey County where the vast acreages, already mentioned in *The Pick of the Bunch* have been laid out by great firms such as Paul Masson and Mirassou. The areas of still fairly young vines are so huge that they put me in mind of those almost endless vineyards in the south of France in the *departements* of Languedoc and Herault. The vineyards that I could see from the car around Soledad all appeared to have overhead irrigation and my mind boggles at the thought of the expense this must have entailed.

Since this was also the Rhodes' first visit, we did not feel too badly about dragging them on this long journey. From Soledad the road winds up towards the Pinnacles National Monument, through wilder and wilder country on the dirt roads which become rougher and rougher as you proceed. The Pinnacles are a range of jagged mountain peaks, the nearest thing I have seen so far to the splendid range immediately behind Gigondas in the Rhône Valley.

This is a very small vineyard on the Chalone Bench of the Gavilan Mountains situated at about 2,000 feet. As will be seen from the notes given below, the production is really minute, but all the wines are Estate Bottled. This district suffers desperately from the lack of water, the average annual rainfall being only from 12 to 15 inches, and so far in this year of drought there have been 8 inches. In very dry years the vines become parched and the production minimal. As explained below, an irrigation system is used.

To quote the brochure: "The most special thing about this isolated, difficult-to-get-to vineyard is its soil. Discovered many years ago by a Frenchman in search of land comparable to that of France, this vineyard grows on the same type of sparse, reddish soil underlain by limestone such as produces the great French burgundies along the Côte d'Or. The production is quite small, for to date each acre of soil will only yield two barrels of 300 bottles of each wine. Thus each bottle is filled with the essence of the soil—the 'goût de terroir' which gives the wine a fullness of bouquet and flavour unique to this vineyard. The wines are made after the classical French methods, i.e., matured in French oak barrels, with nothing added or taken away artificially."

When Dick Graf bought this property in 1965 it was in a derelict condition and the small windowless house, open to all the elements, had become the residence of birds (the feathered variety!) and other wild creatures. Now the house is equipped with pleasant creature comforts, a refrigerator, a dishwasher and even a fine nineteenth century organ, for Dick Graf is also a keen musician. While at Harvard, this delightful young "vigneron" studied the organ and directed the choir and after three years as a naval officer on a destroyer in the Pacific, worked for a bank in Los Angeles. Then he spent a year as a special student at the University of California at Davis where he studied viticulture and enology and he has since visited many of the wine districts in Europe. To supplement his income he is also an importer of winery equipment, corks, casks and so on. Since this vineyard, small as it is, is too much for one pair of hands Dick is helped by his vineyard manager, Paul Shipley.

From the winery there is no other building to be seen, the vineyard on rolling slopes has to be heavily fenced against marauding deer for this is a vast piece of land where all the wild life is protected. On entering the small winery I was much reminded of the cellars of the small peasant growers of Burgundy for there are but a few casks of each wine to be seen. These wines were tasted from the wood:

Chenin Blanc 1971.
  Heaps of bouquet, good flavour with nice fruit acidity, good quality.

Pinot Blanc 1971.
  Good bouquet, well-balanced with a nice flavour. Should make a good bottle.

Chardonnay 1971.
  Fine, full bouquet, delightful taste. Should make a fine bottle.

Pinot Noir 1971 (only one or two casks were made).
  Medium colour, well-bred bouquet, attractive flavour, a good solid wine which leaves a nice after-taste.

Pinot Noir 1970 (only 25 cases of this will be produced).
  Very good colour, distinguished bouquet, full-bodied with plenty of fruit. To be bottled in May 1972.

We then walked a little way up the hill to inspect a newly planted part of the old vineyard and had explained to us the drip system of irrigation which came originally from Israel. There are two small wells on the property but in these arid hills there is insufficient water to supply anything but the house and the winery. so water for the vines has to be brought up in tanks from Soledad. Otherwise in dry seasons such as this in 1972 little or no wine could be made. The system consists of plastic (p.v.c.) pipes attached to the vine stakes at a height of about three feet and at each vine there is a gadget, called an emitter, controlling the flow of water which as required drips into a plastic tube, the bottom end of which goes far enough into the ground by each vine so as to discourage the growth of weeds. This particular system called "Uniflow" can also be used for the distribution of liquid manure.

In the small house there is a counter dividing the kitchen from the dining area so while Dick Graf adroitly prepared and cooked our lunch he was able to partake with us a tasting of some of his wines which are already in bottle. Against most of them is marked the total production and when seeing this, readers will readily understand why many of these finer wines of California are unobtainable in other parts of this huge country.

These wines were tasted in bottle:

Chenin Blanc 1970.
> A good pale colour and a nice fresh bouquet, not absolutely bone dry but it has a delicious flavour. Under 400 cases were made, otherwise how popular this would be both in private houses and in restaurants.

Chenin Blanc 1969.
> Slightly more golden of colour and quite a nutty nose, that nice biscuity smell you find with an older champagne, a full and fruity flavour, but of the two I personally preferred the 1970 vintage. Total production 3,888 bottles.

Pinot Blanc 1970.
> Very pale colour, a lovely full nose, fresh and clean and quite dry, it has a good finish. Needs time to develop. Total production 3,066 bottles, 84 magnums.

Pinot Blanc 1969.
> Again, because of the extra year in bottle, a shade darker, delightful bouquet, good fruit and finishes well. It seems that the Pinot Blanc needs from one to two years in bottle to show at its best and in this case I preferred the 1969 vintage. Total production 5,173 bottles.

Chardonnay 1970.
> Good colour, well-bred bouquet, well-balanced, good quality. Production 486 bottles, 36 magnums.

Chardonnay 1969.
> Quite a full bouquet, not unlike that of a Meursault. Elegant with a delicious taste. Here again, no doubt because of its extra bottle age, I preferred the 1969. Production 1,308 bottles, 84 magnums.

With very good food prepared personally by our host, we drank these four white wines, or rather what remained of them, and two

Pinot Noirs, for the Chalone Vineyard prides itself on the quality of its Pinot Noir.

Pinot Noir 1969 (of which only two casks were made).
Medium colour, attractive bouquet and although only of medium body it has an attractive flavour.
This wine was kept in small oak casks for eighteen months and then was fined with the whites of eggs from the only farm in the valley.

Pinot Noir 1966 (only 1 cask was made and this was the first wine which Dick Graf made on the property).
It has a good dark colour, a concentrated bouquet and a most concentrated flavour. This went down very well with an excellent six year old cheddar which came fom the State of Oregon.

Chalone is yet another of these exciting smaller vineyards of California where eager young, and not so young pioneers have hewn out with their own hands, estates, which in only a few years, have earned a considerable reputation. After six years of rehabilitation, this winery remains in a fairly primitive stage and it is evident that to combat the surrounding forces of nature, considerable courage and enthusiasm have been required from its youthful owner.

Friday, 21st April

The Grand Cru Club

Host: Dr. J. Tupper at the French Club in San Francisco
Members present: Dr. W. Dickerson
Mr. R. K. Adamson
Mr. H. Drescher
Mr. R. Knudson
Mr. B. L. Rhodes
and three guests: Dr. W. Havender
Mr. W. Deiche
Mr. H. Waugh

Each member of this Club takes his turn to be host and apart from

The Grand Cru Club 109

clearly taken a considerable amount of care to see that this would be a good evening.

The aperitif, which one sees a lot of here in California, was a magnum of N. V. Deutz champagne.

The Menu:

> Petite Marmite (in which was to be found a slice of marrow bone together with its contents)
> Sole Doria (i.e., cooked with cucumber)
> Filet of beef with vegetables
> Grand Marnier Soufflé

Two splendid hocks accompanied the fish, both of them imported by Esquin and the responsibility of Karl Petrowsky. Unfortunately, Karl was unable to be present through ill health but the San Franciscan wine lovers have much to thank him for owing to his knowledge and skill in buying the wines of the country of his birth.

Roxheimer Höllenpfad Riesling Auslese Cabernet 1964.
> A perfect bouquet, a fresh truly delightful flavour. One of the nicest Rhine wines I have tasted for a long time.

Winzerheimer Rosenheck feine Auslese 1964.
> A lovely scented bouquet, full, rich and splendid, but really too sweet and overwhelming for the enjoyment of the sole. There was a suitable pause in the service while we sniffed and sipped at our clarets; then the meat course appeared which gave us a break before finalising our decisions.

There was some controversy about the *1961 Ch. Climens* which was offered with the soufflé but with my built-in prejudice towards Climens I was on the side of those in favour.

In either London or Bordeaux, it is all too seldom that one has an opportunity to taste all together a group of the greatest wines of the world, so I regard invitations such as this as among the highlights of my visit to California and am deeply sensible of the honour accorded me. This is the third time the Club has tasted the 1962 vintage and I was fortunate to be present on the second occasion in 1969. It is always useful to know how a fine vintage is developing and our first impression was that the wines are still rather backward, although this was altered the claret provides the dinner and the other wines. Jack Tupper had

The Great Wines of the 1962 Vintage
(Blind Tasting)

Wine	Characteristics	My placing	Points Against	Group Placing
Latour	Colour very dark indeed, fine powerful cedar bouquet, a fine big wine, great quality. Still considerable tannin, still backward. Needs at least two or three years yet to be at its best.	1	30	2
Cheval Blanc	Pale to medium colour, pleasant bouquet, some acidity and not much body	7	51	7
Lafite	Good colour and bouquet, on light side by comparison, but of fine quality	5	44	6
Haut-Brion	Good colour and bouquet, a fine big wine but still has some acidity and tannin to lose	6	42	5
Pétrus	Dark colour, good rich bouquet, a delicious round wine, as sweet as butter	3	1	16
Ausone	Colour between pale to medium, although mellow, by comparison with the rest it was lean and hungry	8	66	8
Margaux	Good colour, fine full bouquet, good fruit and flavour	4	41	4
Mouton-Rothschild	Very dark colour, a deep fragrant bouquet, a fine full-bodied wine. Still has a lot of tannin and will undoubtedly improve over the next year or so.	2	36	3

It will be seen that the points between Margaux, Haut-Brion and Lafite at 41, 42 and 44 were pretty close.

In case it may be of interest to readers, this is the Club record for somewhat after eating the meat.
the 1962's over the past three tastings spread over several years:

Latour	4	1	2	Total:	7
Cheval Blanc	5	7	7		19
Lafite	3	5	6		14
Haut-Brion	7	4	5		16
Pétrus	6	3	1		10
Ausone	8	8	8		24
Margaux	2	6	4		12
Mouton	1	2	3		6

From this Mouton wins by a short head with Latour second, and Ausone, trailing a long way behind the field.

At this particular moment the Pétrus is by far the most attractive to drink, but my personal feeling is that this great superficial charm, if one may so describe it, may not last over the years.

As usual, poor old Ausone comes bottom of the class, but at long last there is a glimmer of light because the 1971 Ausone appears to be much better than usual. It is strange about Ausone because before the war, it was the most expensive of all the wines of Bordeaux. Somewhere among my papers, I have a list of the opening prices of the 1934 vintage and it cost more than any of the first growths.

Friday, 26th April

Miscellaneous Tasting

All good things come to an end and the sadness of leaving our friends in California was made worse by the weather which, having been rather unfriendly for most of our visit, had become more and more resplendent as the days sped by.

For those interested in the niceties of tasting, there is one last batch of notes to be recorded, for, on our last evening, Barney Rhodes set out some Zinfandels which Darrell Corti of Sacramento had sent in for me to try. It turned out to be a good lesson as to how an identical wine can vary through different handling, or in other words, upbringing. All the Zinfandels came from the same source, the Weaver Vineyards, situated at 2,000 feet up in the Gold Rush country among the mountains northeast of Sacramento. They were identical wines but had been handled by different owners; the younger ones, the 1970's were, of course, still in cask.

1970 Zinfandel (Sutter Home Winery), lot No. 1, matured in Nevers and Limousin oak.
Good colour, a strong varietal bouquet, a good flavour.

1970 Zinfandel (Corti Brothers), identical wine, in wood and unrefined.
Good colour, attractive bouquet, better in fact than the other 1970 for it seems to have more polish, if one can use such a word. It also has more body and tannin; this will make a good bottle.

1969 Zinfandel (Sutter Home Winery), lot No. 2, matured in Nevers and Limousin oak.
Good colour and bouquet, not a big wine and it had a slightly "tart" finish, as well as a touch of oxidation.

1969 Zinfandel (Corti Brothers), identical wine, matured in Nevers oak and unfined.
Good colour and bouquet, a fuller wine than the other 1969 and easily the better of the two.

In France, red wines are usually fined at least once before bottling, but of recent years a few of the Californian growers have occasionally experimented by not fining at all and it would appear with some success. Undoubtedly fining does take something out of a wine and when it is rather delicate, as in this case, can make an appreciable difference.

The oxidation in the Sutter Home Zinfandel was very slight and a number of the other people tasting did not pick it up, but having been subjected for so many years to bad bottling in England, my nose, like that of a pointer after partridges, has been so trained to the signs of oxidation, it is not so difficult to pick it out.

Finally, there were two dessert wines which had been found in an old cellar and which had been made around 1886 at the Roma La Boheme vineyard.

Muscat.
Tawny colour and a strong smell of the muscat grape. A delicious flavour and although port shippers may resent the allusion, it was not unlike a rather good tawny port.

Angelica.
A fairly dark colour, a highly concentrated bouquet, rich, almost syrupy, having a taste reminiscent of caramel.

Chicago, 1972
Thursday, 27th April

During our last few days in California, we had been hearing grim stories of the weather in Chicago, the temperature being below zero and accompanied by ice and snow, with the result that we were almost shivering in apprehension. On arrival, we were greeted by a blue sky and the temperature at about 60 degrees; what more could one want!

While enjoying a glass of Taittinger Champagne with our friends Hugo Lorenz, and Richard and Lu Koch, we were asked where we wanted to dine. Promptly, I suggested someplace where we could have prime ribs of beef, because Chicago has always been noted for the quality of its beef. Therefore it was disillusioning to learn that the cattle are no longer raised nearby and that Chicago is no longer a centre for the beef trade. Still on this subject, it is disturbing to hear of the increase of Charollais cattle in America; they may be more commercial to raise, but as well we know from visiting France so often, the meat is not nearly so good as that of Aberdeen Angus or Hereford and so on.

Having disposed of our second bottle of champagne, we arrived at Bill and Charlie's, which we could see was typically American and just, in fact, what Prue and I had been hoping for. In spite of the meat coming from afar, the quality of the prime ribs was all that could be desired. As so often happens though in restaurants of this description, the wine list was really pathetic. However, by dint of really assiduous searching, we managed to unearth some excellent 1966 Châteauneuf-du-Pape, Les Fines Roches. This comes from the estate of my friend Jacques Mousset, so it was a pleasure to find it in Chicago.

Friday, 28th April
Cissac Tasting

When six months ago, Hugo had been in London, we invited Louis Vialard to meet him for dinner and as I mentioned in *Diary of a Winetaster*, Louis is the owner of Château Cissac, which is situated in the commune of that name about two miles to the west of the vineyard of Lafite. The enchanting single storey château was built in 1685 and his family have lived there for the past hundred years. So many of the châteaux in the Médoc are pretentious nineteenth century affairs, surrounded by glamour admittedly, but with precious little charm and few of them have lovely gardens ablaze with flowers in summer, such as one finds at Cissac.

Louis' forbears originate from the Cognac country and married into the family of Mondon; both his grandfather and great-grandfather before him were managers of Ch. Lafite and according to the old archives of Ch. Latour, the manager there in 1785 was a Monsieur Mondon. With this long family association with the local vines, I feel sure that if Louis were to cut himself while shaving one morning, the good red wine of the Médoc would flow, not anything so mundane as common or garden blood!

For some generations now, the great merchants of Bordeaux have mainly lived in the city and there are only one or two old families connected with the very soil of the Médoc who still live there. Ronald Barton of Langoa-Barton is one of them, so is Eugene Borie of Ducru-Beaucaillou and, of course, there is Emile Casteja with ancient family connections who spends the summer months at Batailley. In fact, few of the Médocain châteaux are inhabited at all except during the summer, most of them being used merely for the entertainment of guests at lunch time.

During my perambulations both north and south in California, I found the unprecedented increase in price of the red wines of Bordeaux has made many people, both trade and customers alike, fight shy, not only of the first growths, but of the *crus classés* as well; thus more and more attention is being paid to the good *crus bourgeois*. Everybody now knows that 1970 was an exceptional vintage. one of those all too rare occasions when a really abundant crop was backed by fine quality. Unfortunately, the demand for these 1970's was unusually strong, so that the prices doubled during the course of six months or so and quite a lot of speculation did not help matters either, for during the past few years investment in wine has often proved more lucrative than gambling in stocks. Then along came 1971, a vintage seemingly of rather good quality, but only half of a normal crop, so on account of the general shortage of fine wine the *crus classés* and others have emerged at twice and sometimes three times the price the same châteaux were asking for a better quality vintage a year previously.

When I tasted a few of the médocs, the Saint-Emilions and pomerols in March 1972, I found they had a very good colour, and although it was still too early to judge properly, the 1971's, although certainly not so good as the 1970's, should turn into quite good wines, but at what now appears to be nearly impossible prices. No wonder then the average American consumer is looking to the *crus bourgeois* for future supplies.

For a long time now, the overtaxed English have been turning to these lesser wines of Bordeaux and have become adept at their selection, but this seems to be a new development in the United States, where up to recently, the main demand has been for, if not the first growths, at least the *cru classés*. There will always be a good demand for the first growths, particularly in this huge country of America where there are always newcomers of substance coming on to the vinous scene, but if it is anything to go by, many of my personal friends in California who used to buy the first growths after every good vintage tell me that they ceased to do so after the 1964, or at least the 1966 vintage.

Clearly, my pen has carried me away, because this piece is supposed to be about the tasting of different vintages of Château Cissac which Hugo Lorenz suggested in October 1971! Organised under the auspices of the Chicago Chapter of the International Wine and Food Society and directed by the "spear carriers" of that Chapter, Hugo Lorenz and Richard Koch, the tasting took place in the George I room of the Ambassador Hotel. The 130 members attending were seated at long tables stretching across the room and each person had before him eight glasses filled with claret of an unusually dark colour.

Since in the past, Château Cissac has only been exported to England, with just a little to Belgium, it is virtually unknown in America, so we thought it would be a good idea to arrange a direct comparison of vintages with the well known Château Gloria, a wine which has acquired such a fine reputation under the able management of its present owner, Henri Martin. Many is the occasion when in a "blind" tasting, I have known Château Gloria to surpass even some of the better known second growths. Blind tastings can be very revealing.

The two châteaux were compared vintage by vintage and these are my own notes on them:

Gloria 1966.
Deep colour, a lovely fragrant bouquet, delightful flavour, fine quality.

Cissac 1966.
Deep colour, a full, fruity bouquet, a big, full-bodied wine which needs several years more before it will be ready.

Gloria 1964.
Good colour, attractive bouquet, very good flavour, well forward.

Cissac 1964.
Good colour, powerful bouquet, a big wine with a hint of richness, but still needs another two or three years.

Gloria 1962.
Very good colour, a strong Cabernet bouquet, delicious flavour.

Cissac 1962.
Deep colour, delightful bouquet, again a powerful, full-bodied wine which will continue to improve.

Cissac 1961.
Dark colour, deep bouquet, great concentration of flavour, in fact, a great mouthful of wine. Just enjoyable to drink, but will certainly continue to improve, for it has a long life ahead of it.

Cissac 1960.
Good colour, well developed bouquet, not a big wine, but has kept very well for this vintage.

Although they were clearly different in style, both châteaux showed up very well at this tasting, the Gloria, a true Saint-Julien, being most elegant and distinguished, whereas the Cissac was more masculine and powerful. Louis Vialard prides himself on making his wine in the old-fashioned manner for at the time of the vinification, he leaves the must with the skins for a period of up to three weeks, with the result that of course, as with Latour, Cissac is slow to develop, but long to last.

There is a kind of Rogues' Gallery of the Médoc which produced indifferent wine in 1964, but both the châteaux in question got their grapes in before the disastrous rain began to fall on 8th October of that year, and, as was evident on this occasion, made very good wine.

Dinner with the Koch's
Saturday, 29th April

Hugo Lorenz drove us to Lagrange, just outside Chicago, to dine with Richard and Lu Koch. They have a delightful house filled with antiques and it reminded us of home. Apart from a splendid dinner and delightful company, the evening was specially noticeable for the wine.

To begin with, three remarkable clarets, the first being Lynch-Bages 1962, the second time I have had this charmer during this visit to America. Leaving aside the regrettable lapse from grace in 1964, Lynch-Bages has been consistently good over the past decade.

The middle wine, La Mission-Haut-Brion 1953, came right up to expectations, such a lovely bouquet and a really delicious flavour. This appears to be holding up better than many of the more famous châteaux of its vintage.

Finally, a real masterpiece, Latour 1926, very dark of colour, the bouquet redolent of Latour at its best and it has such a powerful superb flavour. Often while staying at the château one has the privilege of choosing the wine to drink for dinner and sometimes as a great treat, I choose the 1926 for at the moment I think that I prefer it to almost all the other vintages, greybeards included. Little did I expect to have it offered to us in Chicago!

The evening was by no means over however, because after dinner we had not one, but two vintage ports to lick our lips over, both from the house of Graham, a firm whose style I have always liked so much. Considering its age and the journey across the Atlantic via Christie's, the 1924 was really superlative, really on its toes and in excellent condition. Of course 1924 was a very good vintage, not rated so highly perhaps as 1927, yet this particular wine showed fewer signs of age than many of the 1927's I had tasted but a week or so before in California.

Rightly or wrongly, feeling that the 1948 Graham might overshadow the more venerable 1924; our host served it last and what a star performer that turned out to be. Personally, I think he was right, but if anybody is prepared to argue, I would willingly accept to try those two over again, but in reverse order!

Sunday, 30th April

1960 Vintage Port

For quite a long time now there has been a marked predeliction for vintage port in California and, as will have been seen from my notes in the past, many of my friends there can produce as fine vintages to crown their dinner parties as any in England. In fact, I wonder how many people there are in England, even in the Port trade who can emulate Barney Rhodes of Oakland, California, who, from his own cellar, was able to organise a tasting of the now rare 1927 vintage and from no less than eight different shippers.

During the course of this visit to the United States, I have heard more people talking about vintage port than ever before, but it is not only in California but here too in Chicago, because for some time past I have noticed an ardent appreciation developing of this delectable after-dinner ambrosia and this very day has been the culmination of a long standing invitation from Hugo Lorenz to taste and discuss the 1960 vintage. It was, in fact, really a dual invitation, because Richard and Lu Koch had provided most of the food as well as some of the wine.

For some time these three enthusiasts have been collecting vintage port from the Christie auctions, and I also have had the opportunity to procure for them a certain quantity from the cellars of Kinloch's of London. Unless it is very young, to buy vintage port is not nearly so easy as it sounds, because first of all it is essential to know its history and background. Vintage port dislikes being moved around and having its crust disturbed, it will stand a certain amount, to wit this wearysome journey from England to Chicago with all its attendant hazards, but in this instance, for at least half of the wines, it had been their first move from an original bin. After frequent moves, it tends to lose some of its colour and certainly some of its grip.

With the growing appreciation in this huge country of the fine art of drinking this traditionally English tipple, I can foresee the imminent collapse of another of our treasured and time honoured English bastions, for at the present rate of production, clearly there will not be enough to go around. I wonder what those strongholds of this agreeable custom, the London Clubs, will do when faced with this depressing prospect! Smugly, I am glad I have been able to enjoy this nectar for more years than I care to remember. There is one consolation at least, I cannot imagine the average American sommelier wishing to under-

1960 Vintage Port

take anything so complicated as the decanting of a bottle of vintage port.

Among our fellow guests were Louis and his daughter, Danielle Vialard, and Philip Watrous. Phil is the member of the Chicago Chapter of the International Wine & Food Society responsible for their monthly lunches. I do not imagine there can be many French girls who participate in serious vintage port tastings, but being the owner of a *cru bourgeois* herself, Château La Tour de Mirail, as well as the daughter of the proprietor of Château Cissac, Danielle was as well qualified as most people and in fact, acquitted herself rather well.

We had been requested to refrain from eating lunch and to meet in Hugo Lorenz' apartment on the 29th floor overlooking Lake Michigan at around four o'clock. After a glass or two of champagne, we sat down to a delicious cold meal accompanied by 1961 Clos de Tart, a beautifully bred red Burgundy, but one which has not kept anything like so well as it should for such a fine vintage. Then we began on the port, of which there were six anonymous glasses and all we had to do was to enjoy their contents and place them in order of preference. Although, as may have been gathered by now, I am very fond of it, I have never set myself up as an authority on this particular subject, but here, for what they are worth are my notes on the individual wines together with the group placing.

1960 Vintage Port
(blind tasting)

Wine	Characteristics	My Points	Group Placing
Fonseca	Medium colour with a touch of brown at the edges, a good, what one might almost term "spicey" bouquet, good fruit, medium body and very easy to drink	8/10	share 2
Dow	Good colour, quite a nice bouquet, pleasant flavour, but slightly drier than the Fonseca	5/10	5
Sandeman	Good dark colour, a deep fragrant bouquet, good fruit and flavour, but a tiny bit spiritous. This may have been either the journey or its background, or both, because I have tasted better Sandeman 1960 in London	6/10	6

1960 Vintage Port (blind tasting) (continued)

Wine	Characteristics	My Points	Group Placing
Croft	The darkest colour of all, but also edging a little brown, a rich concentrated nose, which is not yet fully developed, a deep, powerful wine	10/10	1
Taylor	Dark but browning a little, very full bouquet, full and very fruity, also a tiny bit spiritous, still young though, and has a long way to go	7/10	4
Graham	Very dark colour, a full very rich bouquet, rich and round with a fine finish, excellent quality	9/10	share 2

In view of the doubtless tumultuous voyage across the Atlantic and then through the Great Lakes, I fully expected these wines to have suffered more from the journey, but not a bit of it; they had the life and "grip" (a great word, "grip," when describing vintage port) as most 1960's I have had the good fortune to taste at home in England.

From time to time, people talk about weekend pursuits; well, I can think of many less enjoyable ways of spending a Sunday afternoon and evening such as this!

Tuesday, 2nd May

Cincinnati

I met Marjorie Valvano for the first time through Katie Bourke of *Wine Magazine* and, as she comes to Europe regularly on buying expeditions, we usually see her on her way through London. Apart from her charming personality, Marjorie is a remarkable person and among the few successful women on the distribution side of the wine business; she buys for and manages the wine department of the huge H. & S. Pogue Company in Cincinnati, Ohio. In spite of her modesty, she has a great command of her subject and consequently runs not only an attractive wine division, but also one with a wide range of well selected wine.

With her husband Bob, an engineer by profession, she met us at the airport and in view of the fact that we had lost an hour (new time zone) we soon found ourselves swept off to lunch at one of Cincinnati's leading restaurants, La Maisonette. This is more than merely a name because Cincinnati justly prides itself on having some of the finest restaurants outside New York. Besides ourselves, Louis Vialard and his daughter Danielle, there were two other guests, Mr. Henry Sonneman, the President of Meier's Wine Cellars and his enologist, Gallo McLean. Such is the size of this vast country and also the extent of my ignorance, that it had never occurred to me that by visiting Cincinnati I would be coming to a wine growing district! It seems that vines were formerly grown on the slopes outside the city, but these have long since given way to urban development. As a new adventure however, the Meiers have planted out about 600 acres on hillsides well exposed to the sun along the Ohio River, about thirty miles east of Cincinnati, although most of their production comes from an island in Lake Erie in northern Ohio where the lake waters temper the winter weather. Up to now, the severe winters in the Cincinnati area have been the problem, impeding the growth of the *vinifera* vine; consequently, in order to obtain better results than the bouquet and flavour of the *Labrusca* grape traditionally grown in America, new hybrids have been planted and it was the produce of these that we were to drink with our meal.

There is so much frost here in winter-time, far more than in the vineyards of California or Europe, that great attention has to be paid to frost prevention. Mr. Sonneman told us that he burns compressed liquid solid fuel bricks made by Mobil in Texas, which burn for six hours before disintegrating. Since he has to use about 200 per acre each night, this must add considerably to the general overhead expenses.

1970 Jac Jan Ohio Chablis (Meier's).
A blend from grape 5276 and grape 5279. Good colour, rather light of bouquet, but fresh, medium dry and agreeable. This was retailing at $2.65.

1970 Jac Jan Ohio Valley Red Table Wine (Meier's).
Medium colour, pleasant bouquet, has fruit, but is very light.

Neither of these wines had that "foxey" taste I had rather expected; however, I was pleasantly surprised by their quality. I am told that hybrids are providing many agreeable wines from other growing areas. From the top of the tower of the H. and S. Pogue Building we had a splendid view of the city and it is much prettier than any of us had somehow anticipated. The winding Ohio and the rolling hills of the surrounding countryside are most effective.

Cru Bourgeois and Cissac Tasting

The rhyme and reason of this visit to Cincinnati was a lecture I had promised to give on the *crus bourgeois* of the Médoc, and to conduct a tasting of some of the wines. When I first planned this, little did I know that I would have Louis Vialard to help me, for his knowledge, wit and Gallic charm greatly enlivened the proceedings.

This further tasting of vintages from Château Cissac followed on from that in Chicago, but as some of the wines involved were different, I trust that a little repetition will be forgiven. In Chicago the comparison was with Gloria, probably the most successful of all the *crus bourgeois* but in Cincinnati Marjorie Valvano produced a selection of other châteaux which widened the scope. It was no mean feat, for one store to provide four such wines in this category.

As it happened, this tasting came at a most appropriate moment, for with the meteoric increase in price of the classified growths there has been considerable disillusionment, and claret lovers who before only thought of the classified growths when buying the wines of Bordeaux, are turning quite seriously to the *crus bourgeois*. In view of the astronomic rise in prices, it would seem that the Bordelais must think all Americans are millionaires. Admittedly there are a great number of well-to-do people and among them inevitably some label snobs, as well as the newcomers to wine who, through lack of confidence, feel that they can only buy the names they know, but on the other hand, there are many who are by no means well off and who do seriously enjoy drinking the wines of Bordeaux. It is this last named group who, with reluctance, are being forced off the *crus classés,* and, if one can judge by the reception of the *crus bourgeois* at this tasting, they will take with alacrity to the good, but lesser wines of Bordeaux.

It will be fascinating to see what the effect will be in, say, 1975, when at their elevated prices the well-known clarets of 1970 and 1971 begin to appear in the liquor stores. Perhaps with the effect of inflation and increasing world demand they will be absorbed, in the true sense of the word, but without the gift of foresight, at the moment it seems hard to believe.

The tasting, on behalf of an enthusiastic group called "The Winetasters," had been most admirably arranged by Marjorie Valvano in the Contemporary Arts Centre, and I do not think that I can do better than to quote her introductory notes on the tasting sheets:

> About the wines—In the whole of Bordeaux there are well over 5,000 vineyards. Less than 200 of these constitute the classified growths—sixty in the

five great growths followed by a collection of other smaller and some less known châteaux which are known as the "crus bourgeois." These latter vineyards often produce wines as fine as those of their reputed superiors, and in many instances, truly great wines. All the wines being tasted on this occasion are "crus bourgeois."

Château Cissac.

In 1895 Monsieur Jacques Mondon, who had inherited his expertise from many generations of wine growers in the Médoc area, acquired two properties in the commune of Cissac, known then as Château Abiet and Domaine de Martiny. This made an estate of some 170 acres, of which only 65 were suitable for vine growing. From then this property has been known as Château Cissac. It is sited in the Haut Médoc district, about one mile to the west of Ch. Lafite-Rothschild. (If I may add a footnote here, Louis' grandfather and great-grandfather before that, were both managers of Ch. Lafite, as we mentioned earlier, and according to some old manuscripts of Ch. Latour which have recently been unearthed, there was a Monsieur Mondon who, in 1785 was the manager at Latour.) Monsieur Louis Vialard, the grandson of the last Monsieur Mondon is the present owner of the property.

Ch. Cissac is made in the old fashioned manner, the must being left in contact with the skins for about three weeks, hence the darker colour of the wine and the fact that it takes longer to mature than a great number of contemporary médocs. In common with the *grands crus* it is put into new oak barrels after every vintage. The vineyard is planted with 75% cabernet sauvignon, 20% merlot and 5% petit verdot.

Château Siran.

Located in Margaux, this property is owned by M. Alain Miailhe. The soil tends to be sandy and the wine is light, but fine and elegant, well representing the style of its commune. Much has been done recently to improve the property and an average of 120 tonneaux (approximately 10,000 cases) is produced each year.

Château Phélan-Ségur (one of the better known *crus bourgeois*).

Located in the northern-most commune of the Médoc, i.e., Saint-Estèphe, where the soil tends to become heavier with a clay mixture which produces wines having more acidity. These are dark of colour, full-bodied, virile and keep well. Phélan-Ségur is a rather large property consisting of approximately 100 acres and produces an average of 15,000 cases per year.

Château Lanessan.

An estate of some forty acres planted in the vine, two-thirds of which are Cabernet Sauvignon and one third Merlot. It is located in the Haut-Médoc and is owned by M. Bouteiller, who is also the owner of Ch. Pichon-Longueville-Baron. The wine is usually full and round with pleasant finesse.

Château Gloria.

Situated in a very good part of the commune of Saint-Julien, this château, under the able ownership of M. Henri Martin, has come very much to the fore since the war. Henri Martin, the Mayor of Saint-Julien and one of the leading figures in Bordeaux wine affairs, is also a manager of Ch. Latour. In blind tastings, Ch. Gloria equals and frequently surpasses many of the *crus classés,* including the second growths.

As will be seen, in each vintage, Ch. Cissac was matched against another *cru bourgeois.* The tasting notes are my own, but the percentages in favour (i.e., with the 1967 vintage, 80% of the hundred people tasting were in favour of the Ch. Gloria) were taken from a show of hands.

1967 Vintage

    Ch. Cissac.
        Medium colour, fruity bouquet, medium body, still immature and undeveloped.
        20% in favour.

    Ch. Gloria.
        Medium colour, certainly darker than the Cissac, lovely bouquet and flavour. More forward too and a fine wine for its year.
        80% in favour.

1966 Vintage

Ch. Cissac.
Good dark colour, good bouquet and lots of fruit, needs another two or three years yet.
60% in favour.

Ch. Lanessan.
Dark colour, full, very good bouquet, a big, full-bodied wine, with plenty of tannin, but appears to have less finesse than the Cissac.
40% in favour.

1964 Vintage

Ch. Cissac.
Fine, dark colour, delightful bouquet, is round and almost rich. Very good now, but has a great future. This is one of the successful 1964's.
90% in favour.

Ch. Phélan-Ségur.
Colour fading to brown, bouquet only fair, medium body, but this bottle, at least, was tiring rapidly.
10% in favour.

1961 Vintage

Ch. Cissac.
Splendid colour, very deep bouquet, masses of fruit and a huge massive wine which still needs some years to mature.
90% in favour.

Ch. Siran.
Unfortunately this bottle was not quite bright, but its contents had a pretty bouquet and a delicious Margaux flavour, ready now.
10% in favour.

It was highly encouraging to see the interest taken in these lesser wines of Bordeaux, and I had the feeling that a number of people were quite surprised.

Later, about twenty of us repaired to the home of Dr. Herbert Francis and his wife Sylvia, for a mouth-watering supper, all prepared by Peter Glaubitz, one of the directors of "The Winetasters." The house, built towards the end of the nineteenth century by a former beer baron in the form of a small teutonic castle, has beautifully proportioned rooms inside and once there we indulged in such gastronomic pleasures as a side of pickled salmon i.e., marinated in salt and sugar with dill weed, which was followed by another succulent dish, sweetbreads cooked with grapes. Dr. Francis is both a friend and firm admirer of Dr. Konstantin Frank, the genius (of Vinifera Wine Cellars) who makes fine wine under almost impossible conditions, so with our culinary delights we sipped Dr. Frank's 1966 Johannisberg Riesling—very clean, very dry, with a real smell of the varietal.

Clearly, a visit to the cellar was essential, so before we sat down to eat, we trooped below to gaze upon row upon row and bin upon bin of fine wines. It was there that our host opened a bottle of Dr. Frank's 1967 Pinot Chardonnay, a lesson for me, because I had always thought that he only made wines from the Johannisberg Riesling grape. This led to the tasting of it as described on pages 129-135. The quality too was a surprise, a fine aromatic bouquet and a delicious flavour and, tired as I was by this time, I could not help being impressed. Our generous host insisted that I take a bottle home with me and this I did in order to compare it with some of the finest Chardonnays from California which I am fortunate enough to have in London.

With our splendid supper, of which the main course was barbecued lamb, we enjoyed magnums of Louis Vialard's 1959 Ch. Cissac and finally with barquettes of strawberries and a soufflé, we were treated to one of Dr. Frank's famous Beerenausleses!

Wednesday, 3rd May

Canada, 1972

After about only four hours' sleep, it was a somewhat subdued party which gathered at Cincinnati airport to catch a 9:15 a.m. plane to Toronto. This was a parting of the ways, because while Louis and Danielle Vialard and I were going to Canada, my wife was branching off to visit her sister who lives in Maine. It is only when one travels as much as we were doing that, by the law of averages, various things go wrong. On this occasion, not only did we have to change planes at Cleveland, Ohio, but also at London, Ontario and it was when we passed through the Customs at the latter place, that we discovered some unpleasant viscous liquid had got loose in the baggage section of the plane and had penetrated our luggage.

When finally we arrived at Toronto, our host, Colonel Allan Burton, proved a proper fairy godfather, or whatever it is, for no sooner had we arrived than my stained suit was whipped off to his cleaning department to be dealt with in a most expeditious manner.

Audrey and Allan Burton live on their delightful farm at Burlington, in the country outside Toronto. Apart from the broad acres of farm land, it is a beautiful estate with a lake in front of the house, fed by a fast flowing stream and on a further lake both swans and wild duck were nesting. Thanks to a very late spring, the countryside had a wintry look, but with the fine weather accompanying us, all the shrubs and magnolia trees were itching to burst into leaf and flower.

Having served for many years with the Household Cavalry of Canada during which time he commanded his regiment, Allan's interest in horses is great, so much so that for many seasons he has hunted in England and is Master of his local hunt. His recently constructed riding school is a "mouthwatering" building for anyone with an interest in equine pursuits.

Among the guests for dinner were our old friends Bill and Marjorie Finlayson, through whom, in fact, I had met my present hosts. The quality of the fare speaks for itself, fresh trout which Allan had caught himself, followed by lamb from his farm, what more could be desired! The wine was on an equally high plane, a Chablis, Le Clos 1967, domaine bottled with the trout; then with the lamb we drank two bottles of Cheval Blanc 1964, a fabulous wine, dark of colour and deep of heart, which can be enjoyed now, as indeed we did, but it will continue to improve for some years to come.

As a château proprietor, Louis Vialard was detailed to attend to the decanting and when he opened one of the two bottles of Cheval Blanc, it was found to be "working" or, if you like, fermenting, but this soon died away and as we drank, the rest of us noticed nothing. This disturbance must clearly have been owing to the season of the year, for the spring was on the very point of bursting. This is a phenomenon which occurs at times, even fairly mature wines can become upset, either in the spring or at the time of the vintage. It struck me as extraordinary though that this should occur so many thousands of miles away from the native heath of Cheval Blanc.

There was more to come though, for with the cheese Allan had provided a bottle of Mouton-Rothschild 1916 (a gift originally from Bill Finlayson). This showed no signs of age and was a fine bottle. It was interesting to see the old Mouton label, a much more simple affair than the modern version. The final *bonne bouche* was a bottle of Warre 1927 and how very good it was. It seems to me that I have drunk more vintage port during this present visit to North America than I ever do during similar periods at home in England.

Thursday, 4th May

The day was spent in Allan's office in Toronto at the top of the Simpson Tower, 32nd floor. The whole floor is devoted to Executives' offices and they are better planned and better decorated than any I have ever seen; most of this, I gather however, is owing to the influence of my host, the Chairman of the Board of Simpsons. From these offices the widespread view of Lake Ontario is magnificent, likewise looking in every direction across the rest of the city.

Apart from the pleasure of coming once more to Toronto, the purpose of my visit was to discuss wine with Allan, who, among his many other occupations, is also chairman of the wine committee of the York Club, no doubt one of the finest, if not the finest club of North America. Late in March, the Burtons and the Hungerfords had dined with us in London and had honoured me by asking me to act as consultant to their club, a fascinating assignment. Jack Hungerford is a friend from my visits to Toronto in the past. I forget what we drank that evening in London, but do remember that we finished on a fairly high note with my last bottle of Wehlener Sonnenuhr Beerenauslese 1949, a wine which had won the German State prize for that vintage.

It was a good thing that I came to Toronto, because there was much to discuss and plan and we were kept hard at it all day long. It was just as well we did all the preparatory work because we had to have everything as much cut and dried as possible before the Committee Meeting arranged for that evening. In my time I have attended many a wine committee meeting in London, both at Brooks's and Boodles, but enjoyable as they undoubtedly are, never have I attended such an amusing one as this turned out to be at the York Club! Between us, we somehow managed to consume quite a number of bottles of excellent vintage port!

An Eye-Opener, London, 1972

The episode to be described was not at all the kind of "eye-opener" you consume when breakfasting at Brennan's in New Orleans, but in fact, something far more exciting. It was a sequel to many experiences in America.

I should endeavour to excuse myself before I begin, because it is hardly the right thing to do to write up one's own tasting, but as in this case the circumstances were so unusual, I hope that I shall be forgiven.

It all stems in the first place from my enthusiasm over the astonishing progress which has been made by the owners of some of the smaller vineyards of California. There is neither the time nor the space here to go into this, but suffice it to say that up to date the progress in quality has not yet been matched by quantity; stocks are still so hopelessly inadequate that there is insufficient to supply even the connoisseurs of California. Quality, like all the good things of life, is rare and difficult to find. Regretfully therefore, what follows here may really only be of academic interest.

To begin with, I feel I must express my gratitude to the growers, especially those in the Napa Valley, who have been unfailing in their kindness to help me in the study of their wines. My feelings are so sincere that I cast around to find some method of showing my appreciation, and suddenly the way became clear.

In London, I have a good friend, namely Bobby Montgomery Scott, the personal aide to Mr. Annenberg, the American Ambassador to the Court of St. James's, and in 1971 prior to my departure to San Francisco I suggested to him that his ambassador might like to have in his cellar a few cases of the really fine wines of California, those barely heard of outside the inner wine circles of that State and which, because of their scarcity, are virtually unobtainable.

A week or so later when I reached the San Francisco area, I made some enquiries and found that my plan was equally acceptable to the growers and that various golden keys to treasured cellars could be turned and, over and above that, the wines would be presented free, although that had not at all been our intention.

I am eternally grateful to the late Walter Peterson for unlocking these doors for me and for assembling the consignment together. Walt Peterson was one of the most erudite and enthusiastic wine men that I have ever met in my entire career. By profession a chemist in the Shell organisation, his hobby was wine and he founded and ran The

San Francisco Wine Sampling Club about which I have written on numerous occasions. Walt had retired early from business, a year previously, so that he could devote himself more to writing on wine, a task he accomplished not only delightfully, but with such great knowledge. His untimely death has been a serious blow to a great number of people.

I also have to thank Dick Peterson (no relation) of Beaulieu Vineyard, for it was he who assembled and despatched the cases to New York for eventual shipment to England, but somehow, somewhere along the line most of the cases disappeared; somebody must have known they were on to a good thing, so a second consignment had to be organised and that finally arrived in London in January 1972, some eight months later.

Since I knew that these wines were unique, I had asked if Mr. Annenberg would allow me to have one bottle from each case, so that I could arrange a tasting in London for a few of the leading authorities, my reason being that although they had on many occasions been able to taste the commercial wines of California, I was certain none of them had any idea of the quality of the wines which were to be presented on this occasion.

Knowing how upset wine can be after any journey let alone the one across the Atlantic, I arranged for the tasting to take place some months later after my return from the United States. This would give it plenty of time to settle down and show at its best. As it turned out, it was as well that I did so, for the result was incredibly successful.

In England, we have in our wine trade a group called "The Masters of Wine," and you can only become a Master of Wine by passing a fairly stringent examination, both written and practical. I felt that at this tasting in particular, the Masters of Wine should be well represented and among those who attended were Geoffrey Jameson, the chairman of the Committee of the Masters of Wine, Michael Broadbent of Christie's, Colin Fenton of Sotheby's, both of whom I am proud to claim as ex-pupils, and Christopher Tatham of The Wine Society. Among us lesser mortals were Hugh Johnson, author of that splendid *World Atlas of Wine*, Mrs. K. C. Bourke, editor of *Wine Magazine* and Heather Bradley, London Representative of the *New York Times* as well as my own humble self.

Before going any further I would like to thank Mr. Annenberg for so kindly presenting all those bottles and Bobby and Gay Montgomery Scott for allowing the tasting to take place in their lovely house.

There were however, one or two interlopers among the bottles, because towards the end of my visit to California I had spent a day visiting Chalone Vineyard, a remote mountain vineyard in Monterey County which is owned by a most enterprising young man called Dick

Graf. So impressed was I by his white wines that there and then, I arranged for an assorted case to be despatched to me by air, for I felt sure they would be worthy of this tasting. Also, while passing through Cincinnati, at the hospitable table of Dr. Herbert Francis, I was introduced to the 1967 Pinot Chardonnay of Dr. Konstantin Frank's Vinifera Wine Cellars. It was of such remarkable quality that I accepted gladly the extra bottle that Dr. Francis thrust into my not unwilling hands! Also included in our tasting were a bottle of Louis Latour's 1969 Puligny-Montrachet and a bottle of 1957 Ch. Lascombes château bottled; these were intended to afford a basis of comparison for our European palates. Furthermore, in order to avoid any kind of prejudice, I had removed the label from the Puligny-Montrachet and had re-labelled the bottle as 1969 fine white Burgundy.

These then, are the wines that we tasted on 6th June, 1972 and they are accompanied, for what they are worth, by my own tasting notes.

White Wines

Chenin Blanc 1970, Estate Bottled, Chalone Vineyard (Monterey County)
Clean fragrant nose, fresh, dry, good fruit acidity and has considerable charm. A good wine in any context.

Pinot Blanc 1969, Estate Bottled, Chalone Vineyard (Monterey County)
Fairly full bouquet, nice flavour, tiny, tiny trace of bitterness at the finish, but good nevertheless.

Johannisberger Riesling 1970, Estate Bottled, Souverain Cellars (Napa Valley)
Pretty perfumed bouquet; an attractive almost fragrant taste. A totally different style of wine from the others but most agreeable.

Chardonnay 1969, Estate Bottled, Chalone Vineyard (Monterey County)
Good colour, a tremendous full rich nose, a huge wine full of fruit and body. Good fruit acidity too, a great success.

Chardonnay 1969, Mayacamas Vineyards, Estate Bottled (Napa Valley)
Delightful scented bouquet, good fruit, well-balanced and fine quality.

Pinot Chardonnay 1969, Beaulieu Vineyard (Napa Valley)
Lovely nose, good fruit, good quality.

Pinot Chardonnay 1968, Estate Bottled, Freemark Abbey (Napa Valley)
Darker colour, fine rather rich nose, full flavoured, delicious taste. For me, this finished only a short head behind the Chalone Chardonnay!

Pinot Chardonnay 1967, Vinifera Wine Cellars (near Hammondsport, New York)
Very pale colour, a lighter wine but excellent. It was remarkable how well this compared with the others.

Chardonnay 1969, Puligny-Montrachet of Louis Latour
Fine fragrant nose, good fruit, dry, clearly of fine quality. It is no disparagement to say that it did not come out on top.

Red Wines

Pinot Noir 1968, Estate Bottled, Heitz Wine Cellars (Napa Valley)
Colour medium, agreeable bouquet and flavour and although different, was not in the same league as the other red wines.

Cabernet Sauvignon (Bosche) *1968,* Freemark Abbey (Napa Valley)
Very dark colour, very fine rich nose, full-bodied, well-balanced, a good depth of fruit and flavour, a great wine. Will improve.

Cabernet Sauvignon (Martha's Vineyard) *1966,* Estate Bottled, Heitz Wine Cellars (Napa Valley)
Rich and very fragrant bouquet, enormously full and rich, very great quality. This will get better and better.

Cabernet Sauvignon 1964, Estate Bottled, Ridge Vineyard (Cupertino)
Very, very dark colour, full rich nose, a very big wine, still full of tannin. Needs 3 or 4 years at least.

Late Harvest Zinfandel 1968, Estate Bottled, Mayacamas Vineyards (Napa Valley)
Black, black colour, a rich varietal bouquet, enormously round, rich and most powerful. Ready perhaps in ten years' time!

Château Lascombes 1957
Good dark colour but going brown, rather dry, has fruit and flavour but did not stand out specially against the California wines.

Schramsberg Blanc de Blanc 1967, Estate Bottled, Schramsberg Vineyards (Napa Valley)
Schramsberg is among the very best American Champagnes, and among local connoisseurs is regarded as the Krug or Bollinger of America. Most American champagnes are easily discernable from their bouquet and flavour but somehow Jack Davies, the maker of Schramsberg, has managed to produce a delightful wine not at all dissimilar from the French variety.

In Europe no sparkling wine made outside the district of Champagne can legally be called champagne, but the French authorities have yet to win their battle over American Champagne. Wine sold under that label in the United States is made both on the east coast and California, some of it is good and much not so good.

Although Schramsberg is on sale in London, rather sadly it has to be labelled as California Sparkling White Wine—it deserves a better fate!

Although for some time I, personally, have been convinced of the quality of these fine California wines, I was anxious also to obtain the completely untrammelled opinion of the really experienced tasters gathered together on this occasion; therefore as each arrived, he was subjected to a minor test. On a separate table away from all the bottles were placed three innocuous glasses of wine (i) 1969 Chalone Chardonnay, (ii) Dr. Frank's 1967 Pinot Chardonnay and (iii) Louis Latour's 1969 Puligny-Montrachet and the tasters were asked to state their preference.

While it was unanimously agreed that the quality of all three was first rate, everyone without exception chose the Chalone Chardonnay as the best of the three, though opinion was divided between the other two. What was so interesting though is that nobody identified the Puligny-Montrachet as being white Burgundy and nobody the New York State wine. It was comforting to have my own opinion so amply confirmed. This result also speaks volumes for the high standard obtained by Dr. Konstantin Frank, particularly when one considers the extreme difficulties with which in New York State he has to contend in relation to the more equable climates of California and Burgundy.

At a later date, a noted Burgundian negociant who is also a vigneron, was put to roughly the same test and unhesitatingly he took the Chalone Pinot Chardonnay to be the Puligny-Montrachet. His surprise was great!

Since the Chalone Chardonnay had such a delightful, almost honeyed bouquet and flavour it reminded me of a fine Corton Charlemagne. Indeed, it had crossed my mind to bring a bottle of Louis Latour's 1969 Corton Charlemagne with me instead of the Puligny-Montrachet, but since my remaining bottles of this superb wine are so few, my innate stingyness prevailed over my better instincts and in any case, we were not to know how well the American wines would stand up to the test.

Apart from the impressive Chardonnays, the group of tasters was also particularly captivated by the charm of the Chalone Chenin Blanc. Up-to-date, I have been inclined to regard the Napa Valley rather in the same light as, say, the Médoc of Bordeaux, the holy of holies where the very finest quality is produced. One of the exciting aspects of this tasting is that the white wine universally acclaimed as the best did not come from the Napa Valley at all, but from near Soledad in Monterey County, about three hours' drive south from San Francisco, whereas the Napa Valley lies some sixty miles to the northeast of the city. This opens up all sorts of possibilities for the future of California wine, and no doubt before long we shall hear of other hitherto unknown vineyards coming into the limelight.

By and large, the red wines were felt to be less successful than the white, but it was generally agreed that they stood up remarkably well against the château bottled 1957 Château Lascombes. Incidentally, one of the reasons why I chose the Lascombes is because this château is so well known in the United States. Besides the 1968 Late Harvest Zinfandel which, by virtue of its nature is in a class by itself, I was pleased to find my previous tasting of the Cabernet Sauvignon Bosche and Martha's Vineyard completely confirmed, for these two are splendid wines. It may well be that because of my acquaintance with them my enthusiasm for them was more intense than that of some of my companions.

As a "bonne bouche" to our tasting, our host and hostess, Bobby and Gay Montgomery Scott invited us upstairs to the drawing room to enjoy a glass of 1967 Schramsberg Blanc de Blanc American champagne. Such is the quality of this Schramsberg that it was the only wine that President Nixon took with him to Peking; the good or bad result of this is that poor Jack Davies, the owner of the winery, has run completely out of stock. It would now appear that London is the only city in the world where at this moment a little is still available!

In conclusion, in case this story of mine may raise false hopes in many a wine lover's breast, it has a sadder side and that, of course, is the acute shortage of stock, for in an average vintage it is doubtful whether much more than about 100 cases are made of some of these wines. Thus, this really fine California wine is not yet for the average consumer, but if one can judge by the way things are going, maybe it will be for his sons and grandsons who succeed him.

JMB
Old street in Berncastel.

Germany, 1972

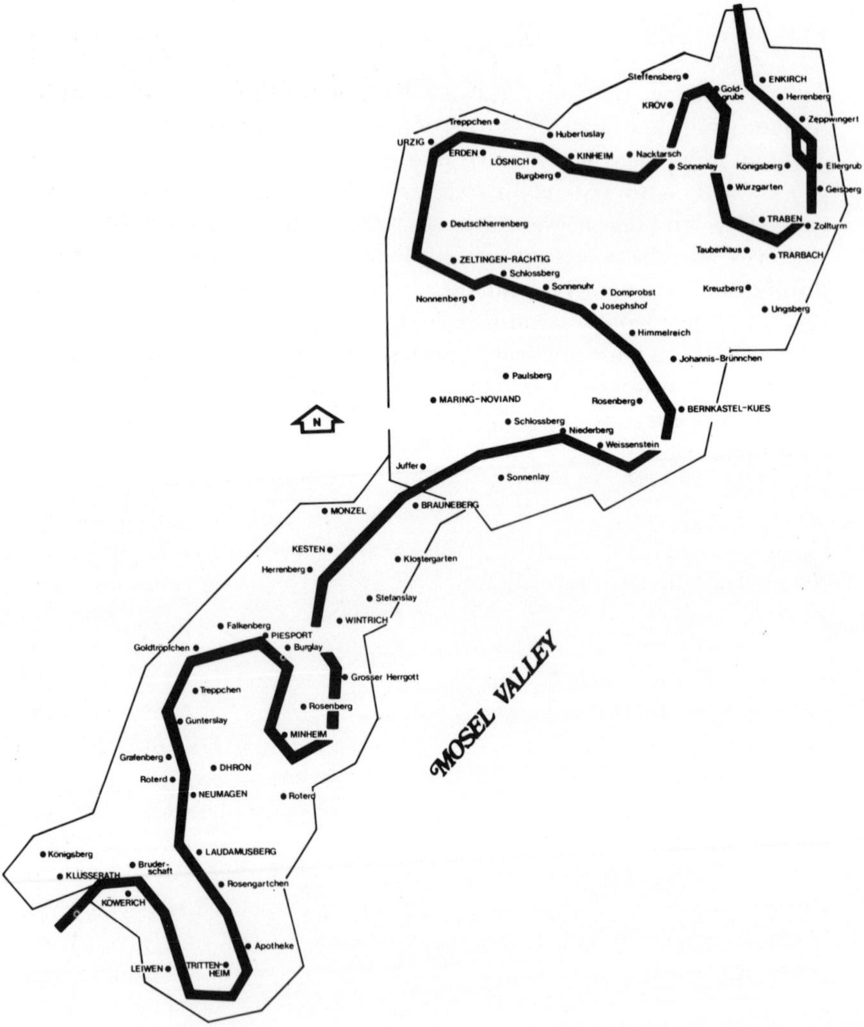
Steffensberg
Gold-
grube
ENKIRCH
Herrenberg
KROV
Zeppwingert
Treppchen
Hubertuslay
URZIG
ERDEN
LÖSNICH
KINHEIM
Nacktarsch
Sonnenlay
Königsberg
Ellergrub
Burgberg
Wurzgarten
Geisberg
Deutschherrenberg
TRABEN
Zollturm
Taubenhaus
TRARBACH
ZELTINGEN-RACHTIG
Schlossberg
Sonnenuhr
Domprobst
Kreuzberg
Nonnenberg
Josephshof
Ungsberg
Himmelreich
Johannis-Brünnchen
Paulsberg
MARING-NOVIAND
Rosenberg
BERNKASTEL-KUES
N
Schlossberg
Niederberg
Weissenstein
Juffer
Sonnenlay
MONZEL
BRAUNEBERG
KESTEN
Herrenberg
Klostergarten
Stefanslay
Falkenberg
WINTRICH
PIESPORT
Goldtröpchen
Burglay
Grosser Herrgott
Treppchen
Rosenberg
Gunterslay
MINHEIM
MOSEL VALLEY
Grafenberg
DHRON
Roterd
NEUMAGEN
Roterd
Königsberg
LAUDAMUSBERG
Bruder-
schaft
KLÜSSERATH
Rosengartchen
KÖWERICH
Apotheke
LEIWEN
TRITTEN-
HEIM

The Moselle 1971: A Great Vintage

Sunday, 25th June

Although tiring, the journey from London to Trier is fairly simple. At Southend, close to the mouth of the river Thames, your car is loaded on to an antiquated looking aeroplane, no fear of hi-jackers here, and you fly with it to Ostend in Belgium. This was my wife's first visit to the German vineyards and with us, we had Dr. Otto Loeb, the great authority on the wines of the Moselle. The journey from Ostend through Belgium and Luxembourg is rather dull but mainly by autoroute. Our first stop was to lunch high up in the Ardennes at a restaurant called La Barrière de Champlan and this was an unfortunate experience because the food was mediocre and the service deplorable. The second was to stretch our legs in Luxembourg in order to admire a little that fair city. The last part of the journey was the best, because our route lay along the upper Moselle, with vineyards steeply banked on either side, the left bank being Luxembourg and the right Germany. From a grey, windy morning, the weather had gradually improved throughout the day and, as though to welcome us, the vineyards were looking their best in the early evening sunshine.

Trier is the capital city of the Moselle area and our destination was the recently re-built Porta Nigra Hotel. This is as bright as a new pin and most comfortable, and what a contrast to the dreary old Victorian mausoleum it has replaced. Externally though, it is quite hideous and how the City Fathers could permit anything so incongruous to be erected opposite the Porta Nigra, the town's most imposing piece of Roman architecture, is hard to believe. Somewhat dark and forbidding, but nevertheless immensely impressive, the Porta Nigra was built by the Romans in the second century to form a gateway to the original city. Thus Trier is not only a magnet for the lovers of wine, but also for those interested in history and archaeology, for this truly delightful town is crammed with ancient remains.

It must be confessed however that our journey was not in search of ancient architecture, but of fine wine, to taste and seek out some of the already famous 1971 Moselles. About a month before, Colin Fenton of Sotheby's London, had met Otto Loeb who had just returned from a visit to Trier, and the latter had mentioned that some of these Moselles were what he termed "Harry's wine!" The last time I had come here with Otto was in January 1965 and on that occasion our purpose had been to buy the 1964 vintage and what splendid wines we were able to discover together. People in my firm had tried to persuade me that January was much too early for such a venture, but with Otto at my side, I knew all would be well. As it turned out, we were among the very first, if not the first buyers on the scene; consequently we had our pick of the finest casks of the 1964's and were able to buy these excellent wines at roughly the same price as the previous unfashionable vintage of 1963, for at that moment it was not fully appreciated how good the 1964's were. It is well to mention here that unlike the produce of the châteaux in Bordeaux, the more eminent categories of German wine can and do vary from cask to cask. I well remember the surprise of the Kendermann firm when I arrived there the following week, to hear that I had been tasting so early and a year or so later Hans Walter Kendermann told me that he had then rushed in to buy the 1964's of the Moselle and that thanks to me they had "made a killing!"

The year 1964 was an exceptional vintage for the wines from the Saar and the Ruwer valleys and it was only recently that I finished my last lovely bottle of Maximin Grünhauser Herrenberg Spätlese of that year. In one way the wine region of the Moselle resembles that of Bordeaux, i.e., not every good vintage is equally satisfactory for all districts, that is to say there are times, as with the 1962 vintage, when the médocs were more successful than the Saint-Emilions and there are also occasions when the wines of Saint-Emilion and Pomerol are better than those of the Médoc. So it is with the wines of the Moselle proper and those from its tributaries, the Saar and Ruwer rivers. When the Saar and Ruwer wines are good, as in 1964, 1966, 1969, they are very, very good, but in other vintages, no doubt on account of their steely character, they are less agreeable than the more ample wines of the Moselle.

What was so exciting about this particular visit was the news that the 1971's are even better than the 1969's, 1966's and 1964's and are certainly the best Moselles since 1959. Mother Nature is sparing with the bounty she bestows on these northern vineyards of the Moselle and the Rhine and it is not often that she relents and so permits the wine growers to produce something really outstanding. For example, since the end of the war, the only really remarkable vintages have been 1945, 1949, 1953 and 1959.

A few words about Dr. Otto Loeb here may not come amiss. The son of a prominent wine merchant of Trier in 1898, he was educated at Cologne University where he obtained his doctorate, his thesis being the first history ever written of the wine trade of the Moselle. His family business concentrated solely upon fine quality wine, and to this day there is a road in Trier named after his father. On account of the trouble with Hitler he came to England in 1937 and founded his firm O. W. Loeb & Co. Ltd. in 1938. Overcoming war-time difficulties with little or no stock to sell, he re-visited Germany in 1948, for the first time since he had left in 1937. When the Glyndebourne Opera started again in 1950, Otto had a lot to do with the supplies of wine and German ones in particular. Otto is a brilliant taster who probably knows as much about the fine wines of the Moselle as anyone in existence. Like his father before him he has never been interested in anything but good quality and, to give but one insight into his character has always resolutely turned his face from either buying or selling any wine bearing the label of Liebfraumilch. One of the things which must have afforded him considerable pleasure was when in 1960 he was made a citizen of his native Trier. He was also honoured in 1968 when through the German Ambassador he received the *Verdienstkreuz*, first class, an award so far presented to only three people in the wine trade.

I myself have known this gentle, artistic personality since the late forties and during my years with Harvey's used to sally forth to buy wine with him. He has retired now but his love for his native wine lures him back like a moth to the flame, for in wine as in music he has an unerring taste.

Although in the past I had been to California on several occasions, it had been chiefly in the role of a salesman and it was not until 1969 that I was able to go there independently to indulge in the study of California wine. It was during this time that I realised what an agreeable impact Otto had made among the wine cognoscenti in and around San Francisco, and consequently during the past three or four years I have had the opportunity to taste finer German wines in California than at home in England. While they are all true devotees of the wines of France, at the tables of some of my Californian friends, the Rhodes', the Adamson's, the Dickerson's, Robert Knudson and the Ichinose's, I have tasted many of the finest German wines imaginable, all stemming from the firm of Sigmund Loeb of Trier. As well as his adopted race, the English, the Californians have much to be thankful for.

Monday, 26th June

Although in Trier there is a cornucopia of interesting things to see such as the Roman baths, the Roman Basilica, fine historic buildings and so on, Prue gallantly accompanied me to the tasting and to help me with my notes. This took place in the offices of Sigmund Loeb and there, together with Otto and his manager, Herr Josef Steinlein, we set to work. There were no less than forty-two wines from which to choose, far too many for my capacity, so the 1969's and 1970's had to be eliminated, our target being the masterpieces of 1971; even so by the time we had completed our task, we had tried no less than close on thirty of them. This is not quite so bad as it sounds however, because our tasting was divided into morning and late afternoon sessions with the best wines reserved for the finale. Moselle, being one of the lightest of all wines with an alcoholic strength averaging only about nine degrees, is far less tiring to taste than others.

The majority of all the wines before us were already in bottle so that from this point of view it was a good moment to see them, but really the best time to have bought them would have been a few months earlier, because here, as in Bordeaux, the prices are greatly on the ascent. All the same, it was almost an agreeable experience because it is not often that one has such a lovely vintage to taste. It was like the 1970 clarets all over again, except that young Moselle is a sheer delight and however enthusiastic one may be, it is not possible to say that about young claret.

Here then are my notes and it will be seen they are more detailed on the wines which took my fancy:

1971 Vintage: Group A

> *Falkensteiner Hofberg Kabinett, Erzeuger-Abfüllung Friedrich-Wilhelm-Gymnasium* (Saar).
> Lovely bouquet, light, fresh and charming, good fruit acidity and a pleasant individual taste.
>
> *Waldracher Meisenberg Kabinett, EA Pfarrgut* (Ruwer).
> Attractive bouquet, has more body than the Falkensteiner, very good quality.

Kaseler Kehrnagel Kabinett, EA Bischöfliches Priesterseminar (Ruwer).
Bouquet still undeveloped, but a lovely taste, good fruit acidity.

Eitelsbacher Karthauser Hofberg Burgberg Kabinett, EA W. Tyrell (Ruwer, formerly Rauten Strauch).
This was a little disappointing, perhaps it will improve with more age in bottle.

Group B

Kaseler Nies'chen Spätlese, EA v. Beulwitz (Ruwer).
A really attractive bouquet, light and elegant and has great distinction.

Ockfener Geisberg Spätlese, EA Friedrich-Wilhelm-Gymnasium (Saar).
Not much bouquet yet, a slightly heavier wine than No. 5 lacking the fine finish, quite good all the same.

Oberemmeler Abteihof Spätlese, EA Reichsgraf v. Kesselstatt (Saar).
Delightful bouquet, good quality, but could have more life.

Kaseler Hitzlay Spätlese, EA Reichsgraf v. Kesselstatt (Ruwer).
Very fine bouquet, plenty of body, could have more fruit acidity.

Josephshofer Spätlese, EA Reichsgraf v. Kesselstatt (Moselle).
Great style on bouquet, more fruit acidity than No. 8, attractive but not outstanding.

Group C

Trittenheimer Apotheke Spätlese, EA Steinlein-Schmitt (Moselle).
A beautifully perfumed bouquet, agreeable flavour.

Eitelsbacher Marienholz Spätlese, EA Bischöfliches Konvikt (Ruwer).
Bouquet not yet developed, a delicious steely flavour, good fruit acidity.

Ayler Kupp Spätlese, EA Bischöfliches Priesterseminar (Saar).
Not much bouquet yet, good flavour with finesse, preferred No. 11, though this will undoubtedly taste better by 1973.

Eitelsbacher Karthauser Hofberg Kronenberg Spätlese, EA W. Tyrell (Ruwer).
An individual bouquet, but the rest of it rather disappointing, no doubt, because these wines develop slowly.

Kaseler Nies'chen Auslese, EA Erben v. Beulwitz (Ruwer).
Fragrant bouquet, fairly full and well made, could have more fruit acidity.

Group D

Ockfener Geisberg Auslese, EA Friedrich-Wilhelm-Gymnasium (Saar).
Nice bouquet, lovely flavour, good fruit acidity, but a bit too sweet for my taste.

Wiltinger Kupp Spätlese, EA Bischöfliches Priesterseminar (Saar).
Flowery bouquet, delightful flavour and most distinguished, but a little too much acidity. This acidity will disappear after a year or two in bottle.

Dom Avelsbacher Altenberg Spätlese, EA Hohe Domkirche (Moselle).
Delightfully fragrant bouquet, delicious flavour, good fruit and good fruit acidity. Fine quality.

Dom Scharzhofberger Spätlese, EA Hohe Domkirche (Saar).
A fine distinctive bouquet, a fine wine, nevertheless a little disappointing. I expected more from this name, but perhaps it is still too early to appreciate this wine properly.

Group E

Falkensteiner Hofberg Auslese, EA Friedrich-Wilhelm-Gymnasium (Saar).
Good bouquet, a lot of character, medium sweet, fine quality.

Piesporter Goldtröpfchen Auslese, EA Reichsgraf v. Kesselstatt (Moselle).
Pretty nose, full fragrant flavour, on the sweet side.

Graacher Domprobst Auslese, EA Friedrich-Wilhelm-Gymnasium (Moselle).
Fragrant bouquet, round, flowery and quite full-bodied, very good quality.

Ayler Herrenberg Auslese, EA Bischöfliches Konvikt (Saar).
Attractive bouquet, slightly sweet, but a lovely flavour, fine quality. It comes from one of the best sites in the Saar valley.

Wiltinger Kupp Auslese, EA Bischöfliches Priesterseminar (Saar).
Distinguished bouquet, a great big wine, good fruit acidity, very fine quality.

Group F

Eitelsbacher Karthauser Hofberger Kronenberg Auslese, EA W. Tyrell (Saar).
Nice flowery bouquet, a lovely distinguished flavour, but not so exciting as its long name would imply!

Trittenheimer Apotheke Auslese, EA Steinlein-Schmitt (Moselle).
Lovely bouquet, rich and fine with great character.

Piesporter Goldtröpfchen Auslese, EA Bischöfliches Konvikt (Moselle).
A lovely bouquet, a real "bouquet garni," a mouthful of fragrance, fabulous quality.

Dhronhofberger Auslese, EA Bischöfliches Priesterseminar (Moselle).
Distinctive bouquet, a great mouthful of delicious flavour, rather rich.

Urziger Wurzgarten Auslese, EA Bischöfliches Priesterseminar (Moselle).
A most distinguished bouquet, fine flavour, good fruit acidity, fairly rich, richer in fact, than the Dhronhofberger Auslese.

Since there was such a large number of wines, the tasting was split up into little groups in accordance with the price brackets and although the prices are not given here (in any case they would no longer apply) our preference within each group may be helpful.

In Group A, we liked best the Kaseler Kehrnagel Kabinett with the Waldracher Meisenberg Kabinett second. In Group B, Ockfener

Geisberg Spätlese first, Kaseler Nies'chen Spätlese second. In Group C, Kaseler Nies'chen Auslese first, Eitelsbacher Marienholz Spätlese second. In Group D, Dom Avelsbacher Altenberg Spätlese first, Dom Scharzberger Spätlese second. In Group E, Wiltinger Kupp Auslese first, Ayler Herrenberg Auslese second and in Group F, Piesporter Goldtröpfchen Auslese first, with Trittenheimer Apotheke Auslese second.

Fortunately perhaps, we all have a different sense of taste, but in a fine vintage such as 1971, my personal predilection veers towards the wines from the Saar and the Ruwer valleys. It is as well to emphasise that this is entirely a matter of personal taste, because the Moselles are also fabulous in 1971.

This had been the first really warm day that any of us had experienced during this miserable summer, so in view of the heat, we waited until the evening for our excursion up the Ruwer valley. The Ruwer surprises everybody because of its diminutive size, one feels a river of such vinous importance should have more "body," but not a bit of it; it is merely a stream a few yards across. However, the beautiful slopes of the valley, either vine clad or wooded, make up for the small dimensions of the river from which they take their name.

This small area is literally studded with gems, for no sooner do you turn up the valley than you are confronted by the vineyard of Eitelsbacher Marienholz and this is swiftly followed by the steep slopes of Maximin Grünhaus and the precipitous incline of Kaseler Nies'chen, as well as the great hump of a hill covered by the vines of Kaseler Kehrnagel. All around and especially on the hills above Waldrach, haymaking was in full swing, the farmers all seizing the opportunity to get their hay in under ideal conditions. Incidentally, it was as well they did, because the fine weather was only to last for forty-eight hours, but meanwhile the pure air was redolent with the sweet smell of freshly made hay. The vineyard owners were also, alas temporarily, encouraged by the weather, because, owing to the lamentable spring and early summer, the vines were from two to three weeks behind in their development. In fact, the flowering was only just commencing.

We returned to an inn amongst the vines, high up on the hill close to Eitelsbach and there, gazing across the valley to the slopes of Maximin Grünhaus, we ate our supper in the heavily scented evening air. I must now confess this meal was washed down with some very good local lager, Bitburger Pils and we found it most refreshing after all the tasting which had gone on during the day.

Tuesday, 27th June
Nähe, Rheingau, Rheinhessen Pfalz

The main purpose of this visit to Germany was so see for ourselves how good were the 1971 Moselles and as the time allotted did not permit a visit to the Rhineland, Herr Steinlein had very kindly collected a range of samples for us from some of the leading growers. Although this was by no means a comprehensive tasting, it gave us an idea of the fine quality of the Rhine and Nähe wines of this vintage.

1971 Vintage: Nahe: **From the estate of Reichsgraf von Plettenberg**

1. *Kreuznacher Kahlenberg Riesling Spätlese.*
   An attractive fresh bouquet, pleasant flavour, fairly dry.
2. *Kreuznacher Kapellenberg Riesling Spätlese.*
   Good bouquet, well made, a little richer than No. 1, but could have more life.
3. *Kreuznacher Brückes Riesling Spätlese.*
   Good bouquet, fairly full-bodied, medium sweet, good quality.
4. *Roxheimer Hollenpfad Riesling Auslese.*
   Attractive bouquet, fine flavour, finishes nicely, good quality.
5. *Winzenheimer Rosenhecke Riesling Auslese.*
   Fragrant bouquet, lovely flavour, fine quality.

Among these Nähe wines I liked No. 3 best with No. 5 second.

Rheingau: From the estate of K. H. Eser

6. *Geisenheimer Kilsberg Riesling Kabinett.*
   A nice full bouquet, good flavour, good quality, quite dry.
7. *Geisenheimer Klauserweg Riesling Kabinett.*
   A nice rather sweet bouquet, good fruit, but a little dull.

8. *Winkeler Jesuitengarten Riesling Spätlese.*
   A distinctive flowery bouquet, attractive flavour, fine quality.
9. *Johannisberger Holle Riesling Spätlese.*
   Considerable finesse of bouquet, a fine full-bodied and slightly richer wine.
10. *Johannisberger Goldatzel Riesling Spätlese.*
    A lovely bouquet, fine flavour, well-made, good quality. Fairly dry.

Although it was not the most expensive, I thought No. 8 outstanding with No. 9 second.

Rheinhessen: From the estate of G. Gessert

11. *Niersteiner Spiegelberg Riesling Spätlese.*
    Pleasant bouquet, plenty of fruit and flavour, medium sweet and quite a nice finish.
12. *Niersteiner Olberg Riesling Spätlese.*
    Fruity bouquet, here is something for those who like a big mouthful of wine! Quite sweet, but good quality.
13. *Niersteiner Klostergarten Scheurebe Auslese.*
    A most perfumed nose, rather a scented wine altogether, not my personal taste. (*N.B.* Clearly there must be many people who like Scheurebe wines, but among the cognoscenti there must also be some who do not regard this special bouquet and flavour as really serious!)
14. *Niersteiner Auflangen Riesling Auslese.*
    Delicious bouquet, good quality, fairly rich, but has a slightly bitter finish.
15. *Niersteiner Rehbach Riesling Auslese.*
    A lovely bouquet, has pronounced fruit and flavour, well-made and fairly dry, good quality.

Amongst these I liked No. 12 best with No. 11 second.

Pfalz: From the estate of Dr. Bürklin-Wolf

16. *Wachenheimer Mandelgarten Riesling Kabinett.*
    Good full, but well bred bouquet, good flavour, well-made and a good finish. Very good quality.

17. *Ruppertsberger Reiterpfad Riesling Spätlese.*
    Rich but good bouquet, nice flavour, medium dry.
18. *Wachenheimer Gerümpel Riesling Auslese.*
    Pronounced bouquet which is full of character, full of flavour too, quite a rich wine, fine quality, very promising.

All of these Palatinate wines were lovely, but if one has to choose, they came in this order, 18, 16 and 17.

Although there were fewer of them, I found the Rhine wines more tiring to taste than the lighter Moselles. The same differences of effect also apply when one is tasting young wine in France, the red wines of Burgundy being more fatiguing than those of Bordeaux.

After a suitable rest, Herr Steinlein drove us through Trier towards the valley of the river Saar, a river whose width is more in keeping with the renown of its wines. One cannot fail to be attracted by the pleasing architecture of many of the houses in this part of Germany, somehow they give an impression too of tidiness, but above all, their slate tiles catch the eye for many of them have lovely mansard roofs which more often than not are interspersed by nice dormer windows.

The road along the lower reaches of the river at first is rather dull and it is not until you get among the vineyards near Kanzem that the scenery improves, for there on the left hand side of the road are the steep and beautiful slopes of Kanzemer Altenberg. After passing the vines of Wiltinger Kupp, we stopped the car to examine some of those by the roadside. Although it appears that the quantity may be fairly good, they were at least two weeks behind in the flowering. What is needed now is really favourable weather for the rest of the season, otherwise the prospects for the next vintage are anything but cheerful.

Our vinous route led through Ayl whence on the far side of the valley can be glimpsed the picturesque village of Ockfen, noted, of course, for the fine wine called "Ockfener Bockstein." We passed through Saarburg overlooked by its castle and climbed ever upwards through a side valley with its broad meadows devoted to agriculture and there again haymaking was in full swing, the roads being crowded with carts laden with fragrant new hay. Finally, near the summit we came to the village of Kastel, untouched by time, but there the air was not quite so perfumed because in front of many of the houses lay their private heaps of farm manure! From the war cemetery at Serriger Klaus, there is a stupendous view of the winding Saar and across to the vineyards of Serriger Vogelsang and Schlossberg.

On our way home, we stopped for supper at a delightful inn called Hotel Lauer and there, in a garden filled with roses in flower and orange blossom, we were able to enjoy a view of the famous Ayler Herrenberg and in the distance the vines of Wiltingen. When travelling and tasting in France, it is hard to resist the temptations of the table, but here in Germany, unless you like pork and endless veal, they are far easier to resist. All the same, at this inn, we enjoyed greatly the wine owned by the proprietor, namely 1971 Ayler Scheidterberg Kabinett, delightfully fresh with just the right amount of fruit acidity. This expression "fruit acidity" can perhaps ring the wrong note for the uninitiated, but with fine Moselle, especially in a great vintage, it provides a freshness and adds enormously to the charm of the wine.

Wednesday, 28th June

Maximin Grünhaus

For many years I have been a firm admirer of the wines of Maximin Grünhaus and as mentioned earlier on, it was only recently at home that I finished my last delicious bottle of 1964 Maximin Grünhauser Herrenberg Spätlese. With this delightful memory in mind, it was with considerable anticipation that I had been looking forward to the morning which Otto Loeb had arranged for us to spend with the versatile Herr A. von Schubert, the owner of this well-known property. Naturally, I had fully expected to taste some fine wine, but I have a feeling that with this vintage of 1971, Herr von Schubert has once again excelled himself. His whole range from all the different casks was of such exceptional quality that this, for me, was a red letter day, one to be compared on the same high level as the occasion when I tasted the great pomerols and Saint-Emilions of 1970 with Jean-Pierre Moueix in Bordeaux.

Unfortunately, we arrived rather late. There are a number of new roads around Trier and somehow we found ourselves on an autobahn from which it was almost impossible to break away and, as a result, it took us well over half an hour to return to our starting point in Trier. Such are the blessings of progress!

When finally we reached our destination, we found that Herr von Schubert had kindly set out a selected range of his 1971 vintage and that we had the honour of being the first foreigners to taste his wine. On account of the time of the year, that is to say the period of the flowering of the vines, our host explained that one or two of his wines were showing a little disturbance, i.e., a slight secondary fermentation, but when accustomed to tasting very young wine, you take such things in your stride. It was, of course, a wonderful opportunity for me to have tasting alongside no less an authority than Otto Loeb, for his assessment of quality here in his native surroundings, is to say the least, impeccable. Since he was born in 1898 in Trier, his knowledge and experience of the whole region of the Moselle is second to none and I am sure all lovers of Moselle will look forward to reading his book on this subject when it is published in London in September 1972.

In all, there were fifteen wines to be tasted, the first two of which, under the new law, are described as "Qualitaetswein" bestimmter Anbaugebiete (for which the abbreviation is Q.b.A.). This means virtually lesser wines to which it has been permitted to add sugar. It seems to me that these new German wine laws are so complicated that few people can understand them, including even the growers themselves not to mention foreigners! For instance, with some of the finer wines, instead of as in the past, using words which we more or less can understand like feine Auslese, or feinste Auslese, there is now a string of six or seven numbers and nothing could be more unromantic than that! But who are we to complain when this has clearly created some kind of heaven for the civil servants who manage vinous affairs.

Maximin Grünhaus is a single property comprising over 100 acres of vines, but since all the slopes are not the same and do not necessarily face in the same direction, various qualities of wine are made and these are sold under different names, such as Abtsberg and Herrenberg. The label itself is delightfully old fashioned, yet attractive and varies according to the part of the vineyard the individual wines come from, i.e., the slopes and their exposure to the sun, and since the property was once a monastery, these names have certain religious connotations. Abtsberg, for example, means wine reserved for the Abbot; Herrenberg that for the brothers who sit at the top table and Bruderberg that for the lay brethren!

The 1971 vintage of the wines of Maximin Grünhaus

1. *Herrenberg QbA.*
    Fresh bouquet, pleasing, medium dry.

2. *Abtsberg QbA.*
    A better bouquet, more complete and attractive than the Herrenberg QbA.

3. *Bruderberg Kabinett*
    Clean bouquet, nice individual flavour.

4. *Herrenberg Kabinett Fuder No. 11.*
   Pleasant bouquet, good flavour, good quality, some acidity which with time will no doubt disappear.
5. *Herrenberg Kabinett Fuder No. 10.*
   Fragrant bouquet, pleasant flavour, nice finish, the best so far.
6. *Abtsberg Kabinett Fuder No. 17.*
   Difficult to taste now, it has still to settle down, but clearly it will make a good wine.
7. *Abtsberg Kabinett Fuder No. 12.*
   This also needs time to settle down. It has a good bouquet with fine breeding and a delightful flavour. Great quality here and this will make a fine wine.
8. *Herrenberg Spätlese Fuder No. 109.*
   Fine bouquet, lovely flavour with perhaps just a shade more natural sugar than the previous wine.
9. *Abtsberg Spätlese Fuder No. 57.*
   Fine clean bouquet, delicious taste, fine finish, excellent quality.
10. *Abtsberg Spätlese Fuder No. 118.*
    Heavenly bouquet, beautifully balanced, fine finish, outstanding quality. This will make a great bottle.
11. *Herrenberg Auslese Fuder No. 134.*
    Fine bouquet, slightly fuller and rounder than Fuder No. 118.
12. *Abtsberg Auslese Fuder No. 38.*
    This also needs a little time to settle down. Fine bouquet though and a lovely flavour, good fruit acidity. Preferred this to 11, 12 and 14.
13. *Herrenberg Auslese Fuder No. 112.*
    A really beautiful bouquet, showing great distinction, slightly richer and fuller than the others, but has good fruit acidity. Preferred this to 14.
14. *Abtsberg Auslese Fuder No. 78.*
    Great finesse of bouquet, a really tremendous round wine of tremendous quality, yet it still remains light and elegant.
15. *Abtsberg Auslese Fuder No. 77.*
    Fine fragrant bouquet, round and complete and has more depth than the Fuder No. 78. This is quite marvellous.

All of these fifteen wines were finely made with the right amount of fruit acidity, in fact, we found the majority of them quite spectacular. Seldom does one come across a range of such outstanding quality as this.

In the very great vintages and these, alas, occur all too infrequently, wines in the categories of Spätlese and particularly Auslese, are inclined to be richer than usual and while I am no real enthusiast for absolutely bone dry wines, normally I do not really enjoy even medium sweet ones with the early courses of a meal. Consequently, during these few days in Germany, I found myself, and I think that I can speak for Otto Loeb as well, preferring in general the Spätleses of 1971 to the Ausleses, and of the former, we both seem to like best the drier ones. There is an added advantage to this in that in these days of rising prices, the Spätleses tend to be less expensive! All the same, such is the excellence of these representatives of Maximin Grünhaus, I can imagine the medium rich and fuller of these Ausleses accompanying sweets and dessert dishes to perfection. In fact, the last three wines at this tasting were of such quality that they reminded me more of beerenausleses than Ausleses.

Down the Moselle, and J. J. Prüm
Thursday, 29th June

Usually Prue and I are strongly averse to guided tours of any description, but when Otto suggested taking one of the river steamers recently inaugurated which ply on the Moselle from Trier down to Bernkastel, we agreed with enthusiasm, especially since the excursion was to be crowned by a visit to the family estate of Johann Joseph Prüm. These river steamers have been in operation since the locks and canalisation system was created some eight years ago and a useful illustrated map of the river can be purchased on board.

The journey began on a grey, misty morning close to the red granite cliffs on the left bank which overshadow the narrow strip of the Trierer Augenspeiner vines. Otto commented sadly that the other bank which in his youth, was all fields is now covered by houses, factories and a huge new hotel. Soon we passed the outlet of the river Ruwer which, hard as it is to believe, even at its outlet, can be no more than ten yards wide.

The fine vineyards of the middle Moselle begin at the village of Schweich and the first one of any reputation is Longuicher Probtsberg.

Some good wine is also made at Mehring further down; in fact, from that district there came an excellent Trockenbeerenauslese of 1959, but this was only possible in that year. Not much Trockenbeerenauslese was made at that time, but since then, presumably for commercial reasons, the quantity has been increased, which is perhaps a pity. As a direct result of the structure of the locks and the consequent raising of the river level, some of the houses at Mehring and even its bridge had to be raised to prevent flooding. If one can judge by the number of barges passing up and down, some of them large enough to carry up to 15,000 tons, this undertaking has clearly been a considerable success, a boon it would appear, particularly for the industry of Lorraine.

The river bends sharply by Poelich to reveal majestic scenery leading to the vineyards of Detzem and Thoernich. The river below Mehring is as wide as the Rhine and strangely enough, some wines from there bear a resemblance to the lighter ones from the Saar valley. It is well known that the vines of the Moselle thrive on slatey soil. This fact is brought very much to one's notice by the towering slopes composed of what look like pure slate chips which loom up as the boat approaches Klüsserath. There seems to be as much slate here as there are pebbles at Châteauneuf-du-Pape! In this area, the best vineyards are Klüsserather Bruderschaft and Koenigsberg.

At Trittenheim, where our friend Herr Steinlein makes some fine wine, the vineyards cling to steep slopes on the far side of the river, the best known of these being Apotheke. A little further on is Neumagen, the place where the poet Ausonius caught his first glimpse of the Moselle, even in those days busy, as is only to be expected, I suppose, with ships laden with casks of wine. In view of his connections with Bordeaux, Ausonius appears to have been quite an enthusiastic traveller. There are a number of fairly well-known vineyards at Neumagen, but they have a distinctive flavour which is not to everyone's taste.

At Dhron there is, of course, the great vineyard of Dhroner Hofberg, which belongs to the Priesterseminar and the scenery here is as beautiful as the wine itself. It was at this point that I thought it would be a good idea to order a bottle of Sekt, Deinhard's Cabinet; a great success it was too and put us in fine fettle. I can think of many worse things than travelling down the Moselle with a good glass of bubbling wine in one's hand!

We were now approaching some of the more famous parts of the river, because it is between Dhron and Erden that the great vineyards of this region lie. The village of Piesport, so noted for its famous Goldtröpfchen, extends along the river front and is as attractive as the wine itself. The finest vineyards lie on the splendid slopes behind the village on the left bank of the river. It seems that there was a local dispute over where the bridge was to be sited; so as not to be outdone, the discomforted faction built their own, thus there is not one bridge here, but two! Just a little further on, the boat passes by magnificent cliffs of slate with vines clinging to them wherever possible. This part is known as the "Lorelei" of the Moselle and it would seem that some of the vines can only be approached by boat. The vineyards also lie along the right bank of the river whence the wines produced can be called Piesporter Michelsberg, but most of the growers of Piesport offer their wines under the label of Goldtröpfchen.

As the steamer glides towards Wintrich, your eyes are drawn to the magnificent slopes towering up above. The best vineyards here are Ohligsberger and Geierslayer and they belong to the estates of Freiherr von Schloremer and Adolph Huesgen. Before the canal was created it was very difficult to navigate the river at this point for there are rocks and other impediments below the surface of the water. In this area between Wintrich and Brauneberg there was considerable strife during the wars of religion; the Catholics were banned so the population around here remains mainly Protestant; also in those times, this was regarded as the best district of all for quality and in fact, Brauneberg was originally named Mondoux, or Dusemond, which infers sweet wine. The great vineyards of Brauneberg lie on the far side of the river from the village and the best known of these is, of course, the Brauneberger Juffer.

The waterfront houses at Lieser have a charm of their own, but the effect is marred somewhat by the ugly mansion of the Schloremer family where the last Kaiser used to stay. Some fifty years ago before the most important vineyard here was split up, the wines of Lieser were better known for quality than they are now. However in those far off days the proprietor used to keep his wine in cask for at least three years and at times even as long as eight! Nowadays, the pendulum has swung the other way and the growers bottle much earlier. For instance, a large number of 1971's were already in bottle by March, four or five months only after the vintage and at the time of writing, in June, it seems that most of the wines with some exceptions, such as those of Maximin Grünhaus, are all in bottle. There may however be two sides to this question, because by bottling so very soon after the vintage, too much can be taken out of a wine.

This river journey ends in a blaze of splendour at Cues and Bernkastel which lie opposite to one another. Cues, which takes its name from the famous philosopher and priest Cusanus, founder of Cusanos hospital for the sick and aged, nestles attractively on a hillside whilst opposite, the famous vineyards of Bernkastel are dominated by the ruins of a dramatic castle called Landshut. Thenceforth downstream all the way to Zeltingen, stretches a chain of villages, all famous for the quality of their wine, but we were not to see them from the boat because it stopped at Bernkastel.

Even if the visitor does not take the boat he must most assuredly see the tiny market place in Bernkastel. Very small, it is a pure gem of antiquity and is crowded with delightful old houses dating back to the Middle Ages; also, if he happens to like fish, he must certainly order the blue trout at the Hotel Zur Post. It was easily the best dish we ate during this visit to the Moselle.

The rest of the day was spent in Wehlen tasting masterpieces in the home of Manfred Prüm and his mother. For all lovers of fine Moselle, the name of Johann Joseph Prüm is a household word and this tasting of a range of their 1971's provided ample proof, if such a thing is necessary, of the outstanding quality produced by this estate. J. J. Prüm is a name that I have known all my life, but more especially for its eminence since the end of the last war. The present occasion was all the greater, because we were tasting wines from such an unusually good vintage, a vintage which may easily rank as among the best of the century. Manfred himself said that he considered the better categories of his wines to be superior even to those of 1959 and 1953 and were as good, perhaps as those of 1949. In 1949, very few, if any estates on the Moselle produced quality equal to that of J. J. Prüm so perhaps other sources of information would not compare the 1971's with vintages earlier than 1959 and/or 1953. In any case, this is a specious argument and the agreeable fact remains that these 1971's are very, very good.

Here is the range of wines we tasted and for those who may be interested, numbers four to six were already in bottle. This is indeed a change of method, because in the old days the wines of J. J. Prüm were kept in cask for a number of years, but nowadays those in the categories up to Spätlese and Auslese, are bottled within six months of the vintage.

1970 and 1971 Vintages: Johannes Joseph Prüm

1. *1970 Bernkasteler Badstube Kabinett.*
    Scented bouquet, medium dry agreeable flavour, needs about two years to be at its best.

2. *1970 Wehlener Sonnenuhr Kabinett.*
   Very nice bouquet, plenty of fruit, good acidity, more depth than No. 1.
3. *1970 Wehlener Sonnenuhr Spätlese.*
   Good bouquet, fruit and flavour.
4. *1971 Bernkasteler Badstube Spätlese.*
   Attractive scented nose, far more depth and quality than the first three, (admittedly 1970's) in fact twice the wine, it has elegance and delightful fruit acidity. Here is a good example of a fine Spätlese.
5. *1971 Wehlener Sonnenuhr Spätlese.*
   Flowery bouquet, splendid flavour with a delightful finish, good fruit acidity, not unlike an Auslese.
6. *1971 Graacher Himmelreich Auslese.*
   Fragrant bouquet, medium sweet, tastes like a great armful of flowers, should such a thing be possible!
7. *1971 Wehlener Sonnenuhr Auslese.*
   Great big bouquet, another mouthful of flowers, but even finer, has both power and depth. Good fruit acidity too and really fine.
8. *1971 Wehlener Sonnenuhr feine Auslese.*
   Lovely bouquet, gorgeous flavour coupled with fruit acidity, medium rich.
9. *1971 Wehlener Sonnenuhr feinste Auslese.*
   Splendid bouquet, fabulous flavour, quite rich, but has good fruit acidity.
10. *1971 Wehlener Sonnenuhr hochfeine Auslese.*
    Slightly darker shade, rich, but fragrant bouquet, a real mouthful of flowers and honey, very great quality, at the moment a little overwhelmed by its fruit and sugar, but in 4 or 5 years the balance of these with the acidity will equal out.
11. *1971 Graacher Himmelreich Beerenauslese.*
    An enormously rich bouquet, a fabulous rich flavour, very great quality.
12. *1971 Graacher Himmelreich Eiswein feinste Auslese.*
    A slightly golden colour, lovely nose, heaps of fruit and a very special flavour.

13. *1971 Wehlener Sonnenuhr Trockenbeerenauslese.*
Slightly golden colour, a heavenly rich concentrated bouquet, an enormously rich, round wine of quite amazing quality.

If these wines are like this now, one can only wonder how they will show when they have obtained some maturity. I fear that mere tasting notes fail to convey their true splendour! When on a level of excellence such as this, it seems monstrous to comment on them in any way which could be presumed unfavourable, but as I think I have mentioned earlier on, when a vintage is as great as 1971, the wines have an added richness which doubtless suits many palates. With food, I personally prefer however a fairly dry wine and that is why for my own consumption I chose one of the lesser stars, the Bernkasteler Badstube Spätlese and with this, I know Otto was in agreement.

Without wishing to be unduly repetitive, it is difficult, in fact, invidious, among such a galaxy of stars to select one from the other, nevertheless, my preferences were the Wehlener Sonnenuhr Auslese (No. 7), which no doubt, would go splendidly with either salmon or sea trout, and then in ascending order, numbers 9 and 10 and specially 11 and 13. As may be seen, and good as it was, both Otto and I preferred both the Beerenauslese and the Trockenbeerenauslese to the Eiswein. For those who may be interested, an Eiswein is usually made after the less successful vintages when the sugar content in the grapes is not too high, otherwise the juice in them would not freeze. It is only possible to make such a wine after a severe frost, i.e., one of at least 5 degrees below zero, then the frozen grapes are picked while the frost is still in them and taken to the press very early in the morning, that is before they have had time to unfreeze.

It was therefore all the more unexpected to find an Eiswein appearing after a fine vintage such as 1971, the fact of the matter is that this was only possible because during the night of November 19 the temperature fell to 10 degrees below zero, but that was the only occasion. In any event, to contemplate making an Eiswein is to take a considerable risk for without the necessary weather conditions, it is possible to lose the entire crop concerned.

These medium rich to rich wines of this year will make fabulous partners for the dishes which terminate a meal, such as dessert and, for the cognoscenti, for sipping with reverence after the meal has ended. I feel sure that not everyone will agree with me here, but I always think that a great Beerenauslese or Trockenbeerenauslese is greatly superior to the much vaunted Château d'Yquem from Bordeaux, excellent as the latter can be. Incidentally, over the past decade or so, there has been a falling away of demand for the richer after dinner white wines in France, England and America but it is encouraging to know that tastes are changing over again. These great wines of the 1971 vintage from the Moselle will act as magnificent ambassadors for this style of wine and I am convinced that once they appear, at any rate on the American market, their reception will be rapturous, for that is where the "T.B.A.'s," as they are called in California, mostly go.

I fully expected this to be the end of the tasting but found that Manfred Prüm had slipped away to produce a *vin d'honneur* in the form of Graacher Himmelreich Kabinett and as this was followed by a whole succession of older but equally interesting vintages, the following notes on them may not come amiss.

1955 Graacher Himmelreich Kabinett.

A very pale colour, well developed but very fresh bouquet, a fresh flavour too and very dry. We all took this to be something much younger.

1956 Wehlener Sonnenuhr Eiswein.

Pale colour and such a pretty bouquet, a delicious flavour with a medium dry finish. Very well balanced. In 1956, one of the poorest vintages of the century, the making of an Eiswein was fully justified, but it took a good ten years for this particular one to mature.

1943 Wehlener Sonnenuhr Auslese.

A lovely golden colour, a delightful rich bouquet, a full, fruity flavour but with quite a dry finish.

1943 Wehlener Sonnenuhr Feine Auslese.

A pale golden colour, a fragrant but older bouquet, as it seemed older than the previous wine, mistakenly, I took it for a 1937.

1951 Wehlener Sonnenuhr Feine Auslese.

Pale golden colour, a fresh fragrant bouquet, a fine depth of flavour. In spite of a faint trace of age, it was so fresh, it might have been much younger.

1953 Wehlener Sonnenuhr Auslese.

Lovely pale colour, flowery bouquet, a delightfully fresh flavour, medium dry and remarkable for its age. At last I got the vintage right!

1961 Wehlener Sonnenuhr Eiswein.

Very pale colour, a young but elegant bouquet, a delicious taste and not too rich.

1964 Wehlener Sonnenuhr feine Auslese.
Very pale colour, bouquet not really developed yet, lots of fruit and flavour, medium dry, it was so fresh it could have been much younger.

1959 Wehlener Sonnenuhr feinste Auslese.
A lovely fragrant bouquet, full, round and rich, really fine quality. What a wine with which to finish an evening such as this!

As I have mentioned earlier on it is not too often that there is a great vintage for German wine, so to be able to come here and taste these splendid wines of 1971 before they are dispersed among the markets of the world has been a most rewarding experience.

Miscellaneous Essays

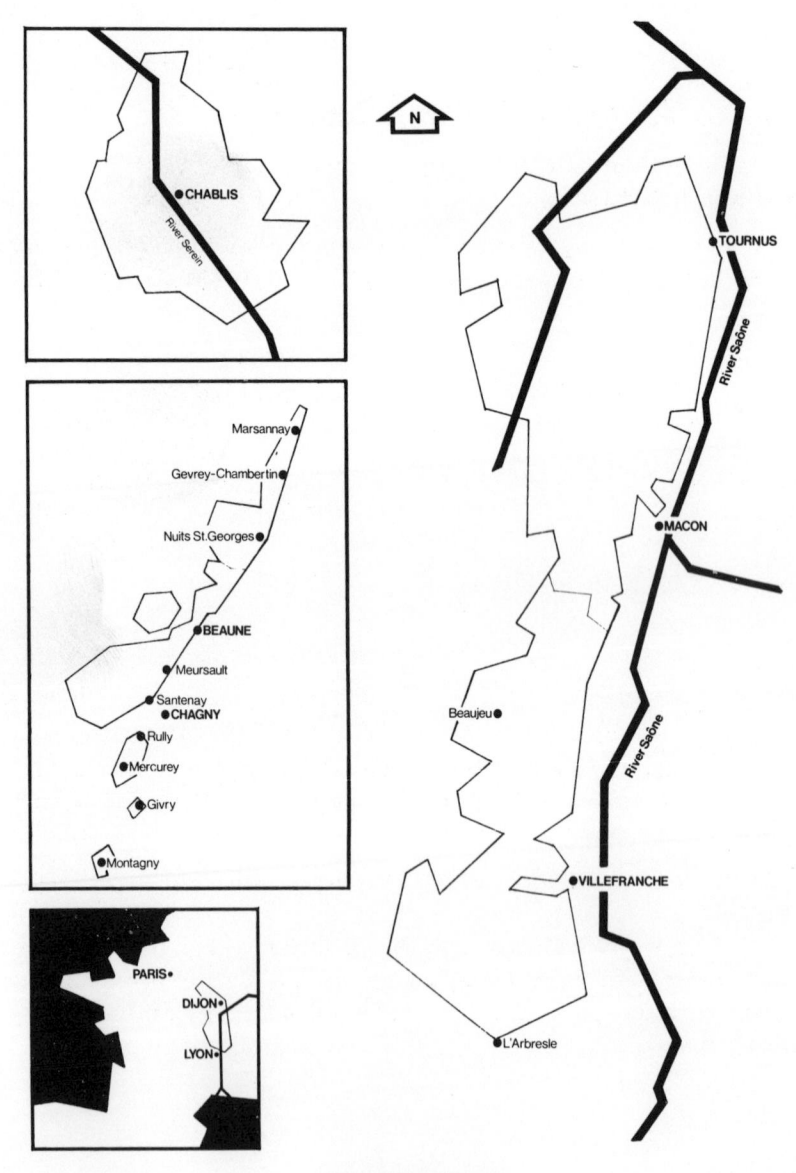

BURGUNDY

1st August, 1971

Sundry Tasting Notes: 1961 Bordeaux

Au Jardin des Gourmets
Host: Joseph Berkmann

These wines were tasted in London, prior to our 1971 visit to France, but we place them here to relate to the 1961 tasting which follows:

Palmer.
> Deep colour, fantastic nose, a lovely, lovely flavour, such a sweetness, really a marvel.

La Mission Haut Brion.
> Fine colour, trace of brown, deep bouquet, a tremendous depth of flavour, superb quality. More backward than the others.

Gruaud-Larose.
> Deep, still immature colour, lovely bouquet, heavenly flavour, a great wine.

Pétrus.
> Very, very dark colour, a huge rich bouquet, enormous depth and weight, really "chewy," one could almost eat this and seems almost larger than life. Fabulous.

Apart from the first growths, these must be among the very finest of the 1961's.

As, in a way I had expected, the Palmer has the edge over the Gruaud-Larose and really, I suppose, La Mission is a greater wine than the Palmer, although at the moment being more backward it is not showing so well.

"La Noblesse" of the 1961 Bordeaux Vintage

I must have met Eddie Penning-Rowsell first of all around 1947/8 and we have been friends ever since. On many, many occasions since I have stayed with him and his nice wife, Meg, in the country, first in Wiltshire and afterwards at Wootton in Oxfordshire. As may be clearly seen from the regular articles he writes in the *Financial Times,* he is our most informed journalist on the subject of wine and is also the author of by far the best book written so far on claret, i.e., *The Wines of Bordeaux.*

As well as being an exceedingly good cook, Meg is also a great gardener, so the really fresh vegetables you eat at the Penning-Rowsell table are a great experience. Gastronomically speaking, our Scotch beef, our mutton, our fish and our vegetables are among the finest primary produce in the world. To take but one example, the quality of our Scotch beef is far superior to that of the much vaunted Charollais. So far so good, but the tragedy lying behind all this is that as a race, we are in general, such poor cooks. Given a good English cook though, such as Meg, and fortunately there is an increasing number of enthusiasts of her calibre, what he or she can do with these fine basic ingredients is not easily surpassed.

Even when I first met him, Eddie had the basis of a fine cellar, though in those days, he was just as penniless as I was. Beginning just before the war and, duty permitting, continuing during those five years of conflict, he acquired a nucleus of 1899 and 1900 clarets, many gems of the twenties and quite a wide selection of the best of the delectable 1929's. At that time, such treasures were not so prohibitively expensive as they are now. The 1929's were at their very peak when they were around twenty-years old and well do I remember enjoying with Eddie such masterpieces of that famous vintage as Léoville-Poyferré, Latour, Pichon-Baron and so on.

Through the years, not only has he been adding to his collection, but has turned Meg and his growing family into considerable authorities on the subject, with the result that from time to time, he can invite some friends to partake in a classic tasting, although tasting is hardly the right word for these epic evenings. Last year, at the time when they reached their twenty-fifth birthday, it was the turn of the classics of 1945, but unfortunately I missed that through being abroad although I did attend the 1959 tasting.

On this particular occasion, 11th March 1972, we were honoured with the leading wines of 1961, surely the finest vintage since 1945.

As mentioned in *Diary of a Winetaster*, I had tasted, some two years ago, these fabulous wines with Henri Woltner at Château La Mission Haut Brion, but had never actually drunk them one against the other, and, in view of their scarcity, I do not suppose many other people have either!

Besides ourselves and Eddie's son Edmund and his wife, the other guests were Dr. and Mrs. Miles Weatherall. We started off on the right foot with a really remarkable dry sherry; the colour was pale golden and the bouquet fresh with no hint of age anywhere, it was quite excellent and in perfect condition. There is nothing unusual about this though until you hear the rest—it came from the cellar of Sir George Meyrick Bart, at Hinton Admiral in Hampshire, and at a recent Christie's sale it was described as being "packed in July 1885" and was bottled by a long since defunct City wine merchant called Claridge. It seemed almost incredible that this fresh tasting sherry in our glasses could and must be, well over 100 years old!

Meg's cooking was eminently suitable to the fine wine, Gougeres to begin with (small balls of choux pastry filled with cheese), roast chicken and assorted cheeses, red Leicester, Cheddar and Wensleydale.

The first wine, 1961 Château Ferriere, bottled in England, was only intended as a "rinse bouche" and that is about all it was. Perhaps the château bottling is better, but this was distinctly disappointing. Then followed a galaxy of splendour and, for those fortunate enough to have any of the following in their possession, these notes may be helpful. Although most of these wines will continue to improve, the point which struck us so forcibly, was how these great 1961's have come on during the past few years. For instance, until I actually sipped it, it never occurred to me that the Latour would be even drinkable at this early stage.

Haut-Brion.
> Good dark colour, a most attractive Graves nose, a real Graves taste too, which is quite delicious. A distinctive and an individual wine, which will doubtless get even better and better.

Margaux.
> Good colour, not quite so dark as the others, but then the wines of Margaux usually have less colour than those of the other communes. The bouquet is charming and gracious and it is a lighter wine than the Haut-Brion, but it has tremendous elegance and is really delightful to drink now it seems to have lost most of its tannin.

Lafite.
A fine dark colour, a fragrant aristocratic bouquet, full-bodied and still has quite a lot of tannin, but, when compared with the others, somehow it seemed a little flat on the palate. This was surprising because from my memory of the previous tasting, I had fully expected it to be the best.

Latour.
Fantastically dark colour, powerful bouquet, still backward but packed with flavour, full-bodied and endowed with a fabulous richness. It is better to keep this for a while longer.

Mouton-Rothschild.
Very dark colour, a splendid "Mouton" bouquet, that delightful cedar smell! A great big wine, which because of its tannin, should continue to improve.

As mentioned above, the surprise of the evening was how enjoyable these wines are to drink now, even the Latour. According to the general concensus of opinion, for present enjoyment, the Margaux came first, Haut-Brion second and Mouton third, but as to general preference i.e., with regard to quality, they came in this order, Latour, Haut-Brion, Mouton, Lafite and Margaux. The Margaux was placed last only because there was some doubt as to its staying power. To come fifth in a company of perfection is surely no disgrace for given an almost unsurpassed vintage such as 1961 and the "haute noblesse" of the participants, it is difficult to imagine any higher level for wine appreciation.

Fine Claret for Today's Drinking

With some exceptions the decade of the 1960's was highly favourable to the claret lover, the exceptions being, of course, 1968, 1965 and 1963.

The 1969's are much too young and in any case have not got a great reputation, but the 1967's are good and while some of them, at a pinch, can be drunk now, the majority will undoubtedly be better in, say, 1973 and 1974. Incidentally, during a recent visit to America, I was surprised to find this most useful vintage had been rather ignored by one or two of the merchants on the West Coast—I wonder why.

The 1966's are better admittedly, for they have greater depth than the 1967's, but they are taking longer to come round and are destined for future rather than present consumption. After 1961, this may prove to be the best vintage of the decade.

Fine Claret for Today's Drinking

Also contending for that position is 1964, for apart from the known mishaps of the Médoc, there are still some excellent wines available from that district and of course, the Saint-Emilions and pomerols are very good indeed. Before too long a time has elapsed, I think we shall be hearing more of the 1964's.

The most useful 1960's are now taking their leave with a graceful farewell, never with great pretensions. The 1960's filled a gap most competently. One or two of them, such as Latour, are now really outstanding, but, by and large, they are slipping quietly into retirement.

This leaves us with two vintages, one in the heyday of its life and the other on the threshold of its career; needless to say, they are 1962 and 1961. The reputation of the 1962's has been established for some time, but how wonderful that at long last, we can begin to discuss the 1961's from the point of view of their drinkability! Not that one can call all the 1961's ready, but at least they are becoming within the realm of possibility.

Let us commence with the 1962 vintage, the perfect example of an ugly Bordelais duckling turning into a swan. After it was first made not much was expected from it and then, almost miraculously, the light began to dawn upon us and for a number of years now, we have been enjoying the 1962's immensely. When I say this, I mean of course the médocs, because although you see many of them appearing on merchants' lists, it was nothing like such a successful vintage for the wines of Saint-Emilion or pomerol, especially the former. While normally the Saint-Emilions and Pomerols are rounded comely creatures, in 1962, they have always appeared to me to be a bit flat chested!

On reading again *The Changing Face of Wine,* in my notes taken during the winter of 1966, it is gratifying to see that I predicted an agreeable future for the 1962 médocs and I for one, have been enjoying them ever since. Some of the lesser wines, the *crus bourgeois* are still standing up well, among them in particular are Châteaux Gloria and Cissac. This is a good sign for the vintage in general because the *crus bourgeois* are not usually so long lived as the *crus classés*.

There are too many successes to mention here, but among them certainly are Léoville-Las-Cases, Ducru-Beaucaillou, Montrose, Cos d'Estournel, Palmer Malescot Brane-Cantenac, Grand-Puy-Lacoste, Pichon-Longueville-Baron, Pichon-Longueville-Lalande and La Mission Haut Brion. As for the first growths, they will be handled in more detail later on.

At a dinner held in California in April 1972, the *pièce de résistance* of the whole evening was the Lynch-Bages 1962, a sheer delight and surely at its very best. It was followed by that masterpiece Pétrus 1967, but the latter failed to conquer, being not ready to drink, a prime example here of infanticide. My advice about the 1962's is to strike now while the iron is hot and drink them while they are at their peak.

One can almost draw a graph of a fine vintage; the line begins low down and, according to its character, gradually ascends, sometimes, as with the 1961's, very slowly indeed. Then it reaches what one might describe as a level plateau and, according to its allotted span, there it remains, until it begins to go gradually downhill.

Most of the 1962's appear to be on this pleasant plateau now, but there remain one or two which are still happily in the ascendant. Mouton-Baron-Philippe, is or was last year, a case in point. In July 1971, Philippe Cottin kindly arranged for me a tasting of various vintages at Mouton-Rothschild and here are my notes on this particular wine: "Very dark colour, full, rich bouquet, a lovely rounded flavour, but still not quite mature and if I owned any bottles of this, I would keep them for at least another year." I am wondering now what difference this extra year will have made.

Although during the past thirteen years quite a number of vintages have burst upon the vinous scene accompanied by great fanfares of trumpets, few of them have been really worthy of the paeans of praise from all those trumpeters. 1929 was rightly described as "a vintage of the century" and but for the excessive tannin in the wines, so would have been 1928. Had the wine makers of that era possessed the *savoir faire* of the present generation, the 1928's could well have been similar to the 1961's, wines you have to wait for, yes, but not almost for ever. There are still some fabulous 1928's around of course, but in a number of cases the tannin has outlived the fruit.

The next real classic was 1945, a similar, but less tannic vintage than 1928; some of the 1945's are really majestic to drink now, but goodness, how we have had to wait for them!

The 1953's had their day in the dazzling limelight, but their span of stardom was really too brief for them seriously to be included among the very great years. In fact, in those days the expression "the year of the century" was not exploited as it has been during the past decade. This nonsense began with the 1959 vintage, but somehow, the 1959's have never quite made the grade.

All of this has been working up to 1961, a great vintage in the classic style. It was indeed fortunate for us that the men who were responsible for the vinification of these splendid wines had made such progress in their wine lore, otherwise, no doubt, for many years to come, we would still be waiting for the 1961's to become ready to drink. Not that they are all ready, by any means, but they are making progress.

As a result of severe frost at the time of the flowering of the vines, the 1961 crop was reduced to only about half the normal size, but the subsequent weather right up to the vintage was so perfect as to allow the vines to lavish their finest essence upon their scarce bunches of grapes. The result was wine of an exceedingly dark colour, a full, rich bouquet, combined with a wonderful concentration of flavour. Admittedly, there was a considerable amount of tannin, but not to such a damaging extent as in 1928 and in 1945.

The last time I wrote about the médocs of this great vintage was during the winter of 1969 and at that time the 1961's were still very hard, but I am sure never again shall I have an opportunity to taste no less than twenty-seven different wines of so splendid a year and all at the same time. Since then, it is pleasing to be able to report that the 1961's are definitely on the way to becoming drinkable, sampling and assessing them over the next few years could therefore be really exciting.

As usual, from the point of view of maturity, the lesser wines of 1961 are more forward than the others and for a year or so I have been drinking Château Bourdieu-la-Valade (Côtes de Fronsac), a parcel of which I was able to pick up cheaply at a Christie sale. At the same time, I bought some Chateau Moulinet (Pomerol) and that, too, is enjoyable to drink now.

Recently, I tried the Talbot against the Gruaud-Larose and while the former has not turned out so well as one would have hoped (there was too much acidity in that particular bottle), the Gruaud-Larose was quite superb, so much so that I returned to the Connaught Hotel, London, to have another bottle as soon as I could. The Palmer has lived well up to its fine reputation, for only last week at the Jardin des Gourmets, also in London, I shared a bottle with a friend from California and one can only describe it as magnificent! Surely it cannot possibly get any better. Ready to drink now, this must be one of the best of all the 1961's.

According to my personal taste, the leading wines of the 1961 vintage have changed places a little since I first wrote about them; on that occasion, I put Lafite easily at the top.

This reminds me, I see I have nearly fallen into the trap of discussing the 1961 médocs almost to the exclusion of the Saint-Emilions and pomerols. A grave error indeed that would be, for the great Saint-Emilions and pomerols are really superb in 1961. Only once have I tasted the fabulous 1961 Pétrus and never yet have I had the good fortune to drink it, but that October (1971) in Bordeaux, I did help to drink a bottle of the great Cheval Blanc of that year and these are my notes: "Dark of colour and a fine bouquet, but on the taste, still a little hesitant, or should I say resistant, but of really fine quality. Evidently this needs a few more years to reach its best."

It is now proved that those wise virgins who put aside some of this fine vintage for the future, were fully justified in their judgment. Now, with a clear conscience, from time to time they can open a bottle with the excuse, shall we say, of studying its progress! All this may make frustrating reading for those who were too young to buy the 1961's or even for those who missed the bus, but they have no excuse whatsoever, except a financial one, to overlook the excellent 1970's, worthy successors to the 1961's.

Two Exercises in Gastronomy

Here in London, we have a remarkable restaurateur, a man as passionately dedicated to wine as any I know. At his Soho restaurant, Au Jardin des Gourmets, Joseph Berkmann must have the finest collection of old clarets of any similar establishment in the country. Although the last bottles of the superb 1900 Château Margaux were opened at one of the dinners now to be described, there still remain other prestigious bottles such as Lafite 1875! His range of 1961 clarets is too wide to mention and also in the cellar there is a goodly proportion of the famous Dr. Barolet Collection of pre-war Burgundies. All this is really to explain the background of an unusual series of dinners which this generous host has provided over the past twelve months.

To begin with, there was an evening built around twelve vintages of Latour and this was followed by another at which we discussed a similar number of 1945 clarets. Merely to assemble together such a galaxy of fine bottles is quite an achievement and functions such as these, which are both gastronomic and educational, are few and far between.

The last two feasts, because that is really what they were, took place in the private rooms at the Jardin des Gourmets, and for both of them a number of distinguished guests had come over specially from France. For the Château Margaux dinner there were Bernard **Ginestet**, Peter Sichel (Palmer) and Louis Vialard (Cissac), all from Bordeaux and to represent the "opposition" as it were, we had the pleasure of the company of Philippe Cairol, a noted wine broker from the Côte d'Or.

Our host had placed me next to Bernard Ginestet, the delightful son of the proprietor of Château Margaux and during the conversation, he told me that never before at one meal had he ever been able to taste such a wide range of vintages from his own château.

Gastronomically, the dinner was quite exceptional. After an aperitif of Taittinger Comtes de Champagne 1964, we sat down to the following:

First Serving
- Le Riz de Veau Financière en Croûte
- Les Faisans
- Les Perdreaux
- Les Canards Sauvages
- "Some Grouse"

La Chasse Royale

Second Serving
{ La Selle de Chevreuil
Les Rables de Lièvre, Sauce Poivrade
Choux de Bruxelles aux Marrons
Le Plateau de Fromages
Le Sorbet aux Framboises

Falling, as it did, in the middle of the shooting season, this was an ideal moment for such a serving of game and never before have I known anything to equal it. On account of its extent, La Chasse Royale may, on paper, appear somewhat formidable, but we were only offered small helpings of the best portions of the game concerned. All the same, so good was the fare that some of us, myself included, were seen to be tucking in to second helpings.

The range of vintages of Château Margaux was astonishing and in case some readers may at least have one or two of the more recent vintages from this distinguished property in their cellars, the following notes on them may prove helpful.

Château Margaux

1961: Very deep colour, a gloriously rich bouquet, plenty of depth, fine quality. Not too much tannin, but we shall have to wait a few years to appreciate properly this splendid wine.

1955: Medium colour, well developed bouquet, good fruit but on light side, typical 1955.

1953: (Magnum) Good colour, lovely bouquet, soft, round and charming, must be at its best now. Ch. Margaux was an enormous success in 1953.

1952: Deep colour, fruity bouquet, lots of fruit, but like so many 1952's from the Médoc, is rather hard and severe.

1950: Good colour, attractive bouquet, good fruit, but there was a slightly pointed finish. Delightful as they were, from my own experience, it is time these 1950's were drunk up!

1945: Very deep colour, enormously rich bouquet, a great big rich wine, there is considerable tannin, so it finishes rather hard.

1934: Good colour, distinguished bouquet, plenty of fruit, though it thins off like so many of the 1934 médocs.

1929: Good colour and it still has that delightful 1929 bouquet. Heaps of fruit still, but sadly, has pronounced wrinkles and thinning white hair!

1920: Very good colour, splendid bouquet, despite the fact it has lost some of its sugar, it is beautifully balanced and of wonderful quality. Has kept better than the 1929.

1900: Good colour, old but impeccable, this is a great wine, though I must admit I have had better bottles. At this age, old wines often vary from bottle to bottle.

1893: Fine colour for its age, old but good bouquet, beautifully balanced and a splendid flavour, great quality.

1888: Very good colour, something not quite right with the nose and a slight taste of mildew, something they had not learnt to handle in those days. Complete, all the same.

1887: Medium colour, full bouquet, it was rather thin and dry and should have been drunk long ago. The second bottle was better!

The second of these feasts took place in the same surroundings on December 1st, 1971, but on this occasion was greatly embellished by the presence of ladies. The menu was precisely the same too and for me this was an unexpected treat, because I could eat that Chasse Royale time and again and also was able to prove to my wife that I had not been exaggerating!

Interested as I am in the *crus bourgeois* this meal had a special appeal. The time may not have come yet in America when the classified growths of the Médoc have become too expensive for the man in the street, but this is certainly the case in England and now that the Japanese are beginning to take an added interest, the outlook for the faithful, but impecunious British claret lover becomes more and more gloomy.

In view of these unpalatable facts of life, there are many of us both here and in the United States who are turning and I am pleased to say turning quite happily, to the lesser wines of Bordeaux. Fortunately for us their number is legion and to sort them out can be quite a rewarding occupation. Anyone with the money can buy the great wines, not, in fact, that they are always by any means great, but it takes more skill and indeed is much more exciting to endeavour to pick out the successful ones among the *crus bourgeois,* both of the Médoc and those growths from across the river Garonne in the districts of Blaye, Bourg and Fronsac.

My abiding fear is that one of these days the mass of the tiny properties will be grabbed up by ruthless juggernauts who will destroy this delightful part of the Bordelais trade in order to market it all as blended Bordeaux Superieur, or not so superior, as the case may be.

To return to our hospitable board, there were sixteen of us in all, seated at two tables and our eyes fairly boggled as we discovered lined up before us like guardsmen on parade, no less than ninety-six generous claret glasses—there was scarcely room for our plates! The purpose of the particular meal was to assess the 1967, 1966 and 1962 vintages of four of the most important châteaux which come under the heading of *Crus Bourgeois*. These were Gloria (Saint-Julien), La Tour-de-Mons (Soussans), Cissac (of Cissac) and Les Ormes-de-Pez (Saint Estèphe), and what a fascinating comparison it turned out to be!

Before we got down to work we were requested to place the four wines in order of preference and at the same time to mark them with points from one to ten. I must confess that I became so absorbed in the task before me that most ungallantly, I was unable to converse properly with the ladies on either side. Fortunately, both were well versed in the ways of wine, so I trust they will understand and forgive.

What made the proceedings of particular interest was the fact that three proprietors had all come over from Bordeaux specially to attend this dinner. Henri Martin, well known to many enophiles in America, is the joint manager of the vineyard of Latour, the mayor of Saint-Julien, the owner of Gloria, the President of the C.I.V.B. and is one of the leading men, if not the leading wine man, of France. Monsieur Cazes, the mayor of Pauillac, the owner of Châteaux Lynch-Bages and Les Ormes-de-Pez and last, but certainly not least, Louis Vialard, one of the most able wine makers of the Médoc and one of the few Médocain proprietors who inhabits his château in Cissac the year round. The best that I can do now is to write down the tasting notes and the points which rightly or wrongly, I put against each wine. While tasting them, I could not help thinking of the people who will only drink the "great names" and how it takes an evening like this to prove how ill-advised they are!

1967 Vintage

    La Tour-de-Mons (Soussans)
        Very deep colour, a big fruity bouquet, good fruit, rather rough and still has a little acidity to lose, needs a further year in bottle. 6/10

    Les Ormes-de-Pez (Saint-Estèphe)
        Medium colour, a pretty bouquet, medium body, still a little tannin, but already delightful to drink. 7/10

Two Exercises in Gastronomy 175

Cissac (Cissac)
:   Good colour, fruity bouquet, has style and individual character. Medium body, rather backward and to display its full quality, needs another eighteen months. 7/10

Gloria (Saint-Julien)
:   Good colour, charming bouquet, well balanced, lovely flavour. Will be better in say, 12 months' time. 9/10

1966 Vintage

La Tour-de-Mons
:   Good colour, big nose, although a little rough is full-bodied and well made. Needs another year. 6/10

Les Ormes-de-Pez
:   Deep colour, lovely bouquet, has charm and finesse and is well forward, in fact, is ready now. 7/10

Cissac
:   Good colour and a good full bouquet. This is a big wine which is full of fruit and quality. Has a good future and will probably be even better in two more years. 8/10

Gloria
:   Very deep colour, heavenly bouquet, beautifully made, has elegance and is delightful to drink now. 8 plus/10

1962 Vintage

La Tour-de-Mons
:   Deep colour, well developed and distinguished bouquet, lots of fruit and has a good flavour. 7/10

Les Ormes-de-Pez
:   Very deep colour, fine bouquet, has plenty of fruit combined with depth and distinction. Full of charm, ready now. 8/10

Cissac
:   Very deep colour, a big powerful bouquet, a fine masculine wine excellent now, but will undoubtedly improve still further. 9/10

Gloria
:   Good colour, lovely bouquet and a fine flavour, no wonder Gloria holds its own so well with the great growths of Saint-Julien. 8 plus/10

To sum up, generally speaking La Tour-de-Mons had the deeper colour and though all its vintages were very good, by comparison, at any rate, the others showed up even better. The three vintages of Les Ormes-de-Pez had considerable charm as well as style and appeared to be made for early maturity. The Cissac was quite the reverse, being made in the old fashioned manner, maybe it was more backward in every vintage, but in each case there was a depth and flavour which promised more to come. The Gloria was its usual self, living well up to its well-established reputation—charming and elegant and clearly made by a master craftsman.

Interesting Meals

This one had its roots some four months ago in Bordeaux when Joseph Berkmann, Maarten Van Keulen, Bob Bottomley and myself, accompanied by our respective wives, visited Château Trottevieille (First Great Growth, Saint-Emilion) as the guests of the owner, Emile Casteja. It was the fourth of October and I remember the vineyard close to the château being enlivened by pickers, gathering in the last of the harvest.

We tasted the 1970 vintage from the cask and, as we departed, Emile presented each of us with two bottles of different vintages of his Trottevieille. There and then, we decided we would assemble together in London to enjoy those bottles at a later date.

This happy event took place on a bitter, snow-ridden evening late in January 1972, an admirable setting for the full enjoyment of the round, full-bodied wine of Saint-Emilion. The venue was the Lafayette restaurant, Joseph's attractive new venture in King Street, St. James's, the decoration for which he is personally responsible.

The menu, delightfully simple, began with a good pheasant terrine, the last for some time, no doubt, since we are at the end of the shooting season. The main dish and one of my favourites, was what I believe is called a New England Boiled Dinner and one which I always enjoy immensely when I am in America. For English readers, this consists of something very similar to our boiled silverside, ham and chicken, and is likewise accompanied by all the appropriate boiled vegetables, carrots, turnips, beetroot, celery, onion and so on. These bland but delicious flavours proved most suitable for the appreciation of the wine. Finally, a really good open tart known as La Tarte des Demoiselles Tatin, which has a base of apple, had been specially prepared for us

Interesting Meals

by the chef. Neither my wife nor myself are great enthusiasts for sweet dishes at the end of the meal, but this was too good to resist.

The wines were six vintages of Château Trottevieille, Saint-Emilion and all with the exception of the 1962 were château bottled:

1969: Colour medium, bouquet pleasant and the wine agreeable, but on the light side, with not, I imagine, a long life before it. It must be remembered that 1969 is not a great vintage for the wines of Saint-Emilion and Pomerol.

1967: (From a magnum) Good colour, a fragrant rather rich nose, full and rounded with a good *gout de terroir*. This will make a very good bottle.

1966: (From a magnum) A beautiful slightly sweeter bouquet, good fruit and very good flavour.

1964: Medium colour, a big, full bouquet, plenty of fruit and flavour but as a 1964, it could perhaps have a little more flesh on its bones. Ready now, but should improve still further.

1962: It is impossible to comment on this bottle because it was corked. For me, the loss was not so great as it might have been. I have never been a great fan of the Saint-Emilions and pomerols of this vintage.

1952: Good, but now an ageing colour, the bouquet equally showing some age. Still complete and still a good mouthful of wine. Would say that this needs drinking within the next two years.

We were completely divided as to which was the best wine of the evening, the 1967 or the 1966, finally the 1967 won by a very narrow margin. On the face of it, 1966 is really a better vintage so it was really a little surprising to me that I preferred the 1967. Since these two fine wines were in magnums, they must be more backward than if they were in ordinary bottles. With a year or two more to mature, the magnums will undoubtedly be more enjoyable, but I imagine the same wines from a bottle rather than a magnum would be good to drink from now on.

Episode Five

On 13th March 1972, sixteen of us sat down to another of these fantastic repasts given by Joseph Berkmann and on this occasion it was held at his Lockets Restaurant in Westminster.

It was the fifth of this remarkable series which I have had the honour to attend—twelve vintages of Château Latour, twelve of the leading 1945 clarets, twelve vintages of Château Margaux, a comparison of four different *crus bourgeois* over three good vintages and now this Mouton dinner—truly a memorable occasion.

We Londoners are indeed fortunate that this most enlightened restaurateur should have chosen to make his home here among us. His restaurants, apart from their generally high standard of cooking, have earned a well deserved reputation for their extremely well selected wines. Many restaurateurs merely pay lip service to the wine side of their business, but Joseph is not only an authority, but a true enthusiast.

Foreign visitors who, from time to time, enjoy a good bottle, will find the best cellar in London at Au Jardin des Gourmets in Greek Street, Soho, for many rareties lie therein and what is more, are available at quite reasonable prices. Although not quite so extensive, the wine lists at the other restaurants, the Minotaur, l'Opera, Lafayette and so on, are far better than the average and for those of us who are not on business expenses, his Beaujolais, as well as being outstanding with regard to quality, is well within the reach of the average purse.

As we assembled, we were offered 1964 Taittinger Comtes de Champagne, Blanc des Blancs. The food, mercifully simple to accompany such a galaxy of fine wine, was sweetbreads in Port, succulent Welsh spring lamb with peas in their pods, roast parsnips and new potatoes with parsley. Next came great sticks of lovely fresh asparagus from California with sauce hollandaise and a selection of ideally matured English cheeses.

It is not often that one has the chance to taste the great wines of Mouton-Rothschild, certainly not a range of this breadth, and both their stature and fine quality were of exceptional interest. It is needless to say that all the bottles were decanted, some of them a suitable time in advance, and others, like the 1893 vintage, just a few minutes before it was actually served. Before I go any further however, I must commend Gino Tecchia, the manager of Lockets, for his perspicacity over the serving of the wines. When I have a number to assess, I find the

Episode Five

aroma of the food on the plate before me, however delectable it may be, disturbs my sense of judgment, so some time before our sweetbreads arrived, the first five wines were poured and this gave us ample time for appraisal and, as instructed, an opportunity to mark the wines with points from one to twenty. Similar pauses occurred later throughout this splendid meal and this enabled us to perform our task far more advantageously than usual.

These are my notes on this spectacular array of great wines:

Year	Characteristics	My Placing	Score	Group Placing
1955	Good dark colour, the fine, fragrant typical "cedar" nose of Mouton (this special aromatic bouquet was evident throughout all the vintages), full-bodied with plenty of fruit. Not a really outstanding wine, but then 1955 was not an outstanding vintage	7	15/20	7
1953	Good colour, distinguished bouquet though beginning to show some age, a really delightful flavour, this is a wine with enormous charm	4	18/20	4
1952	Good colour, great depth of bouquet, full-bodied with considerable fruit, but like all the 1952 médocs, is a little severe. Certainly it lacks the infinite charm of the 1953	9	13-14/20	8
1950	Good colour, a powerful bouquet, good fruit too, but it thins out to a slightly sharp finish. This needs drinking up!	11	9/20	10
1949	A beautiful dark colour, a delightfully concentrated bouquet, to which are attached many nuances. A lovely rich wealthy wine	3	19/20	3
1945	Very, very dark colour, a fine scented, almost rich bouquet, still lots of tannin, but is powerful and has a delightful flavour	Share 1	20/20	1
1937	Medium colour, good, but rather dry nose, lots of flavour. Interesting, but somewhat severe	5	16/20	9

Year	Characteristics	My Placing	Score	Group Placing
1934	Medium colour, plenty of bouquet, good fruit, but lacks charm and has a slightly sharp finish. This is in keeping with the other great médocs of 1934	10	11/20	8
1928	Good colour, a dry rather acetic bouquet, thin and passé. This old gentleman has turned a little senile!	12	4/20	12
1921	Good colour, but I found some sharpness on the nose, very good fruit though	8	14/20	5
1911	Colour rather weak for Mouton, but it has a pleasant gentle bouquet. Light, but elegant, fine quality	6	15-16/20	6
1893	Good colour and although ancient, the bouquet was pleasing, this still has heaps of fruit and charm, really remarkable	Share 1	20/20	2

Last and certainly not least of the wines of this memorable feast, our host gave us some of his fabulous Cockburn 1908, one of the finest vintage ports it has ever been my good fortune to drink. I have known this famous wine since before the war and there it was, as good as ever, at the ripe old age of 64!

Some 1961 Clarets

On 3rd July 1972, Joseph Berkmann gave another of his now traditional "wine assessment" dinner parties. Over the past ten years this dedicated man has been collecting fine wine for his group of restaurants, the quality and scope of which must be beyond compare at any rate in so far as England is concerned. I have already been present (described above) as a guest at dinners featuring such great châteaux as Latour, Margaux, Mouton-Rothschild and there is one starring Haut-Brion scheduled for this November. On these occasions the guests are diverted by no less than twelve vintages representing the châteaux in question. Some times, the wines are served "blind" as with the dozen different wines of the 1945 vintage and at others the name of the château is known and the vintages are divulged. Apart from the enjoyment of an incomparable meal in sophisticated company, these series of tastings have been immensely instructive.

Among his many other wines, Joseph Berkmann has been building up a remarkable collection of the now famous 1961 vintage, and including some of the first growths, Mouton, Pétrus and Cheval Blanc, he must have at least 20 different 1961's in his cellars. On account of their great quality and the very small crop, the 1961's were considered very expensive when they first came on the market. However when compared with the absurd present day prices, such as the 1971's are fetching although they sounded very expensive at the time, in retrospect they were remarkably good value. Even so, at that time the first growths and so on were beyond the purses of many true claret lovers, but being devotees at least, they purchased some of the other classified growths, so it is for these enthusiasts that the following notes are written.

Owing to their heavy tannin content, most of the 1961's have been relatively undrinkable, or, at least rather unattractive to drink for far longer than is customary for a less exalted vintage and it is only now after eight or nine years in bottle that one can begin to contemplate their consumption with any feeling of equanimity. Notwithstanding, with much of their tannin still in evidence, many of the 1961's will continue to improve. Inspired no doubt by the "thriftyness" of my Scottish forbears, I have always held to the maxim of not opening my own bottles of this vintage until I have been certain they were ready and thus have always seized the opportunity to drink them in a restaurant, or, better still, by battening upon the generosity of more generous people than myself. In this manner I have been able to watch at least some of their slow progress towards maturity.

With this thought in mind, it may be of some service to other claret lovers to know how one or two of these epic wines are faring in London. It should be remembered that however great the reputation of the vintage may be, not all of the geese are swans and now that the wines are approaching some sort of maturity, a few of the defects are becoming discernable.

Since Joseph Berkmann knows more about wine than most restaurateurs, he knows all too well the dishes to serve with it, so this dinner was quite a classic in this way—Ris de Veau Financiere, the sauce accompanying this was so good, I wished that I had a spoon to sup it up surreptitiously; Selle d'Agneau Provençale, with the herbs mild enough not to disturb the wine, Pommes Boulangerè and Fromages de France; and finally when the wine was despatched, a Sorbet of fresh raspberries à l'Alsacienne.

Following an aperitif of Pommery & Greno 1955 which sadly, was on the decline, about eighteen of us, husbands and wives, sat down to tackle seven 1961 clarets, all of them château bottled. Our glasses were merely marked from one to seven and we had to get on with it from there. We were asked to mark the wines from 1 to 20.

Calon-Ségur, 3rd Growth (Saint-Estephe).
Good colour, pleasant interesting bouquet, good fruit and quite well forward. 13/20

Lynch-Bages, 5th Growth (Pauillac).
Good colour, delightfully scented bouquet, in fact, a strong smell of cabernet sauvignon; in a way, the bouquet resembled that of a really fine tobacco. Heaps of flavour. Very good quality. I guessed it as Lynch-Bages, if not, certainly a Pauillac! 18/20

Montrose, 2nd Growth (Saint-Estèphe).
Dark colour, good but rather a dusty nose. Has fruit, breeding and plenty of tannin. This needs a year or so yet. 14/20

Léoville-Las-Cases, 2nd Growth (Saint-Julien).
Good colour, great finesse on bouquet with a nice sweetness coming through. Good depth of fruit and a lot of tannin. This will undoubtedly improve. 15/20

Lascombes, 2nd Growth (Margaux).
Good colour, powerful bouquet but something unusual about it, this wine has little charm and a lot of acidity. 8/20

Pichon-Longueville-Baron, 2nd Growth (Pauillac).
Very dark colour, a lovely concentrated bouquet, very good fruit and flavour. Fine quality. 19/20

Gruaud-Larose, 2nd Growth (Saint-Julien).
Dark colour, a big heavenly bouquet and a truly delightful flavour, really fine quality. 20/20

All of the above had a good colour, but one or two were a bit darker than the others.

Although I did not put a name to it, I was not surprised afterwards to find that number seven was the Gruaud-Larose. I have only tasted this wine on two previous occasions, but each time was greatly impressed. In fact, the last time at the Connaught Hotel, London, it proved superior to two other médocs, each bearing a far more illustrious name! If there are any regrets about this tasting, it might have been interesting also to have had Palmer included among the contestants. For me, the 1961 Palmer is among the finest wines one could possibly drink. All the same, there were three wines head and shoulders above the others, namely Gruaud-Larose, Pichon-Longueville-Baron and the Lynch-Bages. However the fact that Montrose and Calon-Ségur only received respectively 14 and 13 points does not by any means imply that they are not good, for this is a vintage of unusually high quality and the wines were only marked comparatively.

To sum up, if one can do this after so brief a skirmish with this great vintage, while some of the 1961's are approaching drinkability, others still have quite a long way to go; also as may be seen, not all the 1961's are of such sterling quality as one would imagine.

A Privation of Port

Most of us have at least one extravagance—mine is shooting, but at least this is a comfort to my wife, because it gets me out of the house on Saturdays during the three months of the season and this gives her some time to get on with things.

There are eight of us guns in our syndicate and we shoot over a large estate some sixty miles north of London. Although this used to be a famous partridge shoot in the days when this table delicacy abounded, ninety per cent of the bag nowadays is driven pheasants, most of which are hand reared.

From fifteen to twenty beaters come out every Saturday and a few words about them may come amiss because, in a way, this little story hinges around them; good country chaps whose broad Bedfordshire accent is not always easy to understand. They have an excellent sense of humour and now after the years, one has come to regard them more or less as personal friends. Not much misses their sharp eyes and they know even better than the other guns how well or badly you are performing—real moments of truth! When I first began to shoot with this syndicate, it seems their nickname for me was "the amateur shot," but I was not told this until much later when apparently I had graduated into being called "the pro," comforting of course, but not at all true!

One of the more delightful adjuncts of a day's shooting is the break for lunch, and after a really cold morning exposed to the east wind or whatever it may be, nothing can be more welcome than a warming drink (even if it is a cold one) and something hot to eat. In some places, as for example in France, the shooting lunch can be a rather grand gastronomic affair, but ours is pretty simple, for apart from the enjoyment of the sport, it is the personality of the individual guns which counts for so much and which helps to make it all so agreeable. From its appearance, our venue for lunch is really rather shaming, an ancient delapidated caravan, which from the looks of it must have been someone's pride and joy way back in the thirties! Its stripped interior contains nothing more than an oblong kitchen table with seats around, plus a diminutive calor gas fire, which on really cold days is quite inadequate, but once that is said and done, all the rest is golden, because the tiny cramped atmosphere quickly engenders a marked feeling of conviviality.

Apart from the eight of us, the company is usually embellished by the presence of one or two of the hardier wives, so that at times there can be quite a squash. Each of us brings our own food and in the most varied assortment of baskets and containers imaginable; simple stuff usually, hot soup in thermos flasks, hot "bangers," sandwiches, pork pies and often tid-bits such as splendidly matured stilton and crisp celery from someone's garden, are passed around.

As to the drink, our national habit is here greatly in evidence, for nearly everyone produces a bottle of sherry of some kind or another and a few of us, even a can of beer. What has become a feature of our syndicate though is the Chesky, which a generous member has provided over the years. Chesky, little known in England, is a kind of liqueur which is made in France of a mixture, I suppose, of cherries with a base of whisky. All of us find this preferable on shooting occasions than the more prosaic sloe gin or cherry brandy and certainly it sends you out into the cold with a warm internal glow!

One of the more amusing days of the season is the Christmas Shoot, only half a day in fact, but memorable because on this occasion we concentrate more on the "goodies" for lunch. Our most affluent member usually brings a magnum of Champagne, either Dom Perignon or Taittinger Comtes de Champagne, as well as a Christmas pudding from Fortnum's, accompanied by the essential brandy butter.

There is an anecdote attached to this Christmas pudding, because some years ago now and on the occasion of its first appearance, we all found it both difficult to cut and even harder to chew, in spite of its provenance from Fortnum's; in fact, on the way back to London, my companion, the donor, suffered grievously from indigestion and it was not until the following week when we heard that the others had suffered likewise, we investigated a little and discovered the famous pudding had not been cooked! I believe such a pudding has to be cooked for at least three or four hours before it is ready to eat! Alas, no one had bothered to read the instructions.

On this last occasion, I was instructed that all that was required from me personally was a bottle of vintage port—this was fine, because I could think of a no more agreeable, nor more appreciative company with which to share my very last bottle of Taylor 1927. In order that it would be in the best possible condition, I stood up this famous bottle for days beforehand and before leaving London around 8 o'clock on the morning in question, decanted it most carefully and though perhaps I should not say so myself, in spite of the early hour, it tasted as near perfection as possible.

Since on shooting days, our "affluent" member is kind enough to drive me to and fro, I duly loaded all my clobber, gun, cartridge bag, shooting stick and all that, plus the precious bottle of port, into the boot of his car. All went well, except for the last drive before lunch when I shot a bird which took some time to find, so by the time I reached the car, I found the wine and food had been taken to the caravan where everybody had already started on the champagne, of which, let me add, there was a plentiful supply. By the time the Christmas pudding had been consumed (properly cooked this time), the moment was ripe for the vintage port and, as a pipe opener (as it were) we began with a bottle of Warre 1960, but good as this was, what we had all really been looking forward to was the *pièce de résistance,* the Taylor 1927.

Naturally confident that our "affluent" member had brought the bottle into the caravan together with our food, I then asked him to set the 1927 on the table. There was a deathly hush—he turned quite white and exclaimed "gosh, I gave that bottle to the beaters for their lunch as I thought it was a Christmas present for them."

Since the assembled company were all enthusiastic vintage port lovers, it was hard to convince them that this had really occurred and one even rushed out to endeavour to retrieve the bottle, but alas, it was far too late and all had been consumed. All we could do was to laugh and my great consolation came later on when our head keeper Frank Dickens, a teetotaller himself, told us that one of the beaters had tasted it and exclaimed "Cor, that's a drop of good stuff!"

An Epic Occasion

An epic occasion in California, a dinner to enhance the enjoyment of various vintage ports, all of that famous year 1927. For several reasons this was an unusual event, first because when we think of vintage port, we naturally associate it with Great Britain and there was I in California; second, the abundance of choice, wines from no less than eight different port shippers; and third, the fact that all this awe-inspiring wine came from one individual's cellar!

The British Isles have always been recognised as the traditional home for vintage port and our cold damp climate has proved particularly suitable for its consumption. However, the fact that we no longer take much healthy exercise on horseback together with the elimination of the draughty houses of the nineteenth century and the advent of central heating, the absolute necessity of a glass of vintage port after dinner may have diminished, nevertheless there still remains for us the blissful enjoyment, if as an excuse only, to warm the cockles of our hearts!

The original port shipped to England was merely a red table wine and presumably of no outstanding quality and its consumption, beginning around the fourteenth century, was greatly stimulated by the Methuen Treaty of 1703. This treaty allowed the importation into Portugal of English woollens in exchange for a preferential tariff for Portuguese wine and from that moment, England never looked back! It was not, however, until the end of the eighteenth century that port as we know it today, was evolved, as it were, by the addition of brandy to the recently pressed wine, a procedure which arrested the fermentation and retained some of the natural sweetness from the grapes. Unfortunately (as it was thought at the time) the marriage of the wine with the brandy took some time in which to settle down and it was not until the discovery of the use of the cork and the subsequent evolution of the shape of roughly the present-day bottle that vintage port could be binned away to mature. This vastly important advance occurred soon after the end of the Napoleonic wars and from that day onwards vintage port came into its own. It was found that the wine improved enormously by age in bottle so much so that it soon became the custom for the landed gentry to fill the capacious cellars beneath their country mansions with various vintages, not only for their own delectation but also a pipe or so was laid down for the eldest and other sons. Admirable as this custom may have been, it has been known that when the time came for some young men to claim their inheritance, all or at least much of the port had disappeared! The temptation of all those bottles had proved too great to resist! The laying down of a few dozen vintage port also provided a useful gift for the gastronomically minded godfather, "to bring up the boy in the right tradition!"

On account of the link between the Port Shippers, i.e., noted English families living in Oporto, those bearing such household names as Cockburn, Taylor, Graham, and Sandeman, most of them, be it noted, of Scottish extraction, the bulk of each vintage was shipped in wood to

An Epic Occasion

the various ports in the British Isles and there it was bottled two years following the vintage. So important was the length of the period of maturing in wood that wine merchants used to list their wine thus, Sandeman 1934, bottled 1936.

Unhappily no vintage port could be shipped during the period of the last war and that, I believe, caused the beginning of serious bottling in Oporto. Although they were regarded with some askance by the English wine trade at the time, certainly the Oporto bottled wines filled a useful gap in the post war years. The present trend is for all of it to be bottled in Oporto and one of the reasons for this may be the increasing interest taken in this nectar by the gourmets of the United States.

During the past decade, the American public has taken to the drinking of fine table wine like ducks to water, with the inevitable result that demand has rapidly exceeded supply, thus the price of that delectable commodity has soared. In view of the present trend, I fear the same will soon happen to vintage port.

The dinner to be described was certainly unusual, for where else in the world would one find a wine lover, let alone a port lover, with no less than eight different 1927's in his own cellar? I doubt very much whether this could be emulated even in England, the home of vintage port. There may be and indeed there are people who still have some 1927 left in their cellars, but surely not from eight different shippers.

The owner of this cellar was my Californian host, Dr. Bernard L. Rhodes, to whom I owe all my knowledge such as it is, of the fine wines of California. A man blessed with such a sensitive palate for wine that in a number of blind tastings I have known him to put a name to each of the eight top wines of Bordeaux. Only once at a dinner party have I known him fail to name the vintage and shipper of the port and— that was going back all the way to 1900!

The people attending this gastronomic repast constituted the elite of the connoisseurs of the area around San Francisco and among them were five wine growers, five wine merchants, a professor of enology, as well as a number of physicians and dentists.

I feel that I can do no better than quote from the notice for convening the tasting:

The fabulous 1927 ports have at last begun to slide over the top, more's the pity! While many of us in this country prefer our vintage ports with more bottle age than do today's port connoisseurs in England, even the diehards among us must admit now is the time reluctantly to lay to rest the remainder of our 1927's.

Harry Waugh's annual visit to California seems a suitable occasion to salute eight different shippers '27 ports and evaluate the late results of their winemaking skill. These ports were all bottled in England in contrast to the more recent practice of Oporto bottling for vintage port. Whichever side one sits on the controversial subject of English bottlings of table wines, there is universal agreement that many English wine merchants are superbly skillful in bottling vintage port.

The dinner will be at 7. P.M. on Friday evening, April 14th at Narsai's Restaurant, 385 Colusa Avenue, Berkeley. The setting for the tasting-dinner will be in the private dining room which is partially constructed from a very old redwood tank. After a recent visit to view the construction progress I can tell you that a principal reason for the delay in opening the restaurant is Narsai's striving for perfection, not only in the culinary sphere but in decor and furnishings as well. Towards this end he has acquired the enormous redwood tank and used it with striking success in his design of the new restaurant.

The plan of the "wake" is to have a light dinner with a moderate amount of wine chosen to complement the food, followed by the range of ports. After a brief period to evaluate the wines there will be stilton, celery ribs, dessert and nuts to accompany these "portly old gentlemen."

Narsai David, himself an outstanding chef has recently opened this most attractive restaurant in Berkeley, California. The wine accompanying the light meal which was to lead up to the tasting was imported by Darrell Corti, a brilliant and erudite young wine merchant from Sacramento. This was a 1950 Dão, a big sturdy affair, surprisingly rich, in fact not unlike a fine Rhone wine. I for one, had never before tasted such an old unfortified wine from Portugal.

Before giving the results of our deliberations, a further word or so about vintage port and particularly the 1927 vintage may not come amiss. Without therefore being too long-winded, the most famous years prewar were 1904, 1908, 1912, 1917, 1920 and of course, 1927 and, since the earlier ones are virtually things of the past, only the 1927's are still of interest to us. A fabulous vintage was 1927 and for my part, at its best in the years succeeding the war; that is, when it was about twenty years old. At that time I was a member of the Guards Club and how well I remember enjoying those splendid 1927's from the cellar; the Taylor, the Graham and the Fonseca, three of which we were to meet again that evening some 5,000 miles away and twenty-five years later!

In prewar days it was said that you had to wait about twenty years for port to be at its best, but nowadays, presumably to meet modern requirements, it appears to be made so that one does not have to wait quite so long.

*A "blind" tasting of 1927 vintage port,
April 1972*

Wine	Characteristics	My Placing	Group Placing	Points
Cockburn	Medium to pale colour, slightly fruity nose, medium body, in fact, rather light with the brandy coming through (it is one of the signs of age in vintage port when the spirit begins to be noticeable)	8	6	14
Dow	Rather pale colour, fragrant bouquet, very light of body and fairly dry with the spirit coming through both on the bouquet and palate.	7	8	5
Fonseca	Medium colour, a light "cedary" bouquet, sweet fruity and rather good	3	5	23
Graham	Very dark colour, deep, rich bouquet, a huge wine, full and rich in the mouth, great quality	1	1	74
Rebello Valente	Colour a trifle cloudy, an agreeable "toasted" nose, medium body, good residual sweetness, all the same, the brandy was evident both on the nose and on the taste	5	3	55
Sandeman	Fairly light colour, poor bouquet, a strong flavour, but there was something not quite clean about it, clearly it must have been a bad bottle	7	7	11
Taylor	Good dark colour, a fine big nose, full bodied, lots of fruit, excellent	2	2	60
Warre	Good colour, nice nose, good fruit and still some tannin	4	4	25

Studying the results once again, we were unlucky with the Sandeman and on second thoughts, perhaps I was a little hard on the Cockburn. It must be admitted that some of these 1927's had turned into rather frail old gentlemen, their hair turned from grey to white, but the breeding and distinction were there for all to see. In contrast, both the Graham and the Taylor were surprisingly vigorous.

Burgundian Beneficence

Although Kir is essentially a Burgundian aperitif, it is just as delightful to drink elsewhere and now that the consumption of wine is so much in vogue, it can often make a more compatible "starter" to a meal than some of the stronger potions in more common use.

The real name, of course, is *Cassis au Vin Blanc,* but it has taken this soubriquet from its erstwhile devotee and disciple, the late Canon Kir, who, for many years, was the much loved and much respected mayor of the fair city of Dijon.

This delectable, refreshing, but not too potent pre-prandial libation is encouraged and enjoyed at all the leading hotels and restaurants in both north and southern Burgundy and for that matter, throughout all France, the natural home of gastronomy. However, for some reason difficult to explain, it is little known either in England or the United States. More's the pity for clearly many among us are missing out on something rather good!

The main ingredients of Kir are very simple and above all not too expensive—Crème de Cassis and a bottle of Bourgogne Aligoté. Crème de Cassis is, of course, the essence of blackcurrant juice and, as with the sherry you use for your cooking, the better the quality, the better will be the result. Essentially a Burgundian specialty, Crème de Cassis should be obtainable from most reputable wine merchants, but it can vary greatly as to quality and there is a further gentle warning; it does not keep indefinitely, for after a while it is subject to oxidation. In this manner it resembles very much a fine Fino Sherry, which preferably should be bottled in small quantities at regular intervals and be consumed while it is fresh.

Bourgogne Aligoté comes under the heading of one of the lesser white Burgundies, and is the produce of the vine of that name. However this does not by any means mean that Bourgogne Aligoté is just ordinary wine, because when well selected and well bottled it can be delightful to drink. Into the bargain, it is still reasonably inexpensive, almost a miracle in these days of soaring prices. Vineyards producing this grape are to be found as far north as the Department of the Yonne (the region of Chablis), throughout the Côte d'Or and as far south as the arrondissement of Villefranche in the Beaujolais.

The way to serve Kir or *Cassis au Vin Blanc,* is to put, say, a teaspoonful of your Cassis into a wine glass and then fill it up with a gently chilled Aligoté. Naturally, the amount of Cassis you use is according to taste. Have no fear though, that to enjoy this alluring beverage, you are restricted entirely to Bourgogne Aligoté, because any white Burgundy will do; but once again, the better the quality, the better will be the result. I have enjoyed it hugely with Macôn Blanc, or even a domaine bottled Meursault and, one romantic and never to be forgotten occasion, while staying at that outstanding haunt of gastronomy, the Hotel de la Poste in Avalon, the manager opened for us a *premier cru* 1966 Chablis, to provide a glass of Kir for our aperitif and suggested that the rest of the bottle be finished with his intriguing first course, "les amuse-gueulles"—a series of platters for which this restaurant is especially noted.

There are other delightful variations upon this theme of *Cassis au Vin Blanc* and if you are an appreciative and sufficiently determined gourmet, you will make a detour while driving through the Beaujolais on your way to the south of France, to the village of Fleurie and enjoy a meal at the "Vieux Cep." There you will be given the aperitif of the house which is called La Tassée. Here, instead of a white Aligoté, the wine used is a Beaujolais (red) and, as well as the Cassis, a small portion of Liqueur de Framboise is added, also easily obtainable in most stores.

Finally, the followers of the *Guide Michelin* will at least be aware of that great restaurant, just outside Lyon, called Paul Bocuse, a temple on the same gastronomic level as, say, Les Troisgros at Roanne, or Taillevent of Paris. There you will be offered a similar and perhaps more exotic delight, Crème de Cassis, a touch of Framboise, but not with Aligoté this time, nor with Beaujolais, nothing but champagne!

These agreeable pre-prandial drinks can be enjoyed the year round and the establishment of your own preference among the variations and nuances thereof, can easily provide you with a series of rather stimulating experiences.

Notre Dame, Beaune

What to Drink and What to Buy in 1974

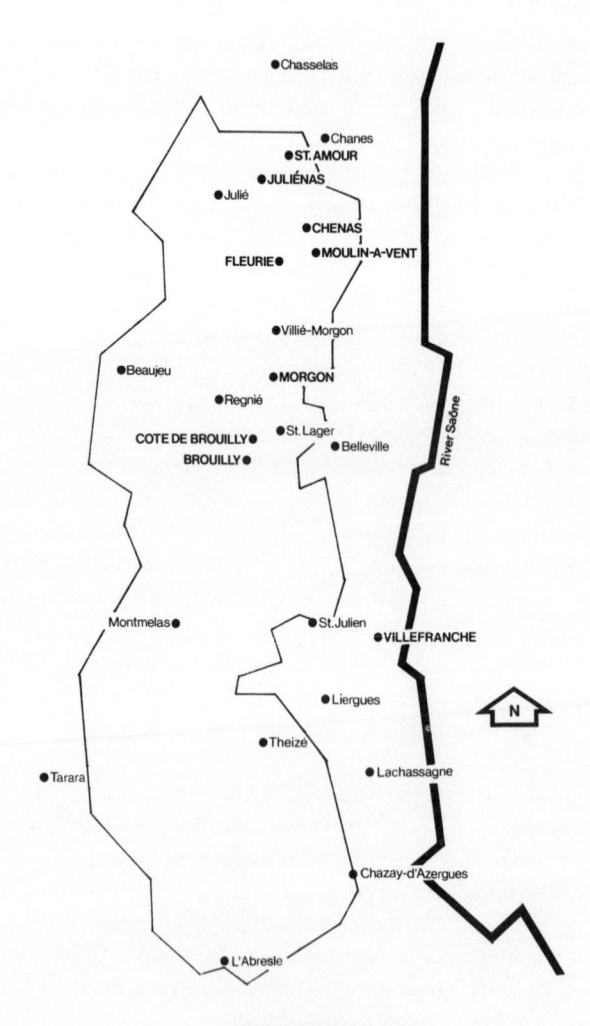

BEAUJOLAIS

What to Drink and What to Buy in 1974

Another year has slipped by and once again we are faced with a fresh view of the vinous scene. As usual, at least for the time being, the white wines cause no great problems, because with a very few exceptions, it is better to drink them while they are young and fresh.

At the moment we are heirs to three good vintages, 1969, 1970 and 1971. All of these can be drunk with enjoyment, although the 1971's, with a little longer in bottle will pick up bouquet and should improve generally.

There is however, a small grey cloud looming on the horizon, therefore it may be advisable to take the precaution to invest in a little stock. The cloud of course, is the 1972 vintage which, following a cold summer culminating in unripe grapes, has produced a number of wines which, to put it mildly, are over-endowed with acidity.

Now that this delectable commodity wine is becoming so expensive, there can be no harm in following the habits of the French, for France after all is the finest country I know in which to enjoy seafood—seafood of every form and description. As a result, through generations of experience, the average Frenchman has become quite an authority on what to drink with shell fish. For such dishes he seems to prefer his wine to come from either Alsace or the region of Muscadet. Here he is wise on two counts, because since these two delightful wines are insufficiently appreciated in the Anglo-Saxon countries, they have not yet become oppressively expensive.

The year 1971 was a particularly good vintage for these two districts; in fact in Alsace they claim it to be the finest vintage since before the war. Admittedly the price has risen, but not nearly so much as they say, of white burgundy—indeed this is fast becoming a luxury item.

The French law of "Appelation Contrôlée" may be a guarantee of authenticity, but not necessarily so for quality. Since a lot of wine of mediocre quality with the correct labels is shipped from France, it is well worth while to buy it from the right source.

My advice in the past to the English beginner has always been first of all to find a good wine merchant and to put himself in his capable hands. To a certain extent this is still true, because many of the fine old

English firms have been established for centuries, though it must be admitted that most of them have deteriorated during the past decade or so since they were taken over by the big brewery companies.

It is a very different matter here in the United States where the entire wine business had to be re-started after prohibition and it is only really during the past ten years or so that the American public "discovered" wine. Inevitably, there must be numerous merchants who, through no fault of their own, have little experience in buying this intricate merchandise and unfortunately knowledge in this respect can only come through experience.

Having just completed the interesting and agreeable task of lecturing to a dozen different branches of Les Amis du Vin in various and widespread parts of the United States, henceforth instead of telling beginners to find a good wine merchant, I shall suggest they join this admirable institution, for the members themselves will soon tell them who the best local merchants are. As an organization, Les Amis du Vin is clearly fulfilling an educational role and is obviously appreciated by the public for there are now over 15,000 members spread all over the country. It is a membership which continues to snowball.

Having found our good merchant, we can continue with the story. The years 1969, 1970 and 1971 were all good vintages for white burgundy, although as stated before, the 1971's will improve with more time in bottle. Thanks to the strong American demand, the price for Pouilly Fuissé has gone through the roof; however all is not lost, because when carefully selected, a Mâcon Blanc, or the new appelation St. Veran, can be equally satisfactory. This of course, is where the skill of your supplier comes into the picture. These three vintages are also a success for the districts of Pouilly Fumé and Sancerre.

Beginners are inclined to get into a muddle over Pouilly Fuissé and Pouilly Fumé, I remember, I did to myself! The former is made from the chardonnay grape and comes from near Mâcon on the river Saone, while the latter is made from the sauvignon blanc and its vineyards lie along a part of the upper reaches of the Loire valley. The sauvignon grape imparts to the wines of Pouilly Fumé, and those of nearby Sancerre, particularly delightful and individual bouquet and flavour and this makes them easy to distinguish.

Before leaving the white wines, if indeed it is not already too late, this is probably the last opportunity to acquire the splendid 1971 Rhines and Moselles, especially the latter. The year 1971 is absolutely outstanding for German wine, possibly the best since the great vintage of 1953. It is all a matter of personal taste, but if you have not already put aside your 1971's and even if you have done so, the wines still to go for are those from the Saar and Ruwer valleys, two rivers that are tributaries of the Moselle. Their steeliness, which can be too severe in poor vintages, gives them an exceptional quality in great years such as 1971. Since these 1971's are so rich, one might almost call them luscious. I prefer the wines of the Saar and Ruwer even to those of the Moselle proper. Many of them are blessed with that most delightful quality of fine German wine, a good fruit acidity.

From the above, it is easy to discern we all have our little prejudices, clearly by inclination I am a "Moselle man," but please do not be misled into neglecting the masterpieces from the Rhine, especially the Rheingau's, for some of them are fabulous. In fact, while writing this article (in San Francisco), I have revelled in a 1971 Rheingau, Rauenthaler Baiken Spätlese from von Simmern, lovely beyond description. Such a vintage may not recur for another twenty years, so do not hesitate, even if you have to pay a little more than you would like, to buy these 1971's from Germany as soon as you can. Always remember it is essential to see that fine wine goes down the right throats—our throats!

One further point, since the 1971's from Germany are by nature so rich, the ausleses can be almost too much of a good thing to drink with a meal, the Spätleses can therefore be bought with complete confidence and they have the additional attraction of a saving for your pocket. In a vintage so fine as this, the Kabinett wines are scarce, but this does not mean they are to be overlooked, here much will depend on the skill of your supplier.

Delicious as they are to drink now, these fine 1971's from Germany will become even better after a further year or so in bottle, so refrain if you can from drinking them all up, they have a good life before them and it may be many years before we shall see their like again.

With regard to the red wines, a sad change has come over the vinous scene for during the past two years there has been a simply devastating increase in price, particularly for red bordeaux, so much so anyone would think the château proprietors there are trying to commit commercial suicide.

The 1970 clarets were expensive enough in all conscience, they were made doubly so by the incidence of the speculators; however on account of the very small crop there is some excuse for the costly 1971's. At least the latter are of good quality; but to claim the 1972's to be of equal calibre must be wishful thinking, yet they are even more expensive than the successful 1970's and 1971's. The Bordelais growers seem to have formed a low opinion of American intelligence! In relation to their quality, about half the asking price of the 1972's might be nearer the mark!

I believe the growers in Bordeaux cannot be aware of the customer resistance that inevitably is building up on the American market. Since the average man who enjoys a bottle of wine does not like to spend much more than four dollars on it, the "crus classés" have already become beyond his reach (French growers please note) and, at the rate things are going even the "crus bourgeois" may well be too expensive in two or three years' time. It appears to me that the average American wine lover is now approaching the situation in which the English found themselves some ten years ago when, thanks to the increasing American interest and thus increasing prices, they were driven more and more on to the "crus bourgeois." With the awakening American interest in this latter category, where do the poor unfortunate English go from there?

The growers in Bordeaux appear to be under the delusion that no matter how much they raise their prices, even if a vintage is not very good, the Americans will continue to buy. You cannot altogether blame them because to date, this apparently has been the case. Now, however, I sense a different feeling in the air and unless the demand continues to increase significantly, importers who purchased the 1970's and 1971's at fifteen dollars a bottle and more, may find themselves stuck with some of their stock. It has taken a number of years to build up the popularity of the wines of Bordeaux and it seems senseless to destroy it by overt greediness.

In consequence, more and more attention is being paid to the produce of Italy and Spain, which is still reasonable in price. To date, the quality of Italian wine has not been so consistent or so satisfactory as it might have been, but this is being rectified, so before long the French growers may well have to look to their laurels: Incidentally, both 1967 and 1968 are good vintages for the Italian wines such as Chianti, Barolo and Valpolicella.

Also during this tour of America, I discovered some dissatisfaction with recent vintages of red burgundy. Modern red burgundy has lost its former lovely dark colour; it develops early and does not last so well as in pre-war days. Therefore if you still have any 1961's or 1962's in your cellar, it is advisable to check them over. It is always pleasant to find an excuse to draw a cork, so here is one for you, ready made!

Some three years ago, a Burgundian broker advised me to tell my friends to drink up their 1966's and his advice proved correct, so according to this way of thinking, the excellent vintage of 1969 should be approaching its best now. In my early days in the wine trade before World War II, I used to hear red burgundy described as the king of wines with red bordeaux as the queen. With the utmost regret, one comes to the sad conclusion that some of its former masculinity has disappeared.

There are always two sides to every coin though, for you can now enjoy your burgundy while it is comparatively young instead of waiting ages for it to mature. An outstanding vintage was 1971 for the wines of the Côte d'Or and, in spite of what has just been written, they have a much darker colour than usual, a lovely bouquet, and a heavenly flavour. The 1971's should be on the market by the time these notes appear, or at least shortly afterwards, so make sure you acquire your share.

Strangely enough, in the generally unsatisfactory vintage of 1972, the red wines from the Côte d'Or appear to have fared much better than those from other places. They are more expensive than the 1971's, inevitably in accordance with modern trends, but they are certainly better than one would expect.

As for beaujolais, which comes from about 80 miles further south, the 1971 vintage is drinking beautifully at the moment; but it should be remembered that the great charms of beaujolais are its fruitiness and its freshness. This latter tends to disappear after the wine has been in bottle for three or four years; it then resembles more the wine from northern Burgundy. You can take it for granted that the local inhabitants have been drinking their 1972 vintage throughout 1973 and from February (1974) onwards, they will be enjoying their still unborn 1973's. By this I mean the regular wine, not the *vin nouveau*. Although the lesser wines of 1972 have inherited the great drawback of their year, acidity, some of the finer ones, the "grands crus" are quite good. In a vintage like this though, so much depends upon how well the wines have been selected.

While the wines of Côte Rotie and Hermitage appear to have escaped unscathed, those of Chateauneuf du Pape, once so rich and full-bodied, seem to have fallen to the lure of commercialism. Nowadays modern Chateauneuf du Pape resembles more the produce of Beaujolais, that is to say it is being made almost for immediate consumption. It has become a pale memory of the former darkly robed, full-bodied nectar we used to enjoy on a cold winter's night.

Now we come to the wines of Bordeaux about which it is usually such a pleasure to write. The prices continue to leap up and up; but in view of the adverse reaction I have noticed while touring America, the day of reckoning may not be too far off. All the same, now is the time to purchase as much of the excellent 1970 vintage as you can afford and as soon as you can, that is to say while your merchant still has some stock left from purchases he made before the prices began to spiral. Since the "crus classés" of 1970 are so expensive, the wines to look for are the "crus bourgeois" of the Médoc, as well as those from the Côtes de Fronsac, Bourg and Blaye; believe me, you will not be disappointed.

Since 1970 was such an outstanding vintage for the districts of Saint-Emilion and Pomerol, there are delightful and less expensive wines to be found from among neighbouring, but less illustrious vineyards, those of Montagne-Saint-Emilion and Lalande de Pomerol.

There has been such a rush for the 1970's in London that in self-defence, merchants to raise their prices, replacements being too costly to consider. Another very good all-round vintage for red bordeaux is 1971; but already because of the considerable increase in price, I have found quite a number of American merchants have decided to leave this vintage alone. The way things are going, it may well be that 1970 and 1971 are the last vintages most of us can afford. Now that the wine is a year old, some château proprietors are saying their 1971 is as good as their 1970 and this is not because they wish to push their wares; the cellars of Bordeaux are pretty well empty. Of the two vintages, I personally think the 1970's have more charm.

To get on to a more agreeable subject, what claret are we going to drink in this coming year of 1974? Of the 1960's that remain, many are showing signs of fatigue and should be drunk up although one or two such as Mouton and Latour remain at their best.

The 1961's, save the lesser wines, such as the "crus bourgeois" (with exceptions like Ch. Cissac), are still for the future and they fully deserve your patience. It is wise not to be too categoric though, because the delightful Ducru-Beaucaillou has been ready for some years now and recently I have thoroughly enjoyed such truly splendid masterpieces as Pétrus, Cheval-Blanc, Palmer and Gruaud-Larose. This last group however, is really to be drunk in a restaurant or at the table of a friend more generous than yourself, while you hoard your own precious bottles miserly under lock and key until they are more mature!

An outstanding vintage for the wines of Saint-Emilion and Pomerol was 1961 and they should in principle be ready before the médocs. All the same, so far, I have seen no signs to encourage me to broach my own bottles of Trotanoy or Magdelaine.

The 1962's have proved an abiding joy and so they still remain, with the exception of a few such as Latour, which is by no means ready. Most of them must be at their best now, so enjoy them rather than hoard.

The 1964's are beginning to come round nicely for after all, they are now nearly ten years old. The Saint-Emilions and Pomerols, which were so successful, are enjoyable now and should become better and better. As for the médocs, this is another matter. Many are extremely good, but others, because the grapes were picked after the rain began to deluge down, were disappointing to say the least. By now, any self-respecting merchant should know which they were, so there is no need to go into that here. I call them the "rogue's gallery," because they have sold successfully regardless of their poor quality. So far as I know, the Saint-Juliens are all very good and some of them even outstanding. Somehow, I think we shall hear more of these successful 1964's.

The 1966's in general, are still pretty well closed up and resistant and although their promise is great, they should not be touched for the time being. This is a fine vintage and well worth waiting for.

Except for a few of the lesser wines, the 1967's—at least those I have tasted recently—are still somewhat immature, but they too will reward you for further patience. I must confess that when I wrote about them last year and the year before, I expected them to be more forward than they are at this writing, but that is half the fun of wine for like the fair sex, it is often so unpredictable! If one can judge from a recent tasting in Los Angeles, I would say 1975 would be nearer the mark than 1974 for their true appreciation and if you can wait longer, they will be even better after that.

The 1968's are now appearing on merchants' lists and no doubt, their praises will be sung, but whatever you may hear this was a miserable ungenerous vintage, one to be used only as a stop-gap. Possibly there will be some agreeable wines at the price, there always are even in poor years, but this is certainly not a vintage for investment.

The same applies roughly to the 1969's, which were greatly overrated when they first appeared on the scene. Much better admittedly, than the 1968's, but that should not be difficult, they have not got very much flesh on their bones. Nevertheless, there are some pleasant 1969's around and these may prove useful until you can start on your 1970's.

On account of their decided charm, a few of the lesser 1970's are already agreeable to drink and will, of course, continue to improve. If therefore you have not bought any so far, it would be wise to look around and see what you can find in the category of the "petits châteaux" of this attractive vintage.

Some of my favourites among the "crus bourgeois" of the Médoc are Gloria, de Pez, Maucaillou, Cissac, Beausite (St-Estèphe), La Tour-de-By, but of course in a vintage such as 1970, there are countless others. At a blind tasting in Bordeaux in October 1972 of the great châteaux of the Saint-Julien district. Ch. Gloria came out on top, which proves the "grands crus classés" are not the be-all and end-all of existence. The trouble with Gloria is that it has become so horribly expensive! Incidentally, and for what it is worth, both the Beau-Site and the La Tour-de-By mentioned above have been awarded gold medals.

In conclusion, it will be seen that disappointing changes have been taking place in the world of wine. Just as we have been inflicted with canned food rather than fresh, so the trend is towards instant red wine with all attendant loss of quality. Fortunately in spite of other unhappy events, this has not yet happened in Bordeaux and let us pray that it won't. At least, in that region there are a number of château proprietors who still insist on making their wine by the old fashioned methods; slow to mature and long to last. My impression is that in America, in spite of all the modern trends, this is what the wine lover, as opposed to the gentlemen whose sole interest lies only in moving boxes, really wants.

Index

All châteaux are found at "Château," indexed by the next principal word. Discussions of particular vintages will be found at "Vintages, Beaujolais," etc.

Abtsberg Auslese Fuder Nos. *38, 77, 88,* 152
Abtsberg Kabinett Fuder Nos. *12, 17,* 152
Abtsberg QbA, 151
Abtsberg Spätlese Fuder Nos. *57, 118,* 152
Acidity (*see* Fruit acidity), 199
Adamson, Robert and Dorothy, 141
Aix-en-Provence, 5, 9
Aligoté, 61, 192-193
Aloxe-Corton, 20, 23, 60
Alsace, 197
Amis du Vin, Les, 198
Appellation de Bourgogne Rouge, 63
Appellation Contrôlée, 5, 76, 97, 102, 195
L'Auberge Bourguignonne, 21
Auberge de Lisle, 64
Auslese, 151, 153, 197
Ausonius, 154
Avelsbacher Hammerstein feine Spätlese, 101
Ayler Herrenberg Auslese, EA Bischöfliches Konvikt (Saar), 145
Ayler Kupp Spätlese, EA Bischöfliches Priesterseminar (Saar), 143
Ayler Scheidterberg Kabinett, 150

Baringo, 99
Barolet Collection, 53, 171
Barolo, 198
Bâtard-Montrachet, 58, 59
Beaujolais, 9, 10-17, 191, 199; (1971) 10, 62; in California, 101-104
Beaujolais blanc, 22
Beaujolais-Villages, 62, 103
Beaune; *see* Côte De Beaune, Hospices de Beaune
Beerenauslese, 128, 157, 158; of Dr. K. Frank, 136
Berkeley Wine and Food Society, 59, 103
Berkmann, Joseph, 25, 163, 171, 176, 178, 180-181
Bernkastel, 155-156
Bernkasteler Badstube Kabinett (1970, Prüm), 156; Spätlese, 157
Bienvenue-Bâtard-Montrachet, 59
Bissonette, Gregory and Katherine, 87
Bitburger Pils, 146

Blayais, *see* Côtes de Blaye
Bloud, Jean-Pierre, 22-23
Bocuse, Paul, 13, 63, 64, 191
Bois de la Garde, 8
Bordeaux, 197-200
Bordeaux Superieur, 174
Borie, Jean-Eugene, 32, 76, 114
Bosche Vineyard, 92, 94, 95, 134
Broadbent, Michael, 130
Bruderberg Kabinett, 151
Bürklin-Wolf, Dr., 148
Burton, Allan and Audrey, 127

Cabernet Sauvignon (Bordeaux), 31, 33, 51, 123, 124, 182
Cabernet Sauvignon (California), 83, 85, 87, 89-91, 93, 94, 95, 97, 132, 134
Cairol, Philippe, 173
California Sparkling White Wine, 133
Calor Gas System, 56
Canada, 126-128
Carpy, Charles, 92
Casks, German wine, 140
Cassis, 3-5, 190, 191
Casteja, Emile, 25, 26, 34, 73, 114, 176
Chablis Fourchaume, 55
Chablis (France), 54-57, 127, 191
Chablis (USA), *Jan Jac Ohio,* 121
Chalone Vineyard, 104-108, 130-134
Chambolle-Musigny, 61
Changing Face of Wine, 167
Chaptalisation, 17, 29, 57
Chardonnay, *see* Pinot Chardonnay
Charente, 50
Charmes-Chambertin, 21
Chassagne-Montrachet, 58
Ch. Ausone, 26-27, 34, 47, 66, 70, 72, 110, 111
Ch. Baret, 73
Ch. Batailley, 25, 34, 73
Ch. Beau-Rivage, 25, 73
Ch. Beau-Site, 25, 73, 201
Ch. Bel-Air Marquis d'Aligre, 37
Ch. Beychevelle, 33, 36, 45, 65, 67, 77, 78
Ch. Bourdieu la Valade, 28, 69
Ch. Bouscaut, 29, 31, 32
Ch. Boyd-Cantenac, 67
Ch. Brane-Cantenac, 36, 65, 77, 78
Ch. Calon-Ségur, 34, 36, 65, 77, 182

203

Ch. Canon-de-Brem, 27, 28, 67
Ch. Cantemerle, 36
Ch. des Capitans (Beaujolais), 10, 11
Ch. Carbonnieux, 31, 32
Ch. de Carles, 66
Ch. Chapelle Trinite, 26, 73
Ch. Chasse-Spleen, 37, 38
Ch. Cheval Blanc, 27, 43, 46, 48, 66, 70, 72, 110, 111, 127, 200
Ch. Chevalier (California), 86-87
Ch. Cissac, 33, 38-41, 114-117, 122-126, 174, 175, 176
Ch. Climens, 109
Ch. La Clotte, 42
Ch. La Conseillante, 38, 42, 69, 72
Ch. Corbin, 42
Ch. Cos d'Estournel, 45
Ch. La Dauphine, 28, 66
Ch. Ducru-Beaucaillou, 32, 36, 45, 77, 78, 202
Ch. Ferrière, 165
Ch. de Fieuzal, 45
Ch. Figeac, 42, 65, 71
Ch. des Fines Roches, 6
Ch. La Fleur-Pétrus, 43, 69, 72
Ch. La Fleur du Roy, 26
Ch. Fombrauge, 55
Ch. Gaby, 27, 28
Ch. La Gaffelière, 42, 43, 68-71
Ch. Gazin, 42
Ch. Giscours, 37, 38
Ch. Gloria, 33, 37, 38, 39, 40, 67, 74, 77, 78, 115, 116, 124, 174, 175, 176
Ch. Grand-Corbin-d'Espagne, 55
Ch. Grand-Puy-Lacoste, 33, 37, 77, 78
Ch. La Grave-Trigant-de-Boisset, 43
Ch. Grand Barail Lamazelle, 38
Ch. Gruaud-Larose, 45, 163, 171, 182, 200
Ch. Haut-Bailly, 29, 31, 67
Ch. Haut-Brion, 29, 46, 66, 110, 111, 165
Ch. Lafite (Lafite-Rothschild), 46, 110, 111, 166
Ch. Lafleur, 44, 69, 71
Ch. La Lagune, 28, 37, 67, 77, 78
Ch. Langoa-Barton, 114
Ch. Lanessan, 33, 38, 40, 67, 68, 124, 125
Ch. Las-Cases, 36
Ch. Lascombes, 131, 133, 134, 184
Ch. Latour, 24, 30, 34, 35, 46, 66, 67-68; *passim*, 73-79, 110, 111, 117, 164, 166, 173; *see also* Forts de Latour
Ch. Latour-Pomerol, 69, 72
Ch. Lefon-Rochet, 33
Ch. Léoville-Las-Cases, 77, 78, 182
Ch. Léoville-Poyferré, 34, 77, 78, 164
Ch. Liversan, 40

Ch. Lynch-Bages, 36, 77, 78, 117, 167, 182
Ch. Magdelaine, 42, 68, 71, 200
Ch. Malartic-Lagravière, 31, 32
Ch. Malescot, 33, 37
Ch. Margaux, 46, 66, 110, 111, 165; tasting 173-175
Ch. Maucaillou, 201
Ch. La Mission Haut Brion, 24, 29, 44, 45, 46, 47, 48, 117, 163, 165
Ch. Montrose, 36, 77, 78, 182
Ch. de Morgan (Beaujolais), 103
Ch. de Moulin-a-Vent (Beaujolais), 22
Ch. Moulinet, 171
Ch. Mouton-Rothschild, 46, 65, 110, 111, 128, 166, 179-181
Ch. Nénin, 45
Ch. Les Ormes-de-Pez, 174, 175, 176
Ch. Palmer, 32, 163, 183, 200
Ch. Le Pape, 25
Ch. Pape Clément, 29, 31
Ch. Pavie, 65, 68, 71
Ch. Pavie-Macquin, 42
Ch. Pétrus, 43, 66, 70, 72, 110, 111, 163, 167, 200
Ch. de Pez, 33, 34, 37, 38, 39, 40
Ch. Phélan-Ségur, 37, 67, 123-124, 125
Ch. Pichon-Longueville-Baron, 36, 67, 77, 78, 124, 164, 182
Ch. Pichon-Longueville-Lalande, 36, 77, 78
Ch. Poujeaux, 37
Ch. Rauzan-Gassies, 34
Ch. Rauzan-Ségla, 34, 65
Ch. Rouet, 29
Ch. Rousset, 28
Ch. de Sales, 42
Ch. Siran, 37, 123, 125
Ch. Talbot, 171
Ch. La Tour-Haut-Brion, 45, 48
Ch. La Tour de Mirail, 119
Ch. La Tour-de-Mons, 37, 67, 174-176
Ch. Trotanoy, 43, 69, 70, 72, 200
Ch. Trottevieille, 26, 73, 176-177
Ch. La Valade, 27
Ch. de Vaudieu, 6
Ch. Vieux-Château-Certan, 43, 65, 69, 72
Ch. Vieux Château Peymouton, 26
Ch. Villars, 28
Ch. d'Yquem, 4, 158
Châteauneuf-du-Pape, 5, 6, 7, 8, 9, 113, 201; white 6
Châteauneuf-du-Pape Petite Bastide, 101
Chénas, 202
Chenin Blanc (White Pinot), 85, 106, 107, 131, 134
Chevalier-Montrachet, 59

Index

Chez La Rose, 14
Chianti, 200
Chicago, *passim* 113-120
Chiroubles, 104
Cincinnati, *passim* 120-126
Clair, Louis, 18
Claret, 12, 25-48, 71-79, 110-111, 114-117, 122-125, 163-183, 197-202
Clos Fourtet, 34, 68
Clos de la Griotte-Chambertin, 61
Clos de la Pousse d'Or, 12
Clos des Ruchottes-Chambertin, 61
Clos de Tart, 119
Cockburn (port), 180, 189
Cognac, 49-53
Cologne University, 140
Concannon (vineyard), 97, 98, 99
Corti Brothers, 112
Corti, Daniel, 111, 188
Corton, Le, 23
Corton Bressandes, 23, 24
Corton Charlemagne, 23, 134
Corton Clos du Roi, 24, 101
Côte de Beaune, 16, 19-21, 57
Côte de Beaune-Villages, 19
Côte de Brouilly, 104
Côte d'Or, 57, 199
Côte Rotie, 201
Côtes de Blaye, 175, 200
Côtes de Bourg, 28, 175, 200
Côtes-Canon-Fronsac, 27-28, 67
Côtes de Fronsac, 27, 28, 170, 173, 200
Côtes de Nuit, 16, 19-21, 57
Côtes du Rhône, 5, 6, 7, 8, 10
Côtes de Ventoux, 6
Cotterell, Julian, 54, 61
Cottin, Philippe, 168
Courtright, Hernando, 100
Crème de Cassis, 61, 62
Croft (port), 120
Crus bourgeois, 33, 37-38, 68, 74, 93, 114, 115, 119, 122, 123, 124, 173, 175, 198, 200, 201
Crus classés, 74, 114, 115, 122, 124, 198, 200
Cruse, Edouard, 35

Danglade, Patrick, 27, 64
Danglade, Roger, 27, 64
Dão, 190
David, Narsai, 190
Davies, Mr. and Mrs. Jack, 133
Davis (California), 105
Decanting, 178, 185
Delmas, Jean, 30, 31, 32
Deutz (champagne), 109
Dhron, 154

Dhron Hofberger Auslese, EA Bischofliches Priesterseminar, 145
Dickerson, Dr. William, 108, 141
Domaine de Bagnol, 4
Domaine de Chevalier, 31
Domaine de l'Eglise, 26, 73
Domaine Paternal, 5
Dom Perignon, 186
Dow (port), 119, 189
Drescher, Harry, 108
Duboeuf, Georges, 13, 63

Echézeaux, 21
Eisele, Milton and Barbara, 91
Eiswein, 158, 159
Eitelsbacher Karthauser Hofberg Burgberg Kabinett, EA W. Tyrell, 143
Eitelsbacher Karthauser Hofberger Kronenberg Auslese, EA W. Tyrell, 145
Eitelsbacher Karthauser Hofberg Kronenberg Spätlese, EA W. Tyrell, 144
Eitelsbacher Marienholz Spätlese, EA Bischofliches Konvikt, 143, 146
Epernay, 24
Eser, K. H., 147
Evoe, 99

Falkensteiner Hofberg Auslese, 144
Falkensteiner Hofberg Kabinett, 142
Fenton, Colin, 139
Fines Roches (Châteauneuf-du-Pape), 8
Fining, 90, 112
Finlayson, William and Marjorie, 9, 11, 12, 13, 127
Fleurie, 9, 13, 22, 63, 193
Folle Blanche (grape), 49, 51
Fonseca (port), 119, 189
Forts de Latour, 74-79
Fragnya, 101
Framboise, 62, 64, 193
Francis, Dr. Herbert and Sylvia, 126, 131
Frank, Dr. Konstantin, 126, 131, 133
Freemark Abbey, 92-95, 99
Fronsadais, 66
Fruit acidity, 144, 150, 153, 157, 197
Fuder (cask), 150, 152

Gardère, Jean-Paul, 74
Geisenheimer Kilsberg Riesling Kabinett, 147
Geisenheimer Klauserweg Riesling Kabinett, 147
Gemello (winery), 99

Germany, *passim* 139-160
Gessert, G., 148
Gevrey-Chambertin, 21, 60, 61
Gewurtztraminer (California), 95
Gigondas, 5, 7
Ginestet, Bernard, 171
Goldtröpfchen, 154, 155
Goût de terroir, 105
Graacher Domprobst Auslese, 145
Graacher Himmelreich Auslese, 157
Graacher Himmelreich Beerenauslese, 157
Graacher Himmelreich Eiswein feinste Auslese, 157
Graacher Himmelreich Kabinett, 159
Graf, Richard, 105, 131
Graham (port), 117, 120, 189
Grand Cru Club, 108-111
Grande Champagne (Cognac), 49, 51-53
Grands crus, 123, 199
Grands crus classés, 203
Grands Echézeaux, 21
Graves, red, 29-31, 171; white, 32
Guards Club, 190
Guide Michelin, 3, 5, 191

Haeni, S., 19
Hauts-Coteaux, 4
Heitz, Joseph, 83, 95
Heitz Cellars, 95-97
Hermitage, 199
Herrenberg Auslese Fuder No. 112, 152
Herrenberg Auslese Fuder No. 134, 152
Herrenberg Kabinett Fuder No. 10, 152
Herrenberg Kabinett Fuder No. 11, 152
Herrenberg QbA, 151
Herrenberg Spätlese Fuder No. 109, 152
Hospices de Beaune, 16
Hostellerie du Vieux Moulin, 16, 17
Hungerford, John, 128

Ichinose, Ben, 141
International Wine and Food Society, 21, 22; Chicago chapter, 115, 119
Irancy (Bourgogne), 55, 56

Jackson, Robert, Ltd., 13
Jacquemont, Louis, 13
Jaeger, William, 128
Jan Jac Ohio Wines, 21
Jardin des Gourmets, 163, 171, 173, 178
Javillier, Raymond, 57
Johannisberger Goldatzel Riesling Spätlese, 148
Johannisberger Holle Riesling Spätlese, 148
Johannisberg Riesling (California), 87, 91, 94, 95, 96, 131

Johannisberg Riesling (New York), 126
Johnson, Hugh, 130
Josephshofer Spätlese, EA Reichsgraf v. Kesselstaat, 143
Juliénas, 10, 14, 15, 104

Kanzem, 149
Kaseler Hitzlay Spätlese, EA Reichsgraf v. Kesselstaat, 143
Kaseler Kehrnagel Kabinett, EA Bischöfliches Priesterseminar, 143
Kaseler Nies'chen Auslese, 144
Kaseler Nies'chen Spätlese, 143
Kenderman, Hans Walter, 140
Kir, 14, 61-62, 192
Koch, Richard and Louise, 115, 117
Knudson, Robert, 141
Kreuznacher Bruckes, 147
Kreuznacher Kahlenberg, 147
Kreuznacher Kapellenberg, 147

Labrusca (vitis labrusca), 121
Lalande de Pomerol, 200
Lassere, 13
Laurent Perrier, 22
Liebfraumilch, 141
Loeb, Dr. Otto, 139, 140-141, 150-151, 153
Lieb, O. W. & Co. Ltd., 141
Loeb, Sigmund, 141
Lorenzo, Hugo, 113, 115, 117, 119

Mackie, Wendell, 83
Macon, 61, 191, 196
Margaux, 123
Martha's Vineyard (Oakville, Calif.), 83, 84, 95, 97, 134
Martin, Henri, 33, 39, 74, 115, 124, 174
Martin, Louis, 88-92
Martin, Louis and Elizabeth, 83
Masson, Paul, 104
Master, Mervyn and Jane, 5, 8
Masters of Wine, 130
Maximin Grünhaus, 146, 150-153, 155
Maximin Grünhaüser Herrenberg Spätlese, 140, 150
Maxim's, 24
May, Tom and Martha, 83
Mayacamas Winery, 84
McCrea, Fred and Eleanor, 83, 87
McLean, Gallo, 121
Médoc, 68, 114, 115, 123, 134, 167, 200, 201
Meffre, Gabriel, 5, 6
Meier's Wine Cellars, 121
Mendocino, 99
Mercurey, 20, 57
Merlot (Bordeaux), 33, 41, 47, 90, 94, 123, 124

Index

Merlot (California), 85, 87, 89-90, 94
Meursault, 12, 19, 58, 193
Mirassou Vineyards, 98, 99, 100, 104
Mondavi, Robert and Marjorie, 84
Montagne-Saint-Emilion, 202
Monterey County, 104
Montrachet, 58-59
Mont Redon (Châteauneuf-du-Pape), 9
Morgon, 13, 63
Moscato Amabile (California), 91
Moselle, 139-146, 153-156, 198
Moueix, Christian, 43
Moueix, Jean-Francois, 64-68
Moueix, Jean-Pierre, 41, 43, 68, 150
Moulin-à-Vent, 102, 104
Mousset, Jacques, 5, 6, 8, 113
Muscadet, 197

Nähe, 147
Napa Valley, 56, 83, 91-92, 94, 129, 134
Nicolini Winery, 100
Niersteiner Auflangen Riesling Auslese, 148
Niersteiner Klostergarten Scheurebe Auslese, 148
Niersteiner Olberg Riesling Spätlese, 148
Niersteiner Rehbach Riesling Auslese, 148
Niersteiner Spiegelberg Riesling Spätlese, 148
Nuits-Saint-Georges, 17, 61

Oberemmeler Abteihof Spätlese, 143
Ockfener Bockstein, 149
Ockfener Geisberg Auslese, 144
Ockfener Geisberg Spätlese, 143
Oporto, 186-187
Oxidation, 62, 98, 190

Paillard, Robert, 18
Palatinate, 149
Papiano (vineyard), 99
Parducci, 98, 99
Paté de foie gras, 63-64
Penning-Rowsell, Edward, 164
Peterson, Dr. Richard, 130
Peterson, Walter and Frances, 129
Petite Champagne (Cognac), 49, 50
Petite Sirah, 94, 97-100
Petit Verdot, 123
Petrowsky, Karl, 109
Pfalz, *see* Pheinpfalz
Pick of the Bunch, The, 33, 84, 93, 104
Piesport, 154-155
Piesporter Goldtröpfchen Auslese, EA Bischöfliches Konvikt, 145; EA Reichsgraf v. Kesselstatt, 144
Pinot Blanc (California), 96, 106, 107, 131

Pinot Chardonnay (California), 85, 87, 93, 96, 106-107, 131-132
Pinot Chardonnay (France), 198
Pinot Chardonnay (New York), 126, 131, 133
Pinot Noir (California), 87, 89, 93, 96, 106, 108, 132
Pollock, David and Margot, 34
Pomerol, 41-45, 47, 69, 71-72, 115, 167, 202
Pommard, 17, 20
Pommery & Greno, 184
Port (vintage), 117-120, 185, 189
Pouilly-Fuissé, 14, 196
Pouilly-Fumé, 196
Pourriture, 47
Premier Cru Club, 123
Prüm, J. J., 153, 156-160
Prüm, Manfred, 156, 159
Puligny-Montrachet, 19, 58, 59, 131-134

Qualitaetswein (Q.b.A.), 151

Rainbird, George, 44
Rauenthaler Baiken Spätlese, 197
Rebello Valente, 189
Reichsgraf von Plettenberg, 147
Rheingau, 147-148, 197
Rheinhessen, 147, 148
Rheinpfalz, 147, 148-149
Rhine, 147-150, 198
Rhodes, Dr. and Mrs. Bernard L., 83, 84, 98, 105, 108, 111, 118, 141, 187
Roederer, Louis, 7-8
Romanèche-Thorins, 13, 62
Roxheimer Hollenpfad Riesling Auslese, 147; Cabinet, 109
Ruppertsberger Reiterpfad Riesling Spätlese, 149
Ruwer, 140, 142-144, 146, 153, 197

Saar, 140, 142, 143, 144, 145, 149, 197
Saint-Aubin, 18
Saint-Emilion, 41, 42, 47, 49, 51, 68-69, 71, 72, 115, 167, 179, 200
Saint-Estèphe 123
Saint-Julien, 45, 124, 201
Saint-Romain, 18
St. Veran, 196
Sancerre, 196
Sandeman (port), 119, 189
San Francisco Wine Sampling Club, 130
Santenay, 19, 20
Sarrau, Robert and Marguerite, 9, 10
Sauvignon Blanc, 198
Savigny-les-Beaune, 16, 17, 20, 60
Schoonmaker, Frank, 97
Schramsberg, 133, 134

Schubert, A von, 150
Scott, Robert and Gay, 130, 134
Semillon (California), 91
Semillon de Soliel (California), 88
Sercial, (1879), 101
Sichel, Peter, 171
Simi Winery, 100
Simonet, Claud, 55
Soledad (Monterey County), 104, 134
Sonneman, Henry, 121
Sonoma (California), 89, 90, 100
Souverain Cellars, 99, 131
Spätlese, 153, 199
Stony Hill Vineyard, 83, 87
Sutter Home Winery, 112
Syrah, 97

Taittinger, 178, 184
Tassee, La, 62, 191
Tastevins, 13, 14
Tastings, blind, 39, 43, 55, 70, 76-79, 103-104; 1961 claret, 182; 1927 port, 189; 1960 port, 119-120
Tatham, Christopher, 130
Tavel, Domaine de Vesticles, 8
Taylor (port), 120, 187, 189
Tecchia, Gino, 178
Thevenot, H., 22-24
Traminer (California), 87
Travers, Robert and Elinor, 84
Trittenheimer Apotheke Auslese, 145; Spätlese, 143
Trockenbeerenauslese, 154, 158
Tupper, J., 108

Uniflow, 106
Union des Crus Classés de Graves, 31
Urziger Wurzgarten Auslese, EA Bischofliches Priesterseminar, 145

Valpolicella, 198
Valvano, Marjorie, 120, 122
Verdienstkreuz, 141
Vialard, Danielle, 119, 121, 126
Vialard, Louis, 38, 39, 114, 119, 121, 126, 171, 174
Villamont, Henri de, 19
Vinifera (vitis vinifera), 121
Vinifera Wine Cellars, 126, 131
Vins nouveaux, 10, 102, 199
Vintages, Beaujolais: 15, 103, 199
—— Bordeaux red: 1961, 163-166, 167, 180-183, 200; 1962, 109-111, 167, 168, 200; 1964, 34, 167, 200; 1965, 44, 47, 1966, 78, 165; 1967, 64-66, 76-77, 166; 1968, 44-47, 201; 1969, 41-43, 47, 201; 1970, 25-26, 31, 36-38, 71-72, 172; 1971, 35, 67-70, 73-74, 202

—— Bordeaux white: 25, 31; 1970, 32
—— Burgundy red: 1966, 198; 1968, 60; 1969, 18, 19-21, 60, 198; 1970, 18, 19, 57, 60-61; 1971, 57, 60
—— Burgundy white: 1970, 55
—— Moselle: 1945, 140; 1949, 140; 1953, 140; 1959, 140; 1964, 140; 1971, 40, 142-146, 151-153
—— Ruwer: 1964, 140; 1966, 140; 1969, 140; 1971, 140
—— Saar: 1964, 140; 1966, 140, 1969, 140; 1971, 140
Viognier (grape), 9
Viognier Condrieu, 8
Volnay, 12, 17, 20
Volnay Santenots, 20
Vosne-Romanée, 21, 60

Wachenheimer Gerümpel Riesling Auslese, 149
Wachenheimer Mandelgarten Riesling Kabinett, 148
Waldracher Meisenberg Kabinett, EA Pfarrgut, 142
Warre (port), 128, 185, 189
Watrous, Philip, 119
Weaver Vineyards, 112
Webb, Bradford, 92
Wehlener Sonnenuhr (Prüm), 156-160
Wehlener Sonnenuhr Beerenauslese (1949), 128; Trockenbeerenauslese (1971), 158
Wente Brothers, 99
Wiltinger Kupp Auslese, 145; Spätlese, 144
Windsor Winery, 100
Wine Magazine, 120, 130
Wine World, 74
Wine and Food Society of Southern California, 100-101
Wine Society (London), 130
Wines of Bordeaux, 164
Winkeler Jesuitengarten Riesling Spätlese, 148
Winzenheimer Rosenhecke Riesling Auslese, 146
Winzenheimer Rosenheck feine Auslese, 109
Woltner, Henri and Hélène, 44-48, 165
Wood, Mr. and Mrs. Laurie, 92

Young wines, 92, 149, 150-151

Zinfandel, 85-86, 89; tasting, 111-112, 132